Faith Seeking Transformation

Faith Seeking Transformation

Rethinking Faith, Theology and Mission in North East India

Yangkahao Vashum

Christian World Imprints

First Published in 2020 by

Christian World Imprints
Christian Publishing & Books from India
C-3, Wazirpur Industrial Area
Delhi-110052
cwidelhi2017@gmail.com
www.ChristianWorldImprints.com
Phone: +91 11 41526079

ISBN: 978-93-5148-469-1 (HB)
ISBN: 978-93-5148-470-7 (PB)

Cover Image: Sunrise signifies new life, renewal, transformation and hope.

Printed in India.

Dedication

To
All the Victims of Covid – 19;
Men and Women on the Frontlines in the
Fight Against the Pandemic
&
Young Readers who are the Future Leaders and
Change-makers of our Society

Contents

Foreword

Faith Seeking Transformation: Rethinking Faith, Theology and Mission in North East India authored by Rev. Dr Yangkahao Vashum is a search into alternative ways of experiencing faith, searching theology and doing mission in North East India. COVID – 19 Pandemic that has created fear psychosis across the globe transcending all divisions between Global South and North, rich and poor, and haves and have nots serves as the historical context of this book. As of today, over 2.5 million people are affected, and nearly five hundred thousand people have lost their lives. The health infrastructure and services exposed the limitations and the Government's commitment to protecting human life. Scientists are working hard to bring out the vaccines and medicines to arrest the spread of the disease.

The lockdown and total shutdown of activities including economic, have made many to lose their jobs, particularly the migrant workers. They were stranded without employment and wages in their workplaces as the countries shutdown their transportation. In India, the sudden announcements of lockdown starting from March 25, 2020, and with it the closure of rail, road and air services created more problems to the migrants than relief from COVID 19. Many after weeks of lockdown stayed under very unhealthy facilities in Government shelter homes with lack of resources and food, many started walking 1000s of miles back home. This resulted in the human catastrophe of enormous size, and the Government was not able to control it. Finally, the Government opened up the rail and road transportation for the migrants to return home. This was not enough, and many lost their lives and those who returned, many of them got infected by COVID – 19. This gave rise to the numbers of infected people in India. The Government because of downtrend in GDP growth, was forced to open the economy after three months of shutdown.

The author describes COVID – 19 as an invisible enemy that has challenged all aspects of human life, i.e., social, religious, economic, political and cultural experiences. The world is going through tremendous pressure of creating resources and opportunities for people to survive particularly those who are in the lower strata of the economy. The invisible enemy has shaken the visibly powerful creatures, the humans. The religious community who had had so much to talk about the enemy have become helpless for their worship places, and worship life was shutdown. Many Christians and other faith communities started thinking, how could God allow such a thing to happen? Rather the faith community was overwhelmed by the intensity of attack of the virus. It was a test of faith. Can God act in such a manner where humans will not be able to worship Him? Nobody ever thought the worship places would be closed for maintaining social distance. How are we going to respond to these challenges from theological and missional perspectives?

The world is gripped in fear, and we live at the edge, some call it the end time. Nothing is going right; not all claims are entirely true. As much as faith is a truth-claim in that we seek God and construct theology, the mission also is driven by our way of not only constructing theology but also doing theology. North East Tribal people's attempt to do theology is a distinct category of "doing theology." In that, it has to answer several questions, and in essence, they are predominantly missional; and construction of theology is superimposition over and above the mission is understood. The Mission in North East context is also faith-seeking and faith-claiming. In that, it is both affirming theology and reengaging in mission in a newer way in this time of the pandemic.

It is true that this pandemic does not discriminate anyone, but vulnerability to the infection is found more among the poor and deprived because of their health and accessibility to the health care system. This world is divided between the rich and poor. While rich nations are exposed to the exponential growth of the COVID 19 and the shortfall in health care, the developing countries provided the best health services to those who can afford private treatment. Ultimately, whether it is poor or rich nation selective facilitation of health is to those who can afford and who can survive, as we hear in the West the old and co-morbid patients were left to fend themselves and many have died due to negligence.

Is this a human tragedy or signs of ecological degradation that has reached the point of saturation? Blame games are on between nations and people. But what is evident is the weaponization of the human habitation and militarization of animal habitation. Unless the human community learn to live as God has designed the Earth, we may see more problems of higher degrees. The humans have enslaved the animals of all sorts for their own aesthetic and exotic appetite, as well as animals, are killed and traded in the market for their flesh, skins, bones, teeth etc. Have we really exploited God's Earth instead of being the keepers of God's Earth?

The voices of indigenous people are significant because they lived in tandem with the jungle. Forest product was their resources from shelter, health to food.

But indigenous people, particularly in North East India, also exploited the resources of the jungle, today we do not see animals, trees and plants of all kinds. While the ancient mythological stories in all tribes are full of animals who were their totemic symbols and carry a prominent religious significance, today it is in a sorry note. We don't see such animals in real life. Instead, they are painted in our costumes and artifacts. Is COVID 19, a reminder to reseek our faith, reformulate our theology and redraw our mission strategy? Are we doing enough to care for our Mother Earth whose creator is God, the Yahweh on whom we construct our theology? Time has come to "doing theology" taking the mother earth seriously.

There is a need to revisit tribal theology. The tribal theology in North East India has moved to the second generation. While the first generation constructed tribal theology, the time has come to critique and see how we can engage tribal theology today in North East Indian context. The first generation tribal theologians eulogized the North East tribal (Primal) religious traditions and culture that they saw everything good. In their zeal to make it distinct from other tribal theologies such as adivasi theology, dalit theology, they almost created too much of categories. They tried to answer who they are not, rather than who they are. The second-generation tribal theologians must now engage in doing contextual theology in that they must critique their own traditions vis a vis Christianization and respond who they are. The author has rightly brought out the context to the fore and outlining the challenges that the tribals of North East India are facing today - the issues of cultural extremism, religious fundamentalism, tribalism, human rights violation, ecological problems, economic issues, globalization, tribal nationalism, development, issues of corruption etc.

All these are pertinent and significant, and they should serve as pointers to transformation. Faith Seeking Transformation must engage in reformulating theology and reorient mission. While theology must root in the context and tribal theology must be the starting point, the mission must begin from home and become inward to address the problems that North East India is facing today. The theologians, church and mission leaders and political leaders must come together to work and address the issues at home in their context. Critiquing faith, theology and mission must be utmost in the agenda we are seeking to appropriate transformation. This book challenges Christians of North East India to seek faith in a newer way that would bring transformation to the North East Society.

Santanu K. Patro
Senate of Serampore College (University)
Serampore

Acknowledgements

Faith Seeking Transformation is a book that calls for rethinking Faith, Theology and Mission in the context of the contemporary world and its realities, and in particular the North East India. This book is a collection of some of my articles presented in various consultations and seminars spanning several years. Most of them have been published in different journals and edited books including *Asia Journal of Theology; Religion & Society; North East Social Research Centre; Centre for Dalit/Subaltern Studies; Journal of Tribal Studies/Tribal Study Centre; Naga Journal of Indigenous Affairs; Indian Theological Journal; Institute of Leadership Enhancement and Ministry Augmentation* and other publications. I am grateful to the editors for granting permission for publication and their invaluable support and encouragement means alot. While most of the articles have been substantially revised in order to avoid repetitions, I have as well retained the original texts for the sake of coherence and clarity for the readers in some of the articles.

This is the outcome of several years of theological reflections as a theological student and teacher who has been engaging in theological education, in molding and training theological students. Secondly, they are the products of my engagements with many scholars, theologians, Christian ministers and activists at different levels and contexts; they have not only enriched my knowledge but broadened my perspectives and sharpened my theological thinking. I thank my students at the Eastern Theological College for sharing their invaluable stories and knowledge. My esteemed colleagues at the Eastern for helping me grow in knowledge and wisdom and for their constant support and encouragement. I am truly indebted to all them – friends, students, teachers, scholars and well wishers. I wish to express my profound thanks to uncles and aunties, the custodians of indigenous wisdom and knowledge, for sharing those priceless wealth of knowledge and wisdom to me.

I would like to thank Prof. Dr Santanu K. Patro, Registrar of the Senate of Serampore College (University) for writing the foreword for the book. Thanks are also due to the Christian World Imprints (CWI) for publishing this book.

I would like to express my profound gratitude to two special friends, Shimreiyo Vashum and Thotreihan Ruivah, who have come forward to sponsor in publishing this book as a sign of our partnership in the ministry of the Lord. They have been a lifelong and true friends of my wife Semmichon and we are truly grateful for their generous contribution.

Also, I wish to thank my wife Semmichon Shimrang Vashum, for her steadfast love and support. She is the force behind the success of this day. My children Mangazan Vashum and Pemting Vashum, for giving me time and space to fully concentrate on my work and ministry by being independent and understanding kids. Above all, I thank God for His grace and mercy!

Yangkahao Vashum
Jorhat, 2020

Introduction

The Context: COVID – 19 PANDEMIC

The whole world is at war again. A different kind of war, of course. And the world is under lockdown. The whole world has just one enemy. The enemy is invisible. And that enemy is called COVID – 19 (Coronavirus disease 2019); the disease caused by novel coronavirus. It all started in Wuhan city in China sometime in December 2019.[1] Since then, within short span of time Covid – 19 has humbled the world. It has singlehandedly brought the world to its knee. It has humbled the mighty, the powerful, the rich, the poor and the weak alike. It does not discriminate anyone on the basis of race, caste, gender, color, age, ideology and religion/faith or no faith. It gives damn thing about the world's boundaries and walls. It has no respect for anything and there is nothing this enemy can't reach or go. The world's most sophisticated arsenals and weapons are of no match before this enemy. The World Health Organization (WHO) declared Covid – 19 as pandemic on March 11, 2020.[2] This is the first pandemic caused by coronavirus and a pandemic that the world has never before seen that can be controlled. The enemy is fast, furious, and ruthless to the core and deadly. It shows no mercy to the victims. So far, Covid -19 has claimed over 7 lakhs lives globally and still counting. According to the latest WHO updates, there are 709,

---

[1] According to the WHO timeline on Covid-19, on December 31, 2019, "Wuhan Municipal Health Commission, China, reported a cluster of cases of pneumonia in Wuhan, Hubei Province. A novel coronavirus was eventually identified," https://www.who.int/news-room/detail/27-04-2020-who-timeline---covid-19 (28/04/2020).

[2] "WHO Director-General's opening remarks at the media briefing on COVID-19 - 11 March 2020," https://www.who.int/dg/speeches/detail/who-director-general-s-opening-remarks-at-the-media-briefing-on-covid-19---11-march-2020 (28/04/2020).

511 confirmed deaths, and 18, 902, 735 confirmed cases worldwide.[3] What is even more troubling is that experts are warning that the disease may linger on for much longer period of time and that developing vaccine may take much longer than expected.[4]

The whole world has come to a standstill. Everywhere, there is lockdown. Roads and streets look deserted. Businesses and the economic power houses have been forced to close down. Schools, colleges and other educational training/ coaching institutions are in lockdown as all the rest of public gathering places such as restaurants, cinema halls and theatres, malls, gyms, sports complexes, etc. Social, political, cultural and all kinds of public gatherings have been closed down. Religious places and places of worship including churches have been closed down as well. Further, almost all domestic and international travels by air, roads, train, sea and other modes of travel have been cancelled and stopped. No one and no power on earth can enforce such lockdown of global scale the way Covid – 19 has singlehandedly commanded. No, no one.

To combat against this invisible enemy, the experts advice that the best response is to take precaution and preventive measures: maintain social (physical) distancing, personal hygiene, stay home and stay safe. In other words, LOCKDOWN is the only answer for now.

The world is mystified and bewildered on the question of the origin of the novel coronavirus. All kinds of theories are floating and are being advanced – from accidental leakage from Wuhan Institute of Virology research lab to animals in Wuhan wet market. According to WHO, the novel coronavirus is "natural in origin."[5] Notwithstanding this assertion, all kinds of theories abound and TV and numerous social media are filled with wild and passionate debates, with no definitive answer insight. In the midst of all this, fake news is flourishing and wildly circulated adding to more confusion and woes, even putting lives at risk. Avalanche of unreliable and false information including the origin of the virus to symptom of the disease to try unproven remedies for curing is spreading around the world to such an extent, that UNESCO, the UN Educational, Scientific and Cultural Organization, has to time and again intervene to "counter falsehood and promote facts about the virus."[6]

---

[3] https://covid19.who.int/?gclid=CjwKCAjw97P5BRBQEiwAGflV6TyR-BKaIUn0Uy2o6LrOZQ_ScgPCaZctWGN5B5-nIwmb3LGw-1A_FBoCYSAQAvD_BwE (08/08/2020).

[4] What happens if a coronavirus vaccine is never developed? It has happened before, https://edition.cnn.com/2020/05/03/health/coronavirus-vaccine-never-developed-intl/index.html (04/05/2020).

[5] "WHO chief reiterates coronavirus had natural origin," in response to President Donald Trump's allegation that the virus has its origin in China's Wuhan Virology Institute. https://www.indiatoday.in/world/story/who-chief-reiterates-coronavirus-had-natural-origin-1673535-2020-05-02 (03/05/2020).

[6] "During this coronavirus pandemic, 'fake news' is putting lives at risk: UNESCO," https://news.un.org/en/story/2020/04/1061592 (04/05/2020).

Faith Response to Covid -19 Pandemic

Coming to the responses of the faith community, from the faith perspectives, there are as well all kinds of reasons and explanations doing the rounds. There are some who openly declare that the pandemic is God's curse to the world because of the wickedness of humanity. Some even declare that God is punishing the world because of the evils of homosexuality and same sex marriages, abortions and other sins. Many more believe that it is God's doing - the fulfillment of biblical prophecies. And they predict, the end time is near! Many more believe otherwise. God is not responsible for the calamities such as this – Covid-19 pandemic. It is human made; humans are responsible. Some believe that although God is not the cause of the disease, God allows things to happen. So, we have here divergent views and explanations about the cause and reasons for such happenings.

Theologically, there is no easy answer to this pandemic. People are asking serious and critical questions. Why all this? Is God behind all this? Why so many people have to die? Why people have to suffer such loss and pain? Are humans responsible for all this? Is this because of human wickedness and sins…? Or could it be possible that things happen as they are in accordance with the laws of nature? No one really has the answer. The world continues to look for answers.

One thing we know for sure, that is, the insatiable human greed and desires for more. The earth and its resources are fast depleting and the earth is pushed to its limit. The ruthless rape of mother earth to satiate human greed and wants continues unabatedly. In the name of development and growth, limitless destruction of natural resources has resulted in the severe ecological imbalances in the world. Humans have been invading the homes and habitats of animals, birds, and other living organisms and creatures constantly as a result they have been pushed to the wall. All these have resulted in destroying the biodiversity which is critical for maintaining ecological balance. Global warming and depletion of ozone layers have devastating consequences resulting in the kind of climate change that we are experiencing today.

Human greed and desires for more know no bounds. Humans have gone even to the extent of producing and selling fake rice[7] and other potentially

---

[7] "Is 'plastic rice' for real?," "The term 'plastic rice' first surfaced in China in 2010. Dubbed the Wuchang rice scandal, Chinese officials unearthed a scam by companies who passed off ordinary rice as premium Wuchang rice by adding flavours to it. The Wuchang rice, known for its unique aroma, is exported to various nations. Chinese traders are believed to have made a huge profit through this scam. In 2011, **a report by** The Korea Times said: "Some distributors are selling fake rice in Taiyuan, Shaanxi Province, and this rice is a mixture of potatoes, sweet potatoes and plastic." Needless to say, the report mentioned in detail the hazards of eating synthetic resin. Thus the term 'plastic rice' came into existence."In India, "The Telangana Civil Supplies Department is being **flooded with complaints** about hotels in the twin cities of Hyderabad and Secunderabad using 'plastic rice' in their food items. Samples have been collected from various hotels to verify the claims. And this is not limited to Telangana alone. Over the past few years, rumours of 'plastic rice' being sold have been doing the rounds and a **public interest litigation was even filed before the Delhi**

hazardous food items for human consumption. Today, there is not a single food produce which has not been contaminated by chemicals, insecticides, pesticides and other hazardous chemicals. Human greed and desires for more has no respect for anyone; it has no respect for life.

Human greed and desires for more know no bounds. The mighty and powerful, the rich and wealthy including the big and powerful Corporations, value wealth and riches more than human life – "The winners take all." They have no qualms about destroying and trampling the poor and the powerless, their rights and dignity; no qualms in robbing and grabbing away the land, forest and other resources to which many poor indigenous people depend their lives. They have no qualms in exploiting the poor and the needy. They profess "might is right" and they are driven by their ambition, "Sky is the limit." And the irony is that the faith community justifies them in the name of prosperity theology/gospel – they claim they receive them as blessings from God!

In the name of advancing human innovation and invention, today, humans have gone even to the extent of becoming like God. Human intelligence is a wonderful gift of God. But, humans are abusing this precious and wonderful gift for their vested interests. Have humans then usurped the place of God as well? Have humans gone to the extent of deciding who should live and who should not which is the prerogative of God alone?

As the world continues to battle against this war – Covid -19 and search for answers (perhaps the world might never know the answer), one thing we know: God is love and God cares. God values life. God is just and righteous. God is compassionate and merciful. God's love is not coercive but persuasive. God suffers with us in our pain and suffering - God is our co-sufferer. The cross of Jesus is the supreme example of God's love for the world and the powerful symbol of God suffering with us. And the resurrection of Jesus Christ is the symbol of hope and life. We know, Covid – 19 pandemic is not the end, how painful and how great the loss might be. Because, we believe in the resurrection! At the same time, we know, we are called to be responsible stewards. We are ultimately accountable and answerable to God.

It must be noted that while Covid – 19 does not discriminate anyone, it will be simplistic and irresponsible to suggest that everyone is equally impacted. It is again, the poor and the needy who have been the most vulnerable and affected lots. They are vulnerable in all fronts. Economically, they are disadvantaged when it comes to testing and getting treatment (unless they are taken care by the government or concerned institutions), to take care of their families during the long drawn lockdown period, etc. Many have lost their jobs and are unemployed. Many are literally struggling for their survival. The rich and well off have always been in a much better off position in all counts; it is true even today. In India, the

---

High Court." https://www.thehindu.com/news/national/is-plastic-rice-for-real/article18761833.ece; https://www.snopes.com/fact-check/plastic-rice-from-china/ (04/05/2020).

poor migrant workers have borne the worst brunt during this lockdown period. Many have been stranded and they are caught in between. Women and children are also among the most vulnerable and affected ones. During the lockdown, cases of domestic violence against women and abuse of children in different forms have alarmingly increased across the globe.[8]

Silver Lining in the Midst of Covid - 19 Tragedy

It is said, "Every cloud has a silver lining." In the midst of the Covid -19 pandemic, as the world continues to experience painful and heart wrenching moments for the loss of their dear and loved ones and as many souls continue to battle for their lives, there are as well some bright side of the pandemic: For once, the earth and everything in it could have the long needed rest for their rejuvenation. The ecological imbalance due to human activities has been reduced. We are experiencing cleaner environment. Noise and air pollution are drastically down. The sky looks clear and cleaner. The air we breathe is cleaner, the water we drink is purer, the rivers and streams look cleaner; the flowers, plants and the whole vegetations look refreshingly beautiful; the birds, animals and all the living creatures and organisms seem to have gotten back their life again – creation is refreshingly alive!

Humanity seem to have learned anew the value of life and the limits of life; the importance and values of relationship; the importance and values of family; the importance and values of rest and health; the importance and values of time.

Humanity seem to have rediscovered their spiritual root and reconnected (spiritually) to their Source and Fountain of life – God! Humanity seem to have rediscovered the importance of prayer life and dependence on God. Humanity seem to have learned some lessons on humility and its values as well as lessons on integrity and justice.

In the midst of this pain and suffering, the world has as well experienced the good side of humanity. Many have demonstrated that humans are caring, kind, loving, willing to risk and sacrifice their lives for others; many have shared generously their resources to others, etc. The world has witnessed the best of humanity in all this as well.

---

[8] "Lockdowns around the world bring rise in domestic violence," https://www.theguardian.com/society/2020/mar/28/lockdowns-world-rise-domestic-violence (03/05/2020); "Implement steps to curb domestic violence during Covid-19 lockdown: High Court to Centre, Delhi govt," https://economictimes.indiatimes.com/news/politics-and-nation/implement-steps-to-curb-domestic-violence-during-covid-19-lockdown-high-court-to-centre-delhi-govt/articleshow/75249397.cms?from=mdr (03/05/2020).

Voices from Indigenous Peoples Around the World: What Can we Learn?

According to Indigenous leaders from around the world who gathered on March 13, in New York City, for a panel on Indigenous rights, deforestation and related health endemics, "COVID-19 and other health endemics are directly connected to climate change and deforestation."[9]

I have reproduced here the statements of the Indigenous leaders who spoke in New York City:

> *The coronavirus is telling the world what Indigenous Peoples have been saying for thousands of years — if we do not help protect biodiversity and nature, we will face this and even worse threats. The coronavirus reminds us that the balance of the Earth is in danger, and we need to maintain our delicate balance of diversity. More than 25 per cent of medicine comes from forests. If we lose our forests, we lose our medicines, too. In our communities, we have respected a certain biodiversity that protects us today. We plant what we eat, and we have the resources and knowledge needed to get through times like this, and this is what we are trying to tell the rest of the world.* [Levi Sucre Romero, a BriBri Indigenous person from Costa Rica and co-coordinator of the Mesoamerican Alliance of Peoples and Forests (AMPB)].

> *The cure for the next pandemic, and even for this one, can be found in the biodiversity of our Indigenous lands. This is why we need to protect our lands and rights, because the future of life depends on it. Indigenous Peoples are at risk for defending diversity, biodiversity, for defending our lands, protecting the environment and trying to stabilize climate change. Health endemics like coronavirus are proof of the destruction of the forests and the climate, and we will continue to fight against deforestation and related viruses, for the balance of the planet.* [Dinamam Tuxá, coordinator of the Articulation of the Indigenous Peoples of Brazil, lawyer and Indigenous social activist].

> *The orientation of our communities is sustainability. While everyone is trying to find solutions on what to do to face climate change, they look to the cities, but no one is looking at what we are doing in the villages and communities. I remember one elder told me, the problem with city people is they eat and drink dead things … they drink dead water in plastic bottles and eat dead food from supermarkets. There is no guarantee that any of it will be safe. If the world worked to strengthen the rights of*

---

[9] "COVID-19 crisis tells world what Indigenous Peoples have been saying for thousands of years," https://www.nationalobserver.com/2020/03/24/news/covid-19-crisis-tells-world-what-indigenous-peoples-have-been-saying-thousands-years (04/05/2020).

Indigenous Peoples, who have learned to live in nature and protect animal and plant species, we would see fewer epidemics such as the one we are currently facing. [Mina Setra, a Dayak Pompakng Indigenous person from West Kalimantan, Indonesia, and deputy secretary-general of the Indigenous Peoples Alliance of the Archipelago (IPAA)].

The world needs to listen to the indigenous peoples and learn from them. Indigenous knowledge and practices have been even proven and supported by science and scientific research.[10] Everything including humanity and the whole of creation are inter-related and connected. What one does therefore affects the rest. We are all connected and destined to be together.

So, what have we learned out of this Covid-19 pandemic? Or to put it differently, what has Covid – 19 pandemic to teach us?

Covid – 19 Pandemic Reminds Us to

1. *Return to the Creator God, the Source and Fountain of our life and the universe; know that our lives are in God's hand:* "Rend your hearts and not your clothing. Return to the Lord, your God, for he is gracious and merciful, slow to anger, and abounding in steadfast love, and relents from punishing." (Joel 2:13); "If my people who are called by my name humble themselves, pray, seek my face, and turn from their wicked ways, then I will hear from heaven, and will forgive their sin and heal their land," (2 Chron. 7:14).
2. *Return to the paths of repentance and seek forgiveness; abandon arrogance, domineering, exploitative, oppressive and discriminatory attitudes and ways of life:* "Seek the Lord while he may be found, call upon him while he is near; let the wicked forsake their way, and the unrighteous their thoughts; let them return to the Lord, that he may have mercy on them, and to our God, for he will abundantly pardon," (Isaiah 55:6-7); "If we say that we have no sin, we deceive ourselves, and the truth is not in us. If we confess our sins, he who is faithful and just will forgive us our sins and cleanse us from all unrighteousness." (I John 1: 8-9).
3. *Return to mother earth, who nourishes and sustains us with her abundant and bounteous produces daily:* "Then God said, 'Let the earth put forth vegetation: plants yielding seed, and fruit trees of every kind on earth that bear fruit with the seed in it.' And it was so. The earth brought forth vegetation: plants yielding seed of every kind, and trees of every kind bearing fruit with the seed in it. And God saw that it was good." (Gen. 1:11-12); "The Lord will make you abound in prosperity, in the fruit of your womb, in the fruit of your livestock, and in the fruit of your ground in the land that the Lord swore to your ancestors to give

[10] *Ibid.*

you. The Lord will open for you his rich storehouse, the heavens, to give the rain of your land in its season and to bless all your undertakings," (Deut. 28:11-12).

4. *Return to the attitude of respect for all humanity and the whole of creation; know that everything is inter-related and connected:* "In the day that the Lord God made the earth and the heavens, when no plant of the field was yet in the earth and no herb of the field had yet sprung up—for the Lord God had not caused it to rain upon the earth, and there was no one to till the ground; but a stream would rise from the earth, and water the whole facc of the ground—then the Lord God formed man from the dust of the ground, and breathed into his nostrils the breath of life; and the man became a living being," (Gen. 2:4b-7). In fact the whole chapter is about inter-relatedness of cosmos, humankind and creation.
5. *Return to choose and value life:* "I call heaven and earth to witness against you today that I have set before you life and death, blessings and curses. Choose life so that you and your descendants may live," (Deut. 30:19); "The thief comes only to steal and kill and destroy. I came that they may have life, and have it abundantly," (John 10:10); "For the wages of sin is death, but the free gift of God is eternal life in Christ Jesus our Lord," (Rom. 6: 23).
6. *Return to the attitude of humility, love and service*: "Blessed are the meek, for they will inherit the earth." (Matt. 5:5); "Do nothing from selfish ambition or conceit, but in humility regard others as better than yourselves. Let each of you look not to your own interests, but to the interests of others. Let the same mind be in you that was in Christ Jesus, who, though he was in the form of God, did not regard equality with God as something to be exploited, but emptied himself, taking the form of a slave, being born in human likeness. And being found in human form, he humbled himself and became obedient to the point of death—even death on a cross," (Phil. 2:4-8).
7. *Return to the life of justice and righteousness*: "Blessed are those who hunger and thirst for righteousness, for they will be filled." (Matt. 5:4); "But let justice roll down like waters, and righteousness like an ever-flowing stream," (Amos 5:24); "He has told you, O mortal, what is good; and what does the Lord require of you but to do justice, and to love kindness, and to walk humbly with your God?" (Micah 6: 8).
8. *Return to the need based life style and sharing of resources; abandon human greed and unlimited wants:* "The earth is the Lord's, and everything in it, the world, and all who live in it," (Ps. 24:1). "Command those who are rich in this present world not to be arrogant nor to put their hope in wealth, which is so uncertain, but to put their hope in God, who richly provides us with everything for our enjoyment. Command them to do

good, to be rich in good deeds, and to be generous and willing to share. In this way they will lay up treasure for themselves as a firm foundation for the coming age, so that they may take hold of the life that is truly life," (I Tim. 6 17-19).

9. *Return to value rest and quality of life*: "And on the seventh day God finished the work that he had done, and he rested on the seventh day from all the work that he had done. So God blessed the seventh day and hallowed it, because on it God rested from all the work that he had done in creation." (Gen. 2: 2-3); "But in the seventh year there shall be a sabbath of complete rest for the land, a sabbath for the Lord: you shall not sow your field or prune your vineyard. You shall not reap the after growth of your harvest or gather the grapes of your unpruned vine: it shall be a year of complete rest for the land," (Lev. 25:4-5).
10. *Return to the attitude of grateful hearts and grateful living before God*: "And let the peace of Christ rule in your hearts, to which indeed you were called in the one body. And be thankful." (Col. 3:15); "The Lord is my strength and my shield; in him my heart trusts; so I am helped, and my heart exults, and with my song I give thanks to him," Ps. 28:7); "Finally, brothers and sisters, whatever is true, whatever is noble, whatever is right, whatever is pure, whatever is lovely, whatever is admirable—if anything is excellent or praiseworthy—think about such things," (Phil. 4:8).

This book is about inviting people to have a serious introspection of our faith, life and the values of our life. It is about rethinking faith, theology and mission in the midst of the deadly Covid – 19 pandemic and contemporary realities. It is about faith seeking transformation! The book consists of 15 chapters and they have been written, some presented and discussed in seminars and consultations at different occasions and times. And most of them have been published in journals and edited books. However, I have substantially revised and updated them in keeping with the change of time and context. As you read them, you will find that each chapter raises critical questions on issues of life, faith, ethics, theology, morality and values of life – on the whole existential questions of our time.

The book begins with/by introducing tribal theology as a contextual theology in the first chapter. It reiterates that all theologies, whether past or present, are contextual. Theology is a human discipline. Every theological articulation or construction is therefore a search for relevance in a given time and situation. There is no theology that is universal or claim to have universal relevance for all people. It raises the need for situating faith and theology in a particular context and situation. It also defines tribal theology, gives its historical context and its development and implications for faith and ministry.

Chapter 2 deals with the issues and challenges of tribal theology as well as delves deeper into the question of the grounding of tribal theology. It argues that tribal theology is grounded on the belief that "God became human and dwelled among us" and "Creation in the image of God." It further argues that Christian faith being an incarnational faith, tribal Christian theology must as well be rooted and incarnated in the cultural soil of the tribal people. It identifies the impacts of the history of colonization and missionization and the kind of theology inherited from the Christian west and others as factors confronting tribal theology. It also addresses the problem of conceptual framework and terminology of tribal theology. This chapter attempts to address the misgivings people have towards tribal theology.

Chapter 3 examines the methodological issues of theology and in particular that of contextual theology. The chapter begins with a brief appraisal of the meaning of method and methodology and some of the methodological assumptions in research in general and theological research in particular. While some theologies are dogmatic and apologetic, those such as liberation and or contextual theology place the emphasis on praxis. It also delineates the difference between traditional theology and contextual theology and espouses the necessity for the methodology of contextual theology for relevant articulation of theology. It examines the various models of contextual theology and argues for taking into consideration postcolonial situation and indigenous people's space and eco-worldview in addressing the methodology of contextual theology.

Chapter 4 deals with the sources of tribal theology. It argues why it is necessary to locate tribal theology in the socio-cultural and political context of the tribal people. Subsequently, it identifies tribal cultural and social heritages together with Christian heritages as important sources for doing tribal theology. For the indigenous people, oral tradition serves as the "Prime Bible." And they include the past and the present, socio-cultural tradition, customs, religious beliefs and practices. They include myths and legend, folktales and stories, wisdom and proverbs, mores and morals, songs and so on.

The succeeding chapters 5-7 locate theology and faith in the context of the entire spectrum of the people's world. They talk about the conceptualization and developing of faith and theology in light of the whole creation as opposed to traditional theology that foregrounds and privileges humanity over creation. Chapter 5 develops a theology of land. It begins with the assertion of the holistic worldview of the Nagas, around which revolves the total being of the people – their personality, thinking and outlook. Their spirituality is intrinsically connected to it. Then a research into the Naga tribal/indigenous concept of land follows. This is followed by a brief study of the biblical understanding of land. Finally, with the resources drawn from tribal traditions and the Bible, an attempt is made to develop a theology of land.

Chapter 6 is an attempt to develop eco-theology that affirms the inter-relatedness and connectedness of the whole of creation in the context of ecological crisis and imbalances perpetuated by human greed and wants. It examines the impact of ecological crisis on the tribal/indigenous people of the Northeast India. For this I intend to examine the socio-cultural and religious traditions, worldviews, creation myths, and rituals and rites of the tribal people. The tribals are known to be close with the nature and their worldview is highly creation centered. The tribals view everything to be in relations. Everything including God-human-world is believed to be inter-related. Therefore, examining and understanding tribal worldview is critical for articulating a relevant and meaningful eco-theology. Further, their traditions of agricultural taboos (rituals) and other related practices offer rich resources for developing such an important theology.

Chapter 7 is an examination as well as an articulation of the theology of rights – human rights in the context of the whole creation and inter-human relationship. It postulates that human rights cannot be conceived apart from the rights of the whole creation. The chapter is broadly divided into two sections. The first section deals with human rights in relation to the rights of the whole creation. The second deals with human rights in the context of human relationships. Traditional Tangkhul practices and beliefs contain a number of values that protect and promote human rights and the rights of the whole creation. Basic to their understanding is the all-important eco-worldview. The chapter ends by affirming that rights are indivisible. They are all interrelated. This is the affirmation of the Tangkhuls and the biblical faith. In this final analysis human dignity can be found only in relationship with fellow human beings and the whole creation.

Chapter 8 deals with the socio-political, economic and religious situations of the people in Northeast India. It particularly looks at the overall situations of the tribal/Adivasi people given the fact that they are the most vulnerable and affected ones. It discusses the conflict situations embroiling the region; looks at the various "insurgency" movements for political independence and self determination and other identity politics, including the recent CAA imbroglio in the nation, especially the region, and at the end offers a religio-theological response to all this.

Chapters 9 argues for rethinking the whole understanding of mission today. Mission has been often narrowly understood in anthropocentric sense in terms of saving human souls alone. Mission is God's mission. And God's mission is for the whole person – spiritual and physical –and for the whole creation and not simply for humanity alone. It affirms the importance of conceiving mission holistically including the understanding of mission mandate. Biblically and theologically, God's mission begins and ends with the plan to save the whole creation and providing life in fullness to all. By way of illustration, the chapter captures and recaptures the holistic redemptive promises (salvation of the whole creation including humanity) of God in the Bible.

In chapter 10, I have dealt at length how climate change and climate justice are intrinsically connected to human attitude and relationship with the whole of creation. From the indigenous people's point of view, climate change the consequence of ecological crisis, is about disruptions of relationships between and among the whole of creation. It is about breaking the balance and harmony that is critical to wholesome relationship of all beings. The chapter therefore, looks at the dimension of tribal worldview and its implications for addressing climate change and justice in our society today.

Chapter 11 explores the theme of liberation in the works of some selected theologians. These theologians come from a wide spectrum of theological traditions representing differing theological view points and time, and as well their understanding of liberation in their theological articulations. The question of the relationship between salvation and human liberation will receive a critical attention in our discussion. The chapter begins with a brief introduction about the emergence of liberation as a theological theme in liberation theology.

Chapter 12 explores and examines prosperity theology and its overall challenge to the understanding of Christian faith and praxis. Prosperity theology or gospel is a collective term for a group of teachings that liken Christian faith with material, and particularly financial success. It is the understanding of faith that centres on wealth and riches, health and happiness as the blessings from God. It emphasizes on the individual ability, gifts, talents and success. They are mostly popular among charismatic preachers and Christians in the so called evangelical tradition. The purpose of this chapter is to offer a theological critique on the overall prosperity theology movement. It also briefly looks at the historical origin and development of prosperity theology, its meaning, and the kind of impact it makes to the overall Christian faith and practice.

In chapter 13, I offer a theological critique against the all pervasive evil called corruption. The chapter begins with defining corruption and understanding corruption, its causes and consequences and its manifestation in various forms. This is followed by theological response to corruption. Ethically and theologically, corruption is a crime and sin. Corruption basically refers to the breaking of integrity, morality, dishonesty of every kind, debasement and depravity in private as well as public life. Corruption is the one most critical issue of our time; it has always been of course. And therefore, it is a critical theological and faith concern for us. And this calls for a serious theological reflection and consideration.

Chapter 14 is a critical exploration into the relation between ethics and development. It raises questions such as what is the pertinence of ethics to debates about development? What is development? In this chapter, I argue that the answer to this question is determined and shaped by one's worldviews and beliefs about the nature of human beings. Our perceptions about life, creation, and the world are deeply influenced by the way we understand ourselves, our communities and the world. This examination is undertaken at the back drop of the Millennium

Development Goals (MDG) report 2000 and Corporate Scandals which have rocked the economic system of the world, affecting disproportionately the poor and the weak. The chapter argues that the modern economy which is based on capitalist ideology and which promotes development as growth and maximizing benefits is the one root cause of the inequalities in the world.

Chapter 15 makes a critical investigation into the churches' response to the challenges of globalization in the Northeast region. Globalization is and has been an all pervasive force impacting our world and society. And of course, it has always been the poor and the weak, who are the worst affected lots. In this chapter, I argue the churches response has not been encouraging. The responses range from no action to making or adopting resolutions/statements against forces of globalization. And that the problems confronting us is at the core a spiritual problem, and that any solution or action plan we propose must be based on the faith and moral values of the people. The chapter ends with some proposals of action plans for responding to the challenges of globalization.

In the spirit of resilience and hope, demonstrated by millions of people in the midst of this terrible and deadly Covid – 19 pandemic, and in solidarity with all those who have been affected by this disease, the book implores us to revisit our faith, theology, mission, ethics and morality and meaning of life and to reexamine ourselves. It calls for faith seeking transformation!

Chapter 1

Introducing Tribal Theology
A Case for Contextual Theology

1. Introduction

Some of you could be hearing the term "tribal theology"[1] for the first time and it may sound to be something new. And you might be wondering what this theology is all about and why it was formed. However, tribal theology should not and need not be a new thing for us to be discovering today. After all, we are all practitioners of tribal theology insofar as we are involved in making the gospel message relevant to our tribal context; insofar as we are engaged in relating the biblical texts to the tribal people's life experiences by way of preaching, Bible studies, and so on. We are all, in this sense, tribal theologians insofar as we are engaged in proclaiming the good news of the Kingdom of God in tribal languages and dialects – adapting

[1] Throughout this book, I will be referring to the Tribals in the North East India and other Indigenous peoples using the terms "Indigenous" and "Tribal" interchangeably. While the Indigenous populations in India are commonly referred to as "Tribals", they are all integral members of the world's Indigenous community. My consistent use of Indigenous-Tribal/Tribe reference affirms that membership and its fundamental relationships and my use of the terms interchangeably will reduce much confusion. Secondly, tribals in the Northeast India are themselves indigenous people, meaning they are the native people of the land. The term tribe or tribal is an imposed term given to the indigenous people of the Northeast India by the colonizers and Western anthropologists and sociologists. Additionally, the Indian Government, for the administrative purposes, has simply categorized the indigenous people in the region as "Scheduled Tribe." The people never called themselves as tribals; they know each other by their own ethnic names such as Sumis, Khasis, Garos, Tangkhuls, Boros, Mizos, Adis, Wanchos etc.

tribal cultural categories for communicating the gospel to the tribal Christians. In any event, whenever there have been attempts to find the meaning and relevance of the Christian faith in the light of people's experiences, we are engaging in tribal theology. In this sense, we are all doing tribal theology; the irony is that we have been in the process of theologising without identifying it as engaging in "tribal theology."

2. Tribals of North-East India

The north-east India is located in the far eastern corner of India sharing an international boundary of 5,182 kilometres (3,220 miles) with the neighboring countries: Myanmar in the east, Tibet and China in the north, Bhutan in the northwest, Nepal in the west and Bangladesh in the southwest. The region is comprised of eight states - seven contiguous sister states of Arunachal Pradesh, Assam, Manipur, Meghalaya, Mizoram, Nagaland and Tripura, and the Himalayan state of Sikkim - which are home to large indigenous/tribal communities comprising of many tribes and ethnic groups with their own languages, ways of life, and histories. As it has been rightly described, the north-east India is a nation within a nation in which more than two hundred twenty ethnically diverse groups live. According to the 2011 census, the region has 45. 58 million population comprising of the scheduled tribes, scheduled castes and general population.[2]

In relation to India, the north-east states are connected with the rest of the country by a narrow strip of land that is often called "chicken's neck" – because it is long and narrow, which is officially known as Siliguri corridor (wide about 22 kms.) of West Bengal. However, this narrow strip of land has come to symbolise much more than virtually meatless part of chicken's anatomy; the real significance of this "neck" is that it symbolises the profound isolation, neglect, and exploitation the people of this region suffer at the hands of the Central government. The alienation, exploitation, and neglect resulting from decades of underdevelopment have produced far-reaching consequences in the lives of the people. The lack of substantial development projects on the one hand, and the processes of globalisation on the other, have created precarious and even deadly situations for the majority of these people.

Ethnologically, the tribals in the north-east India belong to the Australoid, Caucasoid, and Indo-Mongoloid (Tibetan-Burman speaking) racial groups. In general, the tribes can be categorised as comprising two broad divisions – the hills tribes and the plains tribes. The hills tribes consist of various groups of the Mizo-Kuki-Chin family, Nagas, Khasis, Garos, and Arunachalis and they reside in the states of Mizoram, Tripura, Nagaland, Manipur, Meghalaya, and Arunachal Pradesh respectively. Most of the hills tribals have been heavily Christianised

---

[2] http://www.census2011.co.in:80/states.php; Singh, comp., *Basic Statistics of North Eastern Region* 2015, xxvii.

with the exception of Arunachalis who have been isolated and protected from the influence of Christian missionaries by the Indian government. Prior to their conversion to Christianity, the tribals practiced what can be called a primal religion, which is very often incorrectly classified as animism. In contrast, the plains tribals are concentrated primarily in the Brahmaputra and Barak Valleys of Assam, Manipur Valley and plains in Tripura. Most of these tribals have been Hinduised and assimilated into the Hindu culture, but some have been more strongly influenced by Islam, and there are others follow Buddhism and traditional religions.

There is another tribal group known as the *adivasis*, who were either brought to the region by the British, or they migrated to the north-east to work as labourers for tea plantations. Having come from Orissa, Bihar, and Andhra Pradesh, especially most of them either belong to the Munda speaking family or the Dravidian speaking family.

3. Theology is a Human Discipline

Theology is a human discipline. It is human efforts to articulate theology in the light of the faith experiences of the people in a given social context. It must be reiterated that all theologies in the world, whether of the past or the present, are contextual by nature; there is no theology that can claim to have universal relevance for all people and for all time. Every theology is context-based and therefore limited. Every theological articulation or construction is therefore a search for relevance in a given time and situation.

4. Development of Tribal Theology

The term tribal theology and its cognates became popular when it was introduced as a formal theological discipline in theological colleges and seminaries. Tribal theology as a formal theological discipline is, of course, a recent development and phenomenon. The development of tribal/indigenous theology can be traced back to the later part of the 1980s and the early part of the 1990s when tribal theologians such as Nirmal Minz, Renthy Keitzar, followed by K. Thanzauva, Wati Longchar, and others, began looking at theology from the perspectives of the tribal people. Of course, to a large extent, Thanzauva and Longchar are responsible for the shaping and development of tribal theology in the north-east India.

It must also be pointed out that the opening of Tribal Study Centres at the Eastern Theological College in 1995 and Aizawl Theological College in 2000 respectively was a decisive epoch-making history; the setting up of the Tribal Study Centre signaled the emergence of tribal theology in theological arena in the region and within the Senate of Serampore College. It also signaled the seriousness of articulating the tribal Christian faith in the light of the peoples' experiences and social realities. Since then tribal theology has come a long way.

Today, because of the hard labour of many, we have produced and developed highly articulate tribal theology. There is already a wide recognition from within and outside tribal Christians of the development of tribal theology. In fact, one could, without doubt, acknowledge the crucial contribution tribal theologians are making to the overall theological developments in India.

Perhaps, it might be presumptuous on our part to think that it's only those within the Senate of Serampore College who are engaged in tribal theology. After all, there are also many church leaders and theological educators outside the Serampore set-up who are engaged in it.

5. What is Tribal Theology?

It must be reiterated that all theologies in the world, whether of the past or of the present, are contextual by nature; there is no theology that is universal or claim to have universal relevance. Every theology is context-based and therefore limited. Every theological articulation or construction is therefore a search for relevance in a given time and situation.

5.1 Contextual Theology

Tribal theology may be defined as a critical reflection on the faith experiences of the tribal people in the light of their sociopolitical and economic and religious situations. It is a critical reflection on the interaction between the gospel and the tribal culture over the past one hundred years or so and the struggle for liberation from all forms of oppression and domination.[3] Tribal/indigenous theology, like any other contextual theology, takes seriously the socio-political context of the people. It holds creation as well as human situatedness as the starting point of theology with intent to develop a theology that is contextually relevant, meaningful, and empowering to the people. The act of doing theology can be understood as reflections on the faith of our fathers and mothers. However, more often than not, theology reflects the Christian traditions (Bible and Christian traditions) in their strict sense. Very little importance is given to the traditions of our own fathers and mothers except to the degree that they are condemned as evil and devilish. Tribal theology affirms the goodness of the tribal culture. It reiterates the faith that God has been and still is present in the cultural life of the tribal people. It affirms that the Bible together with the life experiences and the traditional cultural resources of the tribal people are the primary sources and datum for developing tribal theology.

5.2 Theology of Culture

As a contextual theology, it seeks to reflect on the faith experiences of the tribal people on the one hand, and to re-appropriate the liberative and life affirming

[3] K. Thanzauva, "Issues in Tribal Theology," in Shimreingam Shimray, ed., *Tribal Theology: A Reader*. Tribal Study Series No. 12 (Jorhat: Tribal Study Centre, 2003), 17.

cultural values for theological reflection on the other. Rediscovery of tribal cultural and religious values is therefore a critical function of tribal theology. This process involves a critical evaluation of tribal cultures and traditions. Additionally, the critical point of departure for this theology is the matrix of tribal worldview. The tribal/indigenous worldview is characterised by the inter-relatedness of all things, and it recognises and values the harmony between humanity and nature. So creation, and not merely human beings, serves as the starting point of tribal theology. The entire reality of life, including our understanding of God and spirituality, has to be seen within the perspectives of our relatedness with all creation. Tribal theology is a theology of culture and liberation at once; after all, tribal theology deals with the totality of life and it seeks for liberation from all forms of bondages.

5.3 Theology of Liberation and Healing

Indigenous theology is a theology of liberation. As a liberation theology, it seeks to take seriously the liberative messages which are essential to the Bible for our faith reflection and articulation. God's act of liberation in the Exodus event and throughout the history of Israel, the prophetic messages of liberation in the Old Testament, and, above all, Jesus' own declaration of his ministry as that of bringing good news to the poor, release to the captives, and sight to the blind, demand that if a tribal theology is faithful to the liberative act of God it must be a theology of liberation and healing. The tribals in the northeast India have been struggling for liberation in all dimensions of life – politically, socially, economically, religiously, and morally.

Politically, the existence of a number of "insurgent" groups who operate in a high state of tension with the pervasive presence of Indian armed forces – often leading to violence and bloodsheds and human rights abuses – mark the extremity of the volatile situation of the region. Factional violence, ethnic clashes, and tribal feuds have brought untold sufferings into the lives of the people in the region. Another problem is that, today, more than ever, the region is faced with the high incidence of HIV/AIDS infections. The prevalence of HIV/AIDS in the region is considered to be one of the highest in India. We need liberation and healing from all the structural, corporate, and social sins in addition to our personal sins and aggressions. We need the spirit of reconciliation and peace to prevail among our people. Therefore, indigenous theology must be a theology of liberation and healing. As part of its holistic vision, tribal/indigenous theology is committed to the "integral liberation of persons and structures" emerging out of the involvement and participation in the struggles of the oppressed and the search for a just and peaceful world.

5.4 Theology of Identity

Tribal/indigenous theology is also necessary for the sake of establishing and maintaining our tribal/indigenous Christian identity; this indigenous Christian identity can emerge only when we are willing to respectfully reclaim our cultures and histories in the light of our faith expression. Basic to our identity as a people is the affirmation that we are created in the image of God. This affirmation is critical in the context when tribal people's attitudes toward themselves are for a great deal influenced by the long history of colonisation and missionisation. In the context when the feeling of inferiority and self debasement and by extension their aversion to anything that is of their past, affirmation of the theology of *Imago Dei* becomes significant. The feeling of inferiority and low self-esteem has been deeply ingrained in the minds and souls of the tribal people for long. As a result, tribals regard themselves as inferior to other fellow human beings. Most of all, such feeling has led many to believe that God has created them inferior to others. In other words, at the extreme, such understanding has led them to believe that God has destined them to be where and what they are now. Being created in the image of God means that we all belong to God and we are all children of God. Being created in God's image means, as tribals, we also share the glory of God's creation.

It is precisely in this sense that we claim that tribal theology is an affirmation and celebration of dignity and worth of every created being. Tribal theology is then an affirmation and celebration of the beauty of God's creation. Tribal theology affirms and celebrates the beautiful cultures of tribal people. It is on this ground that we reclaim the cultural past of indigenous people rather than condemning them as evil and devilish. Indigenous theology is therefore a theology of identity: it raises the question of who we are as Christians. Are we tribal Christians or something else?

5.5 Theology of Social Transformation

One of the emerging visions of tribal/indigenous theology is undeniably the social transformation in the light of Kingdom values. Total transformation of society in the light of the Kingdom values must go hand in hand with liberation. In a way, liberation and transformation are two sides of the same coin – there can be no transformation without liberation and vice versa. While the talk of liberation and transformation from socio-economic and political oppression and injustice is critical, that in itself is inadequate, unless we relate to the issues of creation and ecology. It is critically important to recognise the interconnectedness of all creation including humanity so that we are able to address and engage the issues in an informed and holistic manner.

6. Tribal Theology: Implications for Tribal Christians and Ministry

It is important for us to focus our attention to the implications of tribal theology for theological education, tribal Christians, and local congregations. This will have a great deal of educational and ministerial bearings in the context of tribal Christians insofar as tribal theology endeavors to be relevant and meaningful. I have identified the following areas where tribal theology can have significant implications for theological education, Christian ministry, and tribal Christians.

6.1. Identity of Tribal Christians

This raises the important question as to who we are. Most of us would identify ourselves as Christians. But, the critical question is: are you a tribal Christian or a Euro-American Christian, or something else? Very often we live and behave as though we belong to somewhere else and from somewhere else. Whereas, the fact is that we are tribals and therefore tribal Christians. Tribal theology seeks to inculcate in the minds of tribal Christians this important dimension of our life. Tribal theology helps us affirm that we are tribal Christians and that there is nothing to be ashamed of being one.

6.2. Tribal Worldview and Tribal Christian Spirituality

This is another important area where tribal theology seeks to have a significant impact in the lives of tribal Christians. The tribal worldview affirms the wholeness of life, that is, tribal theology makes no distinction between what is secular and sacred, earthly and heavenly, mundane life and spiritual life. This worldview in this sense is very Christian and goes in line with the teaching of Jesus Christ. True spirituality according to the teaching of Jesus Christ is to live in tune with the values of the Kingdom of God. To practice what we preach and teach in our everyday life.

An objective observation of contemporary tribal Christian life and its spirituality tells us entirely a different story. Influenced by the Western Christian worldview, which tends to maintain sharp distinction between the secular and the sacred, earthly and spiritual life, tribal Christians have compartmentalised their Christian life into secular and religious lives. In other words, tribal Christians assume that what we do in the Sunday worship life has nothing to do with the day-to-day life activities of the week. There are many contradictions in the ways tribal Christians live and behave. Tribal theology attempts to remind tribal Christians that true spirituality makes no distinction between what is secular and sacred, what is worship life and outside the Sunday worship life. Tribal theology reminds that the tribal worldview is not necessarily evil, that rather it goes in line with the Kingdom values that Jesus proclaimed and exhorted His followers to live by. True spirituality must be understood as a way of life – a way of living inspired by the power of the Holy Spirit.

6.3. Tribal Theology and Integrity of Creation

The tribal worldview affirms the integrity of all creation and sacredness of life. It affirms the inter-relatedness of all creation. The well-being of all creation including that of human beings depends on preserving and restoring of the harmonious inter-relationships of all creation. All living creatures, including humans, are meant to work toward maintaining balance and harmony and these are to be seen as the ultimate concern of all beings. Indigenous peoples claim they have reciprocal relationships with all living things, which includes the so-called "inanimate" objects such as rocks, plants, and other natural forms. Everything is imbued with spirit so all is sacred for tribal/indigenous peoples. Because all creation is sacred, the very land we walk and till must be treated with respect and reverence. Therefore, they treat life and creation with respect and reverence. In the context of the so called global warming and ecological and environmental crises, the tribal/indigenous wisdom on maintaining balance and harmony with all creation becomes all the more important. Doesn't the Christian Bible also teach about responsible stewardship of all God's creation?

6.4. Tribal Theology and Worship

Worship plays a very important role in the life of a believing community. However, there is no single pattern or style of worship that could claim to have universal validity for all people and for all times. The style of worship varies from one place and community to another. While some churches prefer to follow liturgical and strict, written worship order, others are more comfortable with free-style worship where minimum order is followed. While some Christians prefer standing at all times, others feel more comfortable sitting or kneeling down during the worship. Moreover, we find Christians whose worship is highly intellectual and the mood of the worship is characterised by minimum emotions. On the other hand, there are Christian worships which are emotionally charged and in such worships people rely on spontaneous response to God's love. In all this, we find that people's culture and tradition influence a great deal in the way one chooses to worship. Usually, Africans, Asians, and other tribal/indigenous communities in the world are by nature quite emotional and this is clearly reflected in the way people worship God. For example, the worship styles of the Afro-Americans and White Americans are very different from each other; while the former prefer free-flowing worship where emotions are expressed freely and profoundly, the worship of the latter is characterised by a quiet and systematic order.

Tribal Christians in the north-east have until this day followed the worship patterns which have been introduced by the early Christian missionaries, whether they were Baptists, Presbyterians or otherwise. It is widely held that traditional Christian worship systems we have inherited from the missionaries are the only valid ways of worshiping God. And even if at all new elements of worship are to be introduced, they must be from the Christian West. Our contemporary worship is thus filled with elements such as praise and worship and others which have come to us from the West.

There is nothing wrong in appropriating new forms of worship in the changing context of our time, appealing to the taste and likings of the young generations of worshippers. However, the view that anything that comes from the West is Christian and anything that concerns with tribal culture and traditions is un-Christian is a serious concern we need to address. Tribal theology seeks to address some of such misconceptions by appealing to the goodness of God's creation manifested in the cultures of the tribal people. After all, what matters in worship is this: "God is Spirit and those who worship him must do so in spirit and in truth."

6.5. Tribal Theology and Indigenous Music

The same goes with the way tribals view traditional, indigenous songs and music. Here again, until recently, traditional songs and music are viewed with suspicion and negatively. Perhaps, most tribal Christians continue to resist introducing indigenous music in their churches' worship. Whereas they have no problem whatsoever with any kind of music that comes from the Christian West. People have no problem listening to or playing the guitar and praising God during the church worship. Whereas, until recently, many tribal Christians were opposed to using traditional instrumental music, such as that from drums and singing of songs in traditional melodies and tunes. Tribal theology endeavors to affirm the beauty and goodness of the God-given cultures of the tribal people and that they are equally valuable in the sight of God; and that they are appropriate for use in praising and worshiping God.

6.6 Tribal Theology and Biblical Interpretation

One important ministerial concern is lack of responsible interpretation of the Bible in a given situation. Traditional biblical interpretation has been heavily influenced by the so-called historical-critical method of interpretation. In the traditional method of interpretation, one first looks at the text critically and followed by the application of the text to the readers' situation. Whereas, contemporary reading of the Scripture, particularly among the Third World scholars, that is gaining currency is the contextual reading of the Scripture. According to this, the context or situation of the reader is primary; one approaches the text from the perspectives of the reader. In other words, the readers' context serves as the primary datum for the interpretation of the Bible.

Tribal theology, here again, works towards finding appropriate methods of reading and interpreting the Scripture which will take seriously the sensibilities and concerns of the tribal people. Secondly, biblical hermeneutics or interpretation has always been influenced by the cultural underpinnings of the reader. Here the cultural milieu of the people and their cultural worldview and orientation play a great role. For example, the Euro-American biblical interpretation has always been greatly influenced by their worldview in which time is given primacy over space. Their view of temporality serves as the basis of their biblical interpretation. Accordingly, the question "when" is always given precedence over "where" in their interpretation. Whereas, the tribal worldview is space and creation oriented. Moreover, whereas the Euro-American worldview has been highly individualistic, tribal/indigenous people are community oriented. And therefore, in the former, salvation is narrowly understood in terms of individual salvation and faith; social and corporate dimension of salvation is less emphasised. For the tribal Christians, a relevant and responsible interpretation of the Bible might be to take into serious account some of these important cultural sensibilities of the tribal people.

6.7 Tribal Theology and Ministry of Healing and Reconciliation

This is another important area where tribal theology attempts to articulate a relevant and meaningful theology of healing and reconciliation, a ministry that is both faithful to the cultural sensibilities of the people and the Christian faith. We all know that factional violence, ethnic clashes, and tribal feuds have brought untold sufferings into the lives of the people in our region. Another problem is that of the high prevalence of HIV/AIDS infections.

7. Conclusion

The purpose of tribal theology is to articulate a living and empowering theology in the light of the given realities of the tribal people. A living and empowering theology like ours can emerge only when we are willing to respectfully reclaim our rich heritage and appropriate them in our theologising enterprise. Doing theology involves an important dimension of defining who we are as a people and a faith community. And this profoundly significant dimension of theology can emerge only when we are truly committed to our traditions and the Bible. By way of concluding, I would like to summarize what tribal theology is in the following affirmations:

- Tribal theology affirms that all human beings including tribal people are created in the image of God; it affirms the dignity and freedom of every human being;
- Tribal theology affirms the goodness and beauty of God's creation; that the goodness of God's creation includes tribal people's cultures and traditions;
- Tribal theology affirms that the beauty of God's creation is found in diversity and not in uniformity;
- Tribal theology believes in glorifying God by using the beautiful cultures and traditions of the tribal people;
- Tribal theology believes in the interconnectedness of all beings and creations;

- Tribal theology believes and affirms salvation of the whole person – physical, spiritual, mental, and social as well; it affirms in God's redeeming work of the whole of creation in and through the cosmic Christ;
- Tribal theology affirms the Bible and tribal cultures including tribal people's experience and context as important sources of tribal theology;
- Tribal theology works toward making the Gospel of Jesus Christ relevant and meaningful to the people; it works toward making tribal Christian faith to be natural, contemporary, relevant and authentic in Christ.

Chapter 2

Tribal Theology
Issues and Challenges

Synopsis

This chapter discusses issues and challenges confronting tribal theology especially from within. Tribal theology is a product of the self theologizing endeavors of the tribal Christians in India, especially in the Northeast India. It is a theology articulated and reflected by the people, for the people and of the people, taking into consideration the contextual realities as well as the experiences of the tribal people. Tribal theology has come a long way and it is still yet to go along way. As a self theologizing expression of faith, without a doubt, tribal theology stands for the maturity of the tribal Christians and their faith. On the other hand, tribal theology still remains quite alien to many tribal Christians. There are still many challenges confronting tribal theology. One single most challenge is on the question of how tribal theology could become a theology of the people accepted, embraced and affirmed by the people as their own theological expression of faith. Undeniably, there is still a huge disconnect between academia and the people at the local congregational level when it comes to the understanding of tribal theology. There are multiple factors for this predicament.

Introduction

Tribal theology is a product of the self theologizing endeavors of the tribal Christians in India, especially in the Northeast India. It is a theology articulated and reflected by the people, for the people and of the people, taking into consideration the contextual realities as well as the experiences of the tribal people. Tribal theology has come a long way and it is still yet to go along way. As a self theologizing expression of faith, without a doubt, tribal theology stands for the maturity of the tribal Christians and their faith. Today, because of the hard labor of many, we have produced and developed highly articulate tribal theology. There is already a wide recognition from within and outside tribal Christians of the development of tribal theology. In fact, one could without doubt, acknowledge the important contribution tribal theologians are making to the over all theological developments in India in general as well.

On the other hand, tribal theology still remains quite alien to many tribal Christians. There is no denying of the kind of distrust/mistrust people have towards tribal theology and those who are associated with it. There is no denying of the animosity generated by tribal theology. People in general even including theological educators, unfortunately, tend to have negative views about tribal theology; this is still the case with the so-called tribal Christians themselves. At the extreme, tribal theology is treated almost like an anathema in many of the local churches in Northeast India. People at the congregational level have preconceived notions and misinformed views about tribal theology. While, many accuse tribal theology of going back to the old tribal religion, many simply regard it as nothing more than a mere theological phenomenon which will fast fade away. There is a serious disconnect between the academy and the church. There seems to be a serious disconnect between the message and the messenger on the one hand, and the recipients of the message on the other. This is no a little ironic in the sense that theology by definition is supposed to serve the needs of the church and community. A theologian is understood as someone who does theology on behalf of and for the sake of the church. The task of theology is to attend to the concerns and aspirations of the believing community – the people of God. Whereas, the believing community at the congregational level, till this day continue to harbor negative views of tribal theology.

This raises important questions: does this mean that tribal theology is merely an academic exercise, as it is assumed by many to be, with no real commitment to the concerns and aspirations of the church and tribal society at large? Could it be the case that the grounding of tribal theology is and has never been clear to the people including the theologians themselves? Have the proponents of this supposedly living and empowering theology failed in communicating the right message to the people at the congregational level? Have the proponents of tribal theology been failing to speak the language of those ordinary masses/villagers for whom and whose behalf theology is being done? What is it that the ordinary folks in the villages are looking and aspiring for which unfortunately many of us have not been able to so far discern and gauge? What is it that majority tribal Christians want their theology to be?

To say the least, the phrase tribal theology has evoked interesting queries both from within and without tribal Christians. What is tribal theology? Why tribal theology? As Christians why do we need another theology? Is tribal theology different from Christian theology? What is the purpose or goal of tribal theology? These are obviously relevant and serious questions which deserve earnest and close attention. In light of all this, it will be prudent on our part to raise hard questions and revisit tribal theology. There are still many challenges confronting tribal theology. One single most challenge is on the question of how tribal theology could become a theology of the people accepted, embraced and affirmed by the people as their own theological expression of faith. Undeniably, there is still a huge disconnect between academia and the people at the local congregational level when it comes to the understanding of tribal theology. There is not just one single factor for this predicament. And to understand this, I would like to identify the following factors for our consideration.

I
The Grounding of Tribal Theology

It is critical to ask, what is the basis of tribal theology? What is the grounding of tribal theology? Tribal theology is defined as a critical reflection of faith on the basis of people's experiences and social realities. Theologians – you and me – might assume that such definition is good and relevant because it talks about critical reflection of faith in the light of the people's experiences. Whereas, one might also ask what does this mean to those ordinary people in the local churches? Does this definition of tribal theology make any sense to them? Even for those educated tribal Christians whose theological views are informed by the so-called "fundamentalist-evangelical" theology, what does tribal theology mean? Secondly, tribal theology calls for retrieving some of the important resources of the cultural past; and those cultural resources serve as important sources for formulating "relevant" tribal theology. Reclaiming our past and its cultural values is critical for the articulation and formulation of tribal theology. However, one might ask, have we been able to make a convincing case for the necessity of such a claim for reclaiming the cultural past to the people for whom and whose behalf we do theology? In other words, what is the theological grounding for such a claim? Have we been able to make a convincing case to our tribal Christians majority of whose theological views are informed by the so-called "fundamentalist-evangelical" theology or other wise?

The Word Became Flesh

Christian faith is about incarnation. Central to Christian faith is the belief that God became human in and through the person of Jesus Christ (John 1:1, 14). God came to the world and lived among us. Becoming human means God literally became human, every bit like you and I, with all the emotional, intellectual, physical and spiritual dimensions. "And Jesus grew in wisdom and stature, and in favor with God and man," (Luke 2: 52). Jesus ate foods, was angry and even cried, got tired, put on human clothing and most of all assumed human culture and lived with and among people. Jesus was born into a Jewish culture, had human parents in the persons of Joseph and Mary from the Davidic lineage. This means that Jesus embraced and affirmed human culture. Even when Jesus was born into Jewish culture and land, and grew up as a Jew, He is more than a Jew because the Word became flesh and lived among us! God becoming human therefore means God shared our human condition and Jesus was like you and I. The only difference is that Jesus is God and a person without sin at the same time. Unlike Jesus, we are creature-humans and at the same time sinners. In the words of St. Paul, "For all have sinned and fall short of the glory of God," (Rom. 3: 23).

What does it mean to say that Christian faith is an incarnational faith in relation to people and culture outside of Jewish context? Specifically, what does God becoming human mean in relation to tribal people and their culture? Jesus represents universal humanity and the Jewish culture to which He was born into as well as raised is a representative of human culture. Therefore, Jesus is a Jew and at the same time He is more than a Jew. Jesus cannot be limited to and by a Jewish identity. He is every human being of and from every culture and tradition. As Jesus ate Jewish foods so also he does eat tribal foods and cuisines, wears tribal dresses, and embraces tribal culture in the manner He did with Jewish culture. The bottom line is this: ***In as much as Jesus is a Jew, He is a tribal as well! He is the prototype of humanity.*** In as much as God incarnated in and through the Jewish cultural soil, God incarnated as well in and through tribal cultural soil. This is the core of incarnational faith. This is the reason why Christian faith is an incarnational faith. The true character of a Christian faith is therefore the incarnation. Tribal Christian faith must be therefore an incarnational faith. This is to say that for the tribals - and for that matter people with any culture and tradition – Christian faith cannot be a foreign religion or faith. It cannot be an imported or imposed faith from outside of our cultural soil. It must be rooted in the people's culture, tradition and social reality. Likewise, tribal Christian faith must be rooted in the culture, tradition and social reality of the tribal people. In other word, Christian faith must be incarnated in and through the cultural soil of the tribal people. Writing in the context of Naga Christians, Renthy Keitzar argues that Naga Christian faith and theological understanding "are still too western or westernised (or too American Baptistic!). Our understanding of the Christ of faith is not fully Jesus the Man, the Son of God, our Saviour and Lord: He is not fully reincarnated as a Naga among Nagas and dwelt among us; so that we Nagas will see his glory, glory as the only Son from the Father (cf. John 1:14). That is what I call Naganization of the gospel and Christian theology."[1] Keitzar further argues:

> Christianity came to Nagaland more than one hundred years ago and, now, the Christian way of life is fast becoming a part and parcel of own culture; but Jesus Christ, the Lord of the Christian church, is not fully adapted to Naga way of life. He still remains an American, keeping Himself aloof from the Naga people, we worship a distant, otherworldly, Jesus or we adore him in *mysterium tremendum.* He has to be reincarnated, be born and brought up as a Naga. Then only we can call Jesus as "my brother, my clansman, my villager, and my tribesman." This will be the correct way of understanding Jesus from the Naga point of view.[2]

In support of his idea, Keitzar cites the following texts from the Bible: John 1:12ff; Romans 8:14-17; Galatians 4:1-7, etc.[3]

Created in the Image of God

Tribal theology claims its starting point to be space, creation and land. Land and space serve as the locus standi of tribal theology. Tribal theologians have made creation and land as the departure for doing tribal theology. However, it must be pointed out that Wati Longchar has done the most in developing tribal theology using the land and space concept as the basis of tribal theology and as its methodological basis.[4] The use of land and space distinguishes tribal/indigenous theology from the human-centered theology of the West. Land and space theology sharply delineates itself from the traditional Christian theology that the tribal Christians have inherited from the West through their missionaries. Land and space theology affirms the integrity of the whole creation and it takes the integrity of the whole creation as its starting point. It also distinguishes itself from the classical Christian theology that is heavily influenced by Western philosophies. Tribal theology rather relies on the worldviews of tribal people as its basis.

While, land and space theology brings in the necessary corrective to the one sided approach of the traditional Christian theology, not enough has been done in relating tribal theology with creation in the image of God. It seems to me that tribal theology has simply assumed and thus overlooked the significance

---

[1] Renthy Keitzar, *In Search of a Relevant Gospel Message* (Guwahati: CLC, 1995), 18.

[2] *Ibid.*, 25.

[3] I am working towards developing a full fledged article on this important dimension of our faith: "The Word became flesh and dwelt among us."

[4] A. Wati Longchar, *An Emerging Asian Theology: Tribal Theology: Issue, Method and Perspective*. Tribal Study Series no. 8. Jorhat: Tribal Study Centre, Eastern Theological College, 2000; *Returning to Mother Earth: Theology, Christian Witness and Theological Education: an Indigenous Perspective* PTCA Series No. 4 (Tainan: PTCA; Kolkatta: SCEPTRE, 2012).

of creation in the image of God. This is too important a thing to be overlooked; tribal theology must reclaim the centrality of this truth in its attempt to come up with a holistic theology of the people. Secondly, it must as well reclaim and affirm the incarnational faith of the church – God becoming human in and through the person of Jesus Christ. Land and space together with God becoming human and our belief that we are all created in the image of God must be taken as the starting point of tribal/indigenous theology. This is extremely important given the history of colonization and missionization of our people in the past and the enduring impacts it made to the tribal/indigenous people. When we carefully examine the reason why tribal Christians are averse to tribal theology, one is not surprised to find the connection it has with the impacts of colonization and missionization: its negative consequences, especially at the psychological level. Additionally, the pietist-puritan evangelical theologies they have inherited from the early missionaries also contributed in their over-all attitude of themselves and who they are.[5] Given this, it will be helpful for us to discuss in brief the impact of colonization and missionization upon the tribals.

II
The Ubiquitous Presence of the Past Historical Experiences: The Struggle Within

Indigenous peoples of Northeast India are at a cross roads where the political, religious, theological and cultural elements which constitute their identity have been influenced profoundly by the years of British colonization and the Indian occupation of the region since 1947 on the one hand, and the overpowering and the ubiquitous presence of the Western Christian image of the "other." Other factors that are compounding the situation include the forces of modernization (civilization) and the recent globalization processes-economic, technological and cultural.

Theologically, to this very day, tribal Christians continue to follow the kind of theology that was brought to their soil by the Christian missionaries over almost two hundred years ago. Indeed, the message preached by those first missionaries was the pietistic-evangelical theology of the seventeenth and eighteenth centuries which emphasized individual sin and the primacy of salvation of the individual soul continues to have strong sway on the Indigenous people's theological outlook. Unfortunately, despite their good intentions and work,[6] the missionaries failed to understand and appreciate the religious and cultural ethos of the people. What is even more unfortunate is that tribal Christians have bought into the stereotypes

---

[5] For a detail discussion refer to Yangkahao Vashum, *Christology in Context: A Tribal-Indigenous Appraisal of North East India* New Delhi: Christian World Imprints, 2017.

[6] The influential works of the missionaries among the tribals in Northeast India include introducing modern education, literatures, Bible translations, medical works and others.

believed and propounded by the missionaries which necessarily negated and despised tribals' own traditional cultural and religious values. To this day, most tribal Christians think that to be an authentic Christian means they must shun anything that is of the past and embrace whatever comes from the Christian West. This way of thinking is so deeply embedded in the tribal Christians' beliefs that they consider their most important obligation as Christians to be their strict adherence to the tenets of Christianity introduced to them by the missionaries.

Quite often when Churches celebrate Jubilees, either silver or golden, the predominant theme for the occasion is "From darkness to Light,"[7] to draw an unequivocal distinction between the pre-Christian era and the Christian era, thereby reminding the tribals, and the world, that they were in darkness before they were brought the "Truth" of Christianity. Such reiteration serves to compound and reify for one and all this baseless contention that their traditions and the ways of their past were nothing but evil and damned. It surely conveys the idea that their forefathers and foremothers were without the presence of God.

Such understanding has led them to undermine and /or reject a great deal their cultural values and traditions. This is reflected clearly by the prevailing worship pattern and styles, including the hymns and songs[8] they sing and the accepted style and form of preaching. Except for the language, everything is meant to be a near exact imitation of Western Christian style and tradition. This obsession with imitating the West is even plainly evident in the church buildings which are built to replicate the gothic architectural style of the West rather than the tribal, or indigenous styles.

Ultimately, however, the most critical problems of tribal Christianity are the uncompromising deprecation and negation of the tribal worldview and the uncritical acceptance by the people of "Western Christian worldview" brought to them by the missionaries. Tribal worldview which is characterized by undifferentiated unity between the sacred and the secular, the worldly and the heavenly, the physical and the spiritual was replaced by Western Christian view which supposedly maintains sharply delineated distinctions of all these supposed binaries. The traditional worldview of tribal community gave way to the view of humanity which valorizes the individual and that individual's salvation, which flatly contradicts the core of Tribal worldview as the inter-relatedness of all beings in creation.

---

[7] "From Darkness to Light" was the theme chosen on the occasion of the celebration of 125 years of Christianity in Nagaland. Nagaland Baptist Church Council, *From Darkness to Light: A Publication of the Nagaland Baptist Church Council on the Celebration of the 125 years of Christianity in Nagaland* (Kohima: Nagaland Baptist Church Council, 1997); A. Yanang Konyak, *From Darkness to Light: A Story of the Baptist Work Among the Konyak Nagas* (Guwahati: Christian Literature Center, 1986). This was also the theme of the Tangkhul Baptist Churches for its Centenary celebration in 1996.

[8] In recent years people have begun to adapt their traditional folk music into Christian worship and singing. The Mizos, Kukis, and Zeliangrongs have done the most in this regards.

Arguably, the most detrimental effect of the uncritical acceptance of "Western Christian worldview," as opposed to the tribal worldview, is the compartmentalization, exemplified by the strong distinction maintained between the so-called secular and sacred, which is fundamental to the West notion of Christian faith. There is clearly a disconnect in tribal Christian life today between, on one hand, the orthodoxy of the Church's doctrines and teaching, and the way tasks and responsibilities of daily life are carried out on the other. Traditionally, tribals view religion as the entirety of a way of life rather than a propositional statement of faith; in other words, each action and every activity were considered religious. They believed that the total sphere of life was permeated by the presence of God and so they lived in the constant consciousness of divine presence. Because of their reverence for all creation and their belief in the primacy of the larger community rather than the individual, the indigenous people's were demeaned and denigrated as people without religion or God by the Western missionaries and colonizers.

Additionally, the strong emphasis on the primacy of individualism has contributed a great deal to the gradual erosion of communitarian spirit and value which are the hall-mark of indigenous people's community life. Correspondingly, whereas the Western ideas of sin and salvation must be understood at the level of the individual, the social and corporate dimensions of sin and salvation lose all significance.

The condemnation of tribal histories and ways of life has had far reaching psychological consequences for tribal people which manifests in feelings of inferiority and self debasement. People are often led to develop the sense of insecurity and inadequacy because of the repeated negation of their ways of life. In addition, an attitude of distrust and distain develops regarding everything that was or is of their own cultural. Franz Fanon in his *Black Skin and White Mask,* describes how the indigenous people in Algeria were faced with just such identity crisis as a result of French colonization.[9] He explained that some Blacks developed self-hatred and negative image towards themselves and attempted to imitate the white colonizers in order to earn acceptance and status in the society. Fanon argues that the process began early, beginning in childhood and continuing sometimes throughout the person's entire life.

For many decades, indigenous peoples in Northeast India have demonstrated this self-defeating identity crisis.[10] In recent years at least, in secular realms, people

[9] Franz Fanon, *Black Skin White Mask* (New York: Grove Press, 1967), 147f.; Cf. Ashish Nandy, *The Intimate Enemy: Loss and Recovery of Self under Colonialism* (Delhi: Oxford University Press. 1983).

[10] In my Tribal theology class at the Eastern Theological College, I would ask my students to introduce their full names, the village they were born into, and also to mention two or three good things about their people/village. To my surprise, well not so surprisingly, rather as expected many of them felt uncomfortable even to mention their names, when they are named in their mother tongue/dialect. Many of them felt embarrassed to identify with their village. And many of them

have begun to realize the necessity of rediscovering their cultural roots in order to redefine their identity as a Naga, Mizo, Khasi, Kuki or Boros. Student and other political/cultural organizations have taken various initiatives aimed at redeeming and promoting their own cultures and traditions. However, such awareness and the subsequent attempts have so far not been translated at the religious/Church level. Even if there are initiatives at the Church level, the concerns and contents of cultures are treated as social affairs and outside the purview of Christian worship life. In general, as previously noted, the Churches continue to affirm traditional theology, worship and expression of faith. In other words, Christianity has yet to take roots in our tribal cultural soil such that it remains very foreign to the people despite the fact that Christianity arrived in our lands over two hundred years ago.

III
Tribal Theology, Tribal Past, and Tribal Christians

Given the mindset, the attitude and the overall outlook of the people as enumerated above, there have been concerns raised against tribal theology on the question of revisiting the tribal cultural past. Some would even go to the extent of accusing tribal theology of going back to the life before Christianity – going back to the old tribal religion. People raise questions such as: we are now Christians and therefore why talk about our past and history? Clearly, the assumption here is that since tribals have embraced the Christian faith, nothing of the past matters anymore. The tribal past is viewed negatively and even to the extent of branding it as evil and devilish. This is a serious concern we need to address. It might be helpful for us to address this issue by looking at some of the approaches people have taken when dealing with the people's past.

Romanticising of the Past Heritage

This refers to the uncritical acceptance of tribal heritage, practices, and traditions. Romanticising often involves recounting the past stories and glories of a community, a sentimental or idealised attachment with the past. A romantic view of the past is a way of reminiscing the past memories but those good memories are found to be inapplicable in contemporary social realities; something that cannot be undertaken or practiced in our contemporary context. Sometimes it is known as glorification of the past. There are people who feel more comfortable living in the past than living in the present; they take refuge in the glory of the past when confronted with the challenges of the present and they dare not look into the future. At least, this approach sees the past positively and is willing to keep alive the glories of the past rather than simply rejecting the past in its totality. However,

---

even found difficult to mention few good things about their people or village. Even when they could describe that their people are generous, hard working, honest, etc. they could not confidently do so.

the tribal/indigenous approach of rediscovering the past cultural values calls for a critical scrutiny of the past; it rejects the uncritical approach to the past.

Total Rejection

At the other extreme is the total rejection of the past; anything that is of the past is considered bad and evil. Influenced by the history of colonisation and missionization, the tribals in the north-east India have viewed the past negatively. They themselves have come to have such understanding which has resulted in a negative outlook of the past.

The Myth of Syncretism

Some believe that the Christian message will be contaminated by the so-called tribal traditions and practices. Syncretism, both in general and in a strict sense, refers to the process of combining philosophy and theology. In other words, it refers to the use of philosophy in the making or construction of a Christian theology. Sometimes, syncretism refers to the uncritical borrowing of cultural elements from the so-called non-Christian traditions into the Christian faith. However, this fear is largely the creation of the Christian West – of those who have no problem appropriating their own cultural or philosophical ideas/values into their faith expression or theology, but they raise serious questions when it concerns with "Third World" people's cultures and traditions. Any attempt to indigenise or contextualise Christian faith or theology using Third World people's traditions in general and traditions of indigenous people in particular, is often viewed with suspicion, if not simply accused of "syncretism."

Critical Approach to the Past

This approach calls for critical examination of the past and its traditions and values; whatever is found to be bad and evil is rejected and good traditions and values are rediscovered. In this regard, K. Thanzauva categorically states, "No culture should be uncritically accepted or rejected."[11] Accordingly, he proposes, "rejection, adoption, and transformation" as the "integral components of the filtering process of culture and of the method of inculturation."[12] Secondly, we look to the past not for the sake of glorifying it but keeping in view what lies ahead of us – the future. We look to the past for appropriating those cultural values that are life affirming and liberative for building our future. We reclaim the past for the sake of dreaming the future, the future that we want to have. In the process, the past must be subjected to critical examination; we look for critical appropriation of the past for the sake of building the future. The past is important for two reasons: our identity and belongingness, and for dreaming the future.

---

[11] K. Thanzauva, *Theology of Community: Tribal Theology in the Making* (Aizawl: Academy of Integrated Christian Studies (AICS), 2004, 8.

[12] *Ibid.*

IV
The Problem of Conceptual Framework and Terminology

This section, briefly looks at the problem of conceptual framework and terminology such as terms like "theology" which are terms we have inherited from the Christian West and the challenges associated with them for tribal Christians.

The Term "Theology"

The term "theology" itself is problematic for the indigenous/tribal people; it is a foreign language and a western concept. Theology as intellectual discipline (intellectual inquiry into faith) is quite alien to the tribals. For them religion is a way of life or a way of living and never an intellectual ascent of faith in God. For them faith is experiential and it has to do with day to day life. James West (Chayenne) calls theology a "non-Indian concept." He writes, "But, theology as an intellectual discipline, sometimes very separated from the everyday life of people, is a very foreign concept to most Indian tribal experience."[13] This is very true as well with the indigenous- tribal people in India. Spirituality or faith is about experiential living and not so much about intellectual ascent of faith. This has certain implications in and for doing "theology" for indigenous-tribal people. One of the serious problems concerns with the difficulty in defining theology as such. While, theology is defined as a critical reflection on the faith experiences of the people, the experiential nature of faith as theology is subordinated with intellectual activity called reflection. In other words, faith or spirituality for that matter, as a way of life is relegated to the secondary and intellectual inquiry becomes the primary focus. This is simply not the way our fore-parents conceived and experienced faith to be. For them, everything is experiential and thinking or reflection is the outcome of their experience.

Whereas, theology as we know it today, primarily begins and ends with intellectual inquiry into or on faith. The experience of the people is treated more as a data for doing theology rather than the theological expression of faith in itself. This is how, for years and years, we have been conditioned to think and understand theology to be. The tragedy is that we have not been able to free ourselves from this conceptual captivity till date. This is therefore one single most challenge confronting indigenous-tribal theologians working on tribal theology.

Oral Culture vs. Written Culture

Another related concern is the dynamics between oral culture and written culture. Here we have two very different cultures as well as orientations. They represent two very different conceptual frameworks, thought patterns and life orientations.

---

[13] James Treat, ed., *Native and Christian: Indigenous voices on Religious Identity in the United States and Canada* (New York: Routledge, 1996), 11.; Cf. George E. Tinker, *Spirit and Resistance: Political Theology and American Indian Liberation*. Minneapolis: Fortress Press, 2004).

Tribals being an oral oriented people have their way of expressing their faith, way of life differently from that of people of written culture and tradition. Theologically, this is another serious concern for tribal people. The loss of oral tradition which comes with their whole life orientation could mean even their understanding of spirituality, faith and life meaning, have had far reaching impacts and consequences. On the one hand, while we bemoan the loss of oral culture and everything that is connected with it, there is on other hand, a legitimate concern of how genuinely one could transmit the stories, and meaning of life contained in those oral traditions. In other words, there is a serious challenge on the question of identifying the true source of the story.

Having said this, I must hasten to assert that the loss of oral culture outweighs everything and anything else. First, the loss of oral culture means the loss of the very life principle and meaning of life of the tribal people. The understanding, outlook and ways of life of a people are deeply embedded in oral tradition. Secondly, people's worldview, their spirituality and the overall orientation of life, which served as the basis of their life existence are all expressed and conveyed through and by oral communication. It is simply to say that tribal people belong to the oral world. It is there that they feel most natural and happy. The demise of oral tradition means the loss of oral spirit and authority in our contemporary society. Spoken words have no value and meaning unless they are substantiated by written documents. Spoken words or oral stories for that matter are therefore simply taken for granted, abused and rendered valueless in today's world.

Tribal theology must work towards rehabilitating the value and authority of oral traditions even when we are confronted with the real challenge of discerning and disseminating what could be known as the true source and content of the story. This is critical for tribal Christians to reaffirm our faith in the spoken words in our day to day life interactions. By doing so, the authority and the spirit of oral tradition are rediscovered and honored. Such understanding will have serious implications for our faith affirmation. For instance, our preaching and or proclamation of the good news of Jesus Christ will become authoritative as well as taken seriously. We live by what we say and preach. Remember, our fore-parents meant what they said and they honored their words; words and deeds go together. Tribal theology therefore, must seriously address this in order to do theology in the true sense of the term, spirit and content.

Conclusion

Tribal theology regards the Bible as the primary source of its theology. It also takes tribal cultural resources and tribal people's experiences as important sources.[14] Theological reflection based on tribal life experiences and traditional heritage is an essential task of indigenous theology. The indigenous peoples are endowed

[14] Yangkahao Vashum, "Sources for Studying Tribal Theology," in Shimreingam Shimray, ed., *Tribal Theology: A Reader*. Tribal Study Series No. 12 (Jorhat: Tribal Study Centre, 2000), 63-77.

with rich cultural and religious resources and, rather than condemning them as evil and demonic, every effort should be made to reclaim these resources for the purpose of theological reflection. In this search for an articulation of meaningful theology we must retrieve the cultural values that are known to be life affirming and liberating. This search will involve processes of recollection, remembering, and sharing with a view to formulating a theology that will ultimately be inclusive, dialogical, liberating, and above all empowering.

The challenges confronting tribal theology are enormous. In as much as it is psychological and attitudinal, it is also theological in nature. It is psychological because, tribal Christians are to a large extent captive to the so called traditional western theological thinking and expression of faith. And for people of such understanding, there do not arise the need for another theology such as "tribal theology" or otherwise. The assumption is that the inherited theology from the Christian missionaries, as well as any other theology that comes from the Christian West, are the only valid "Christian theology." It is further assumed that there is just one norm and method of doing theology as well as method of interpretation of the Bible and therefore, there can be no such theology as "tribal theology" or any other theology for that matter. Such attitude, mindset and understanding predominantly pervade the overall outlook of the tribal Christians and their understanding of tribal theology. The challenge is therefore, to a large extent psychological and attitudinal in nature. Tribal theology, to be effective, needs to be liberated from such challenges; only then will it become a people's theology, accepted and embraced by the people themselves.

Chapter 3

Methodological Issues in Theology
Interrogating the Methodology of Contextual Theology

Introduction

For a theology to be authentic it must be grounded on certain methodological assumptions; additionally, every theology has characteristic features which constitute its very nature. While some theologies are dogmatic and apologetic, those such as liberation and or contextual theology place the emphasis on praxis. In this chapter, I propose to discuss some of the important methodological issues of theology in general and contextual theology in particular. In discussing contextual theology, I will be addressing primarily the methodological issues of tribal theology. The chapter begins with a brief appraisal of the meaning of method and methodology and some of the methodological assumptions in research.[1]

What are Method and Methodology?

Method and methodology are terms which are often used loosely. Sometimes they are used to mean the same thing: method and methodology understood as an approach or working principle. Method and methodology in this sense are concerned with the question of how. How do we go about doing theology? We

---

[1] This chapter is initially my professorial lecture I gave at the Eastern Theological College, Jorhat on August 31, 2018. Part of my lecture is taken from my book *Christology in Context: A Tribal-Indigenous Appraisal of North East India* (New Delhi: Christian World Imprints, 2017). However, I have reproduced here in *toto* with the exception of few changes, for the sake of maintaining the flow of argument.

often ask questions such as what is your method or methodology? By this we mean what sort of approach or working principle do we follow or employ in our research or thesis project. Method refers to the means; the means to an end. It could also refer to the rules followed or to be followed. Method is the system of procedure employed in any body of knowledge and its activity.

Methodology strictly speaking is the science of method. It refers to the body of methods used in a particular branch of studies. In methodology we engage in philosophical discussion about the appropriateness of the various methods involved. In methodological studies, we do not deal with one particular method but rather look at the various methods employed by theologians considering the weak and strong points.

Methodological Assumptions and Presuppositions

Within each discipline there are different methods and every branch of human knowledge has its own method.

1. Method or methods are not considered or developed in a vacuum. It is always assumed that there is already a body of knowledge in/for that particular branch of studies. It is presupposed that within that discipline there exists a body of knowledge. Then only the question of method arises.
2. Each discipline will then develop its own method(s) according to its suitability of the subject matter. Some would argue that the goal or vision of the particular branch of study would determine the method and its development.
   - Historical research: archeological findings as method.
   - Biblical Studies: use MSS, textual criticisms, form criticism, redaction criticism (theological motifs), source criticism, etc.
   - Sociology: social survey, prepare and use questionnaire, etc.
3. Behind all methods there lie certain presuppositions and values; they are not totally value-free. This is because every branch of study has its own objectives and goals – to achieve something ultimately. There is already certain presupposition.
4. History is always fact and interpretations. Further, interpretation differs according to our presupposition, assumption and perspective. For example, Sepoy Mutiny 1857: from rulers (imperial) perspective, it was a rebellion; whereas for the nationalist historians, it's the first war of Independence and not a mutiny. Take the Northeast Indian situation: Naga or Assamese struggles for Independence is regarded by Indians as law and order situation and not a political problem; hence the Independent movements of the region are always branded as secessionist movements.

5. All academic pursuits are value-laden. Following Michael Polanyi's seminal analysis of the role of valuation, Arvind P. Nirmal makes three important observations in regards to the relations between academic disciplines and their value systems.[2] Firstly, all academic disciplines develop their own value systems and these value systems are often used to carry on their pursuit of truth. Secondly, there is a correspondence between the value system of a discipline and its vision of ultimate reality. Finally, the pursuit of truth for any discipline is a gradual and cumulative process in which our intellectual aspirations are "enlightened" and "elevated." So we talk about scientific value, economic value, theological value, historical value, etc. No discipline is therefore value-free.

Methodological Issues in Theology

Theology as a Human Discipline

It is appropriate that we begin by asserting that theology is a human discipline. It is human efforts to articulate theology in the light of the faith experiences of the people. As a human academic discipline, theology has relations with other academic disciplines. Theology heavily relies on human sciences such as sociology, anthropology, cultural anthropology, history and psychology. Of course, social analysis is integral to doing theology. Social Movements as alternative texts that can inform the construction of alternative or counter-hegemonic theological discourses and texts have become integral to theological discourses and articulations. Social theories provide us with new tools to understand people and their situation and society. As such analytical mediation is a significant category in constructing theologies.

Theology thus shares some of the fundamental epistemological and methodological assumptions of other academic disciplines. Theology follows integrated and interdisciplinary methods or approaches of study. Like any other discipline, theology assumes that there exists a body of theological knowledge and that its subject matter is intelligible and knowable. It assumes that theology is corrigible and subject to criticism and revision.

The Object of Theology

The question of the object of theology is a critical one indeed. It is certainly related to the question of theology itself – what is theology? Traditionally in confessional theology, God is considered to be the object of theological investigation. Theology has always been defined as the study of God. But, the question is, can we study God? Is it possible for us to really know and study God? Traditional confessional theology affirms that God's self disclosure in and through the person of Jesus

[2] Arvind P. Nirmal, *Heuristic Explorations* (Madras: Christian Literature Society, 1990), 5.

Christ is the basis of our knowledge of God. A. P. Nirmal argues that the object of theological research is not God but the concept of God. "God can never be studied, but theology, as an academic discipline, is a study. It is a study of the concept of God. It is a study of human thinking about God. It is a study of human words and language about God."[3] Following Gordon Kaufman, Nirmal argues that theology is primarily a conceptual study. To further substantiate his view, he refers to the etymology of theology: *theos-logos* literally means "God Words." Theology is then a study or words about God and not about God-self. If theology is a human discipline and therefore subject to correction and revision then, the object of theology certainly cannot be God-self; it has to be the concept about God, the words and language we employ about God and other related theological concepts.[4]

This raises a serious question on the place of experience and faith in theological consideration. If theology is primarily a conceptual study how shall we then locate the role of experience and faith in theological reflection? To this, Nirmal argues that experience belongs to the religious person and faith to an individual's relationship with God.

Theology, Religion and Faith

Is it right to make a distinction between theology, religion and faith? Don't they go together? How do we understand the relationship between theology, religion and faith? These are some of the mood points one might have to raise. Nirmal distinguishes theology from religion and faith.

> Religion is more comprehensive than theology. It includes not only concepts but also beliefs and practices. Faith is not a concept. It is a relationship – an existential relationship between the believer and what he or she considers to be the Ultimate Reality. In philosophical terms, faith or faith-relationship is "groundless" and non-conceptual. This relationship is abiding whereas theology is tentative....Theology presupposes religion and faith. When religion and faith are articulated, their articulations become theology's data. Theology therefore, is the second or even third order activity – religion and faith being prior to it.[5]

Theology "is the second or even third order activity" after religion and faith. This observation is quite striking. It underscores the primacy of religion and faith over theology. The fact is that before you begin to articulate theologically, religion and faith have to be articulated and only then what have been articulated become theology's data or source. In other words, prior to theological articulations, faith

[3] *Ibid.,* 22.

[4] *Ibid.*

[5] *Ibid.,* 23.

experiences by religious person must take place. How is that possible? Shouldn't the activity of faith experiences by religious person be taken as theological articulation or activity? How can we differentiate the two from each other? Nirmal argues that "the main function of theology is to examine the adequacy of the concepts employed by the believer to articulate his or her faith. It not only examines the existing concepts but also the new concepts. This is what makes theological research possible."[6] He goes on to argue that at the level of religion and faith one should resort to phenomenological method.

Definitions of Theology

In the light of the above discussion on the meaning and nature of theology, it might be helpful here to peruse through the various definitions articulated through the history of theological discourses. Select definitions by different theologians are provided below for our considerations.

Classical Definition

1. Classical definition by Anselm of Canterbury, 11th century English theologian: Theology is "*fides quaerens intellectum*, faith seeking understanding."[7]
2. Thomas Aquinas defines sacred theology as science: "... sacred doctrine is a science because it proceeds from principles established by the light of a higher science, namely, the science of God and the blessed. Hence, just as the musician accepts on authority the principles taught him by the mathematician, so sacred science is established on principles revealed by God."[8]

Modern Definition

1. John Macquarrie: "Theology may be defined as the study which, through participation in and reflection upon a religious faith, seeks to express the content of this faith in the clearest and most coherent language available."[9]
2. Karl Rahner: "Theology is the *science* of faith. It is the conscious and methodical explanation and explication of the divine revelation received and grasped in faith."[10]
3. Owen C. Thomas: "Systematic or dogmatic theology is the methodical investigation and interpretation of the content of Christian faith. It is the

---

[6] *Ibid.*

[7] Anselm of Canterbury, *Proslogion*, translated by M. J. Charlesworth in *The Major Works*, ed. Brian Davies and G. R. Evans (New York: Oxford University Press, 1998), 83.

[8] Thomas Aquinas, *Summa Theologica* I. 1.2. in http://iteadthomam.blogspot.com/2006/05/definition-of-theology.html (accessed on 22/08/18).

[9] John Macquarrie, *Principles of Christian Theology* (London: SCM Press Ltd, 1966), 1.

[10] Karl Rahner, "Theology," in *Encyclopedia of Theology: The Concise Sacramentum Mundi*, ed. Karl Rahner (New York: Seabury Press, 1975), 1687.

orderly clarification and explanation of what is affirmed in the Christian message."[11]

Liberation/Contextual Theology

4. Gustavo Gutiérrez: "Liberation theology is a critical reflection on Christian praxis in light of the word of God."[12]
5. James Cone: "Christian theology is a theology of liberation. It is a rational study of the being of God in the world in light of the existential situation of an oppressed community, relating the forces of liberation to the essence of the gospel, which is Jesus Christ."[13]
6. K. C. Abraham: "Theology is not a systematic explication of timeless truths, nor is it a matter of laying a pre-fabricated system of ideas to a situation. It is a reflection of the faith-experience of people in a given context."[14]
7. Stephen B. Bevans: "Contextual theology as the process of doing theology ...as taking two things seriously: the experience of the past (recorded in Scripture and preserved and defended in tradition) and the experience of the present, that is, context (individual and social experience, secular or religious culture, social location, and social change."[15]
8. Rosemary Radford Ruether: "The critical principle of feminist theology is the promotion of the full humanity of women.... Theologically speaking, whatever diminishes or denies the full humanity of women must be presumed not to reflect the divine or an authentic relation to the divine, or to reflect the authentic nature of things, or to be the message or work of an authentic redeemer or a community of redemption."[16]
9. Wati Longchar: "Indigenous theology... is a people's theology born out of the experiences of various forms of injustice and exploitation in the context of their assertion for right and identity. It is a theology that attempts to express

---

[11] Owen C. Thomas, *Introduction to Theology*, revised edition (Serampore: The Indian Theological Library, Senate of Serampore College, 1989), 1.

[12] Gustavo Gutiérrez, *A Theology of Liberation: History, Politics, and Salvation*, revised edition with new introduction, translated and edited by Sister Caridad Inda and John Eagleson (Maryknoll: Orbis Books, 2000), xxix.

[13] James H. Cone, *A Black Theology of Liberation*, revised edition (Maryknoll: Orbis Books, 1990), 1.

[14] K. C. Abraham, *Transforming Vision: Theological-Methodological Paradigm Shifts* (Tiruvalla: Christava Sahitya Samithi, 2006), 17-18.

[15] Stephen B. Bevans, *Models of Contextual Theology*, revised and expanded, Faith and Cultures Series (Maryknoll: Orbis Books, 2002), xvi.

[16] Rosemary Radford Ruether, *Sexism and God-Talk: Toward a Feminist Theology* (Boston: Beacon Press, 1983), 18-19.

Christian faith in socio-cultural, religious, traditional and liturgical thought patterns of the people."[17]

10. K. Thanzauva: "Tribal Theology is a theological reflection on the tribal Christian experiences of the interaction of tribal culture and gospel over the past one hundred years in this region and of the struggle for liberation."[18]

Examining the various definitions of theology, helps us to see how theology has been understood, articulated and reflected through the centuries. The classical and modern definitions represent more or less the traditional western theological understandings of theology. They are characterized by systematic, coherent and lucid interpretation and presentation of the content of Christian faith. And at times the content of faith is assumed to have been already a "given" thing.

Liberation and or contextual theology, on the other hand, understand theology as a critical reflection on the faith experiences of the people in light of the word of God in a given context. The emphasis is clearly on the act of critical reflection, faith experience, context and praxis.

Given this differences in the way theology has been understood and viewed, there exist varied methods of doing and articulating theology at different historical times and contexts (examples of different theological methods are cited at the later part of the paper).

The Past and the Present –which Validates? The Question of Authority

The question of validation in theology, whether the past or the present, validates theological assertions or claims is a critical issue in theology. This is a question of authority or norms of authority as well in theology. While traditional theology argues the Bible, the confession, and creed – the past as validating any new theologies, theologians like Gordon Kaufman and A. P. Nirmal think otherwise. Kaufman whereas in his earlier systematic theological method, loyalty to the Christian tradition as unique' and 'essential' was precisely what it meant to be a Christian theologian, in his later constructive method he argues that "it is a serious mistake to invoke the *authority* of the major symbols of the tradition as the principal basis for theological work."[19] While loyalty is still considered a marker of what it means to be a theologian, he shifts the focus of this loyalty from the Christian tradition to ultimate mystery, which Christians call God. Secondly, guided by his pragmatic commitment, Kaufman argues for judging theological

[17] Wati Longchar, *Returning to Mother Earth: Theology, Christian Witness and Theological Education: An Indigenous Perspective.* PTCA Series No. 4 Tianan: PTCA; Kolkatta: SCEPTRE, 2012), 86.

[18] K. Thanzauva, "Issues in Tribal Theology," in Shimreingam Shimray, ed., *Tribal Theology: A Reader*. Tribal Study Series No. 12 (Jorhat: Tribal Study Centre, 2003), 17.

[19] Gordon D. Kaufman, *Systematic Theology: A Historicist Perspective* (New York: Charles Scribner's Sons, 1968), 64; Gordon D. Kaufman, *In Face of Mystery: A Constructive Theology* (Cambridge: Harvard Univ. Press, 1993), 48.

claims not simply by how well they either correspond to Christian scripture and tradition or correlate the tradition to the current situation rather to judge these claims according to their fruits. The adequacy of theological claims has to be evaluated not on how it came to be known but whether it empowers people to act more humanely in the world.[20] Kaufman asserts in his work *The Theological Imagination,* "All claims to truth made simply on the grounds of religious authority are in question: theological truth-claims are to be assessed strictly in terms of our present needs and our present moral insight (educated as much as possible, of course, by past experience and by tradition)."[21]

In a similar line, Nirmal proposes that the past must be examined by the new after all any re-search means an examination of the "past" in the light of the "present." Nirmal makes a forceful argument for the reversal of the movement in the following statement:

> Traditional confessional theology has always insisted that critical examination of the Church's theological and doctrinal formulations is necessary. But, it has also insisted that such a critical examination is to be carried on in the light of and by the standards of the "past," i.e., the Scripture, the confession, the creed, the council or the rule of faith. It is this that "validate" new theological formulations. The "past" examines and validates the "present." This has been the movement of traditional theology. I am arguing for reversal of this movement. Any "re-search" means an examination of the "past" in the light of the "present." In a "re-search" it is the "old" that is subjected to examination in the light of the "new." In fact, that is what research is all about. If Scripture were the supreme standard by which all theological and doctrinal formulations were to be examined, why is Scripture itself subjected to historical-critical research? Or is it the "re-searched" Scripture that is to be the standard of all new formulations? But, then biblical research is a continuous process. When and where are we to stop? The same argument could be brought against the other standards of theology. Somehow, traditional theology has missed the point that it is the new that judges the old and supersedes it.[22]

I have quoted this rather a lengthy quotation *verbatim* because it brings out all that one can say about the relations between the past and the present. Nirmal beautifully problematizes and brings to the fore the critical issue of authority that

---

[20]Nathanael L. Inglis, "The Importance of Gordon Kaufman's Constructive Theological Method for Contemporary Anabaptist-Mennonite Theology," *The Conrad Grebel Review*, 34 No. 2 (Spr 2016), 133.

[21] Gordon D. Kaufman, *The Theological Imagination* (Philadelphia; The Westminster Press, 1981), 196.

[22] Nirmal, *Heuristic Explorations*, 25

is often associated with the past - Christian tradition - in theological discourse. While acknowledging the role of the past, Kaufman and Nirmal argue for treating the traditions non-authoritatively. Nirmal appeals to Jesus and His teaching in the Gospels such as that Jesus was critical of the traditions of the time, His new covenant superseding the old one, the newness of the Gospel-wine would burst the old wine-skins, etc., besides other passages in the Bible. Most of all, the old is judged by the new. What is the implication of this for theological research? Nirmal expounds eloquently thus:

> Traditional theology has failed to see that the formulations of the new Gospel of Jesus could themselves become old and obsolete. We should speak not only in terms of the new Gospel but also in terms of the *newness of the Gospel.* The Gospel becomes and happens. It did not just happen once upon a time. It is this *new Gospel-happenings* that need to be theologized. Theological formulations of these *new Gospel-happenings* should critically examine the older formulations and, if necessary, discard them (*the emphasis is mine*).[23]

The Rational Character of Theology

This concerns with the question of the rational and systematic character of theology. Paul Tillich offers the following directing principles for the protection of the rational character of theological conception:[24]

First, theology must be *semantically rational.* This refers to defining properly theological terms and symbols used so that they are adequate and reasonable for their tasks. Second, theology must be *logically rational.* This refers to the use of concepts including dialectical and paradoxical concepts, they must be described in logically correct terms. Third, theology must be *methodically rational.* It must follow a method; it must derive and state its propositions in a definite way. It must be systematic. By "systematic" Tillich means a way of writing theology which follows a certain method, and remains consistent with certain principles.

The Question of Objective and Method

In general a theological method is determined by the objective or the vision. Depending on the goal of studies one decides upon the appropriate method. However, not all theological methods are determined by the goal of studies. This is especially true in the case of theology.

David Tracy in his *The Analogical Imagination*, argues that sometimes it is difficult to know exactly what we are looking for in our theological pursuit. There is no precise object of the study. Nor can we say that we know everything. God's

---

[23] *Ibid.*, 27.

[24] Paul Tillich, *Systematic Theology*, vol. 1 (Chicago: University of Chicago Press, 1951), 53-59.

knowledge is not completely exhausted by Jesus Christ; whereas, in our search we move closer and closer to the truth. God's knowledge is not a closed chapter; God's knowledge is a mystery. Hence, there is no one theology; there is no final theology. All theologies are approximations of the truth of God.[25]

Theological Language: Models and Metaphors

In theology we employ models and metaphors. The God language such as God as Father, Jesus as Shepherd, etc., are metaphors or models. Models have limitations but they are useful as far as they point to the true knowledge of God. For example, God as Father and earthly drunken father can never be compared. Secondly, God as father does not necessarily mean that God has a wife. Despite all this, theological research deals with models and metaphors, "believing that they have at least structural similarity with the object of its enquiry, namely God,"[26] asserts Nirmal. At the same time, he goes on to caution that it is wrong to assume that models and metaphors have "one-to-one correspondence with God." Every metaphor has its limitation in the sense that a metaphor as representative of a person, object or action must never be taken literally. Metaphor, in other words is a form of figurative language used to illustrate the meaning and significance of another subject or object. They are therefore not ends in themselves but means to an end; they point to the ultimate goal. Images are human constructs and therefore have certain limitations.[27]

Again a model that works for some people may not be necessarily helpful for others and context. Hence, we need to employ multiple models or metaphors. In this sense, theology is a multi-model or metaphor discipline/discourse. It is therefore, in this sense, one must understand that the task of theology is essentially revisionist. One must keep examining and revising its models and metaphors relating to the concept of God.

Examples of Theological Methods

Here, I have put together some of the theological methods of select theologians spanning different historical time and period by way of illustrations.

1. Patristic Theology: Apologetic Theology
   The church fathers were known for their defense of Christian faith in the face of the challenges from the critics of Christian faith who were often known as the "heretics." Their theological method is known as apologetic because they defended Christian faith from the critics and

---

[25] David Tracy, *The Analogical Imaginations: Christian Theology and Culture of Pluralism* (New York: Crossroad, 1981), 5f.

[26] Nirmal, *Heuristic Explorations*, 24.

[27] Vashum, *Christology in Contrext*, 144.

skeptics alike. They refuted point by point the charges leveled against Christian faith. Well known among them are Origen, Chrysostom, etc.

2. Middle Ages: Thomistic Method
   The method of synthesis of reason and faith (Medieval synthesis): In this revelation and reason are recognized as valid knowledge of God. E.g. Existence of God can be proved by rational arguments; such theology is known as natural theology. On the other hand, the doctrine of trinity requires faith to understand; faith plays a vital role in such theological understanding.
3. Reformers
   Reformers reject natural theology of Thomism. They did not want neutral knowledge; rather they were interested in the saving knowledge of God. Accordingly, they believed that in theology human reason is not required. To be more specific, knowledge for the sake of knowledge derived from human reason, is not important. Only scripture; the saving knowledge of God derived from the scripture is what counts and nothing else.
4. Paul Tillich
   Method of Correlation: By that he means there is correlation between philosophy and theology. It's the philosophical task to raise existential questions and ontological questions. Theology answers these questions. Questions raised by human situation and answers provided by theology. Theologians' task is therefore to provide answers to these existential questions.
5. Rudolf Bultmann
   Demythologizing method: For Bultmann the basic category is the message/*Kerygma* – the N. T. word. This needs interpretation. The message comes to us wrapped in myths and the first step is then to get to the core message. This requires reinterpretation but not removing the layers of myth. Thus the *kerygma* (message) has to be reinterpreted in the most meaningful language available.
6. Karl Barth
   Revealed knowledge of God: The starting point of theology is God's self revelation in and through Jesus Christ. He is therefore critical of natural theology which claims that God's existence can be proved by human reason. Knowledge of God is possible only because of God's self disclosure.
7. Gordon Kaufmann
   Kaufmann is quite critical of revelation. He thinks just the opposite of Barth and neo-orthodox theologians who claim revelation as the starting point of theology. Rather for him revelation of God should be the ultimate concern of theological investigation and not the starting

point. He argues it is not the question of where theology begins and ends rather the movement – "how one makes the movement from the preliminary to the ultimate, from creatures to God."[28]

In regards to theological method, Kaufmann favors and argues for imaginative construction. In like manner, David Tracy follows imaginative construction as his theological method.

8. Asian Theologians: Inter-religious dialogue – dialogue with people of other faith and ideologies.
9. Latin American Liberation Theology: Praxis method – action-reflection method. Theological method based on involvement in human struggle for liberation.
10. Dalit Theology: A. P. Nirmal: *Pathos* – experience of suffering as the starting point of dalit theology. Experience of suffering is prior to action-reflection.
11. Tribal Theology: Creation-centered theology: Wati Longchar – land/ space as the starting point of tribal theology. K. Thanzauva: Synthetic-praxis model and social transformation in the light of the Kingdom of God as the vision of tribal theology.
12. Feminist theology: Rereading the scripture through the lens of women's experiences and using the tools of critical biblical studies, besides other critical methods of studies.

Interrogating the Methodology of Contextual Theology

What is contextual theology? How is contextual theology different from traditional theology? Generally, every theology is contextual, whether past or present. No theology can claim to have universal relevance for all people, culture, and time - context. Given this, why not all theologies, past and present, be known as contextual theologies? Why only those select theologies, especially the theologies from/of/by Third World, non-Euro-American/Western countries, minorities, etc. are known as contextual theologies? "A contextual theology is one that foregrounds reality and experience," explains Felix Wilfred.[29] The context of the people serves as the basis of contextual theology. Context does not simply mean the geographical context but the social-cultural realities of the people. It refers to the particular experiences of the people. Some of the salient features of contextual theology include the following:[30]

- contextual theology makes no claim for comprehensiveness
- it makes no claim for universality; universality is understood in terms of particularity

[28] Gordon D. Kaufman, *An Essay on Theological Methods* (Missoula: Scholars Press, 1979), 1.

[29] Felix Wilfred, *Margins: Sites for Asian Theologies* (Delhi: ISPCK, 2008), 3

[30] *Ibid.,* 8-17.

- options for the poor, needy and those at the margins
- people as the actors/subjects of theology.

Difference Between Traditional Western Theologies and Contextual Theologies

It might be helpful for us to articulate the differences between the two theologies and their distinctive characteristics in the following categories:

- **Methodology**: **Traditional**: Western worldviews, philosophies, ideas, cultures, thoughts, speculative/abstract, theoretical, rationalistic, objective methods, etc. Theologies from above! **Contextual**: Non -Western worldviews, people's stories/experiences, people's histories, traditions and cultures, people's voices and movements as sources, etc. Praxis: action-reflection, engagement, involvement, struggles, theology from the margins, etc.
- **Context: Traditional**: rich/powerful people's experiences/perspectives, the agenda of the Empire, **Contextual**: people's life: historical, socio-economic and political contexts – rooted in the historical and cultural reality of the people.
- **Experience: Traditional:** Experience of the rich and powerful people (oppressors). **Contextual:** Experiences of the poor, oppressed, marginalized, minorities, etc. "Option for the poor." people's experience of suffering and pain (*pathos).*
- **Content: Traditional:** Good news for the rich? Human centred, spiritual salvation, theologies for the rich and powerful – Prosperity theology/gospel. **Contextual**: Good news for the poor! Holistic salvation (liberation and salvation); eco-theology: cosmic salvation.
- **Claim? – Traditional:** to be "universal" and "perennial". **Contextual:** makes no claim for comprehensiveness and being universal.
- **Bottom line:** Every theological articulation or construction is therefore a search for relevance in a given time and situation.

Models of Contextual Theology

To begin with, it will be helpful to discuss the extent models of contextual theology as we examine some of the methodological issues concerning contextual theology.

Using the work of Stephen B. Bevans,[31] as his starting point, K. Thanzauva, A Mizo theologian, has identified and explicated six different models which are present in tribal theology in the Northeast India. These models are transplantation, fulfillment, translation, dialogical, synthesis and praxis.[32] Transplantation and

[31] Stephen B. Bevans, *Models of Contextual Theology*, revised and expanded edition (Maryknoll: Orbis Books, 2002).

[32] K. Thanzauva, *Theology of Community: Tribal Theology in the Making* (Aizawl: Mizo Theological Conference, 1997), 54-88.

fulfillment models account for context by marking the literal transportation of the gospel message from one place to another, particularly as this was done by missionaries from the Christian West to the non-Christian world, without making any adjustment or change to acknowledge differences in language and culture. The gospel message is proclaimed using the West's epistemological categories and is draped in the cultural garb of the Western Christianity as the "Truth" for all people everywhere. The proponents of these two models hold the native cultures and traditions in the utmost disdain and contempt and believe they must be condemned as demonic and evil. The early Christian missionaries embodied these models and, unfortunately, their powerful influence on the susceptible tribals means that to this day most Christians in the Northeast India subscribe to these models. Tribal Christians have been convinced that their own traditional culture and values are antithetical to authentic Christian faith. The four remaining models described by Thanzauva are not as blatantly antagonistic of the traditional culture and values.

Proponents of the translation model recognize the positive nature of indigenous cultures and traditions; on the contrary, they are in fact disposed to using indigenous cultural metaphors and images to facilitate translation of the gospel message to the native languages. This method could be manifest as a literalistic, word-for-word translation, or it could take a functional and dynamic form. The functional translation looks for the dynamic equivalence rather than the literal meaning of the original word. The underlying assumption of this model is that, "Christianity contains an essential element, a supra-cultural message which can be separated from a culturally bound mode of expression."[33] In other words, the essence of the gospel cannot be altered but must be translated in a way that is meaningful to the reader or listener. This model, in addition to transplantation and fulfillment models, is being widely applied in the Northeast India. Although, the translation model requires the gospel message be made linguistically meaningful to the listener/reader, it ignores the actual cultural context within which the translation will be learned thereby precluding all critical interaction between the gospel message and the people's experience. Two noted adherents of this model are Renthy Keitzar and Zairema.[34]

The dialogical model, which is primarily a contribution of the Asian theologians,[35] recognizes the importance of dialogue between or among more cultures in order to find common ground in matters of faith. Put another way, the relative validity of every culture is presumed as is the necessity for mutual enrichment through dialogue. Indeed, the dialogical model recognizes the

---

[33] *Ibid.*, 67.

[34] Both Renthy Keitzar and Zairema are known for their works on indigenizing the gospel message in the Northeast Indian context.

[35] Some of the well known proponents of dialogical methods are Stanley J. Smartha, M. M. Thomas, S. Wesley Ariarajah, Raimundo Pannikar, and Aloysius Pieris.

compatibility of every culture with Christian faith including the cultures disdained and denigrated by proponents of transplantation models. This model makes it possible to find common ground among ostensibly disparate religious groups in order to promote harmonious and peaceful co-existence. Now, the dialogical model is good as far as it goes, however, it falls short in at least two ways: First is its failure to challenge the existing social and economic inequalities in the society, and second, it shies from addressing the core issues of the respective beliefs.

The synthetic model focuses on synthesizing two or more cultures, particularly Christian traditions and cultures and the traditions of the indigenous peoples from which a new form of Christian expression or theology emerges.[36] In other words, there is a fusion of two or more traditions resulting in the formation of a new theology or faith expression. As with the dialogical model this model recognizes the inherent goodness of culture and it allows for critical interaction between Christian tradition and indigenous people's cultures and traditions. It takes very seriously the cultural context of the people in the formulation of a relevant faith expression and also allows for the critical interaction with other contexts and differing theological expressions. "This model is synthetic in the Hegelian sense of not just attempting to put things together in a compromise but of developing, in a creative dialectic, something that is acceptable to all standpoints."[37] In the Northeast India, this synthetic interaction is occurring in the fusion of Western and traditional music, it has yet to be a dominant factor in theological expression.

The last of the six models is the praxis model which refers to the contextual character of liberation theology and the emphasis on the action-reflection method of doing theology. The praxis model presumes the significance inherent in the socio-economic, political and spiritual contexts. Jon Sobrino rightly states that the praxis model "in its most profound sense is understood as the unity of knowledge as activity and knowledge as content."[38] This model is based on the conviction that, "Truth is at the level of history, not in the realm of ideas"[39] and is concerned with social transformation and liberation in the light of the Kingdom's values.

Appropriate Methodology?

The six models of contextual theology we have examined outline a range of possible approaches to employ in our theological formulation. While some theologians opt to rely on one specific, others have found it most beneficial to combine models; in fact, there are instances in which models overlap one

---

[36] K. Thanzauva, *Theology of Community*, 74-77; cf. K. P. Aleaz, "Gospel and Culture: Some Indian Reflection," in *Indian Journal of Theology* 36, no. 2 (1999), 64-79.

[37] Bevans, *Models of Contextual Theology*, 90.

[38] Quoted in Bevans, *Models of Contextual Theology*, 72.

[39] José Miguez Bonino, *Doing Theology in a Revolutionary Situation* (Philadelphia: Fortress Press, 1975), 72.

another. After his search for a relevant method or methods for the formulation of theology in the north east India Thanzauva has proposed a combination of the synthetic and praxis models which he refers to simply as the synthetic-praxis model.[40] He argues that this method is appropriate in a context like the north east India where marginalization, discrimination and social injustice as well as cultural alienation of the people are rampant and endemic. While the synthetic model emphasizes the cultural identity of the people, the praxis model facilitates the social and economic transformation of the people. Thanzauva further states that by employing the synthetic-praxis method theologians can engage in a much needed critique of the interaction of Christianity and tribal culture and reflect on contemporary conditions, undertake a social analysis of the people's struggle, and initiate the reclamation of past traditions and values.[41]

This synthetic-praxis method Thanzauva proposes is without question a viable model that can be applied in the construction of tribal theology for three reasons. First it takes seriously people's cultures and their distinct socio-economic and political contexts. Second it allows for critical interaction between Christian traditions and the tribal people's cultures and values that results in a new form of Christian expression of faith and theology. And third it requires reclaiming past cultural traditions and values. Now having noted the positive aspects, I would be remiss if I neglected to identify two of the model's shortcomings. One problem is that it assumes that indigenous cultures are essentially identical, failing to recognize the diversity that exists among indigenous communities. Second, it fails to recognize the "differentiated complexities" which are the consequence of the hybridity that is contemporary indigenous peoples' reality. While the synthetic-praxis model is critically important for articulating an indigenous theology, it will benefit considerably with the additional clarity provided by a postcolonial theory of difference for a result that is a fuller and more empowering treatment of tribal theology.

Contextual Theology: A Further Discourse on Methodology

According to Mark L. Taylor, the ethos of postcolonial theology is defined by the combination of the discourse of difference and the discourse of liberating struggle, what he calls it "differentiated liberating struggle."[42] It is "differentiated" because of the fluid and hybrid nature of the postcolonial situation and a "liberating struggle" because of its commitment to liberation from colonizing powers and agents. "In this ethos" Taylor writes, "The discourses of difference are taken up as

---

[40] Thanzauva, *Theology of Community*, 84-88.

[41] *Ibid.*, 84.

[42] Mark L. Taylor, "Spirit and Liberation: Achieving Postcolonial Theology in the United States" in Catherine Keller, Michael Nausner, and Mayra Rivera, ed., *Postcolonial Theologies: Divinity and Empire* (St. Louis: Chalice Press, 2004), 46.

intrinsic to, facilitative of, liberating struggle."[43] In this sense, a postcolonial ethos exists simultaneously with the ongoing anti-colonialist struggles and thereby showing cognizance of the differentiated complexities.

It should now be clear that tribal theology is a form of postcolonial theology in that it emerges out of a people's struggles against the forces of marginalization and oppression. A successful tribal theology will undertake three main functions as it seeks to expose and emasculate the body of global forces which undermine the very existence of its peoples and their cultures. I will discuss these elements in no particular order. One main concern of tribal theology is certainly a "liberating struggle;" struggle for liberation in all its social, political, and economic contexts is a focal point of tribal theology. Just as any other liberation theology, tribal theology inevitably follows the method of praxis and must begin by addressing the existing conditions or situation of the people with the objective to ensure a better and healthier tomorrow. By first engaging the people's experiences of oppression, exploitation and alienations a tribal theology takes seriously the longings and aspirations of the people and it must also be the struggle's motivating force.

Another essential function of tribal theology is to take seriously the history, memories, and experiences of the people. Remembering the past is critical, not merely for its own sake, but to serve as both affirmation and expectation for building and shaping the future the people want. George E. Tinker, an American Indian theologian, articulates this understanding as it would apply in his own context when he states:

> An American Indian theology must be a liberation theology . . . . This American Indian theology will begin with a clear memory of how we got where we are today in order that we might begin to create a future that is healthier than our present.[44]

He goes on to explain that the process of dreaming for the future must be done following, as closely as possible, traditional Indian values and ways of thinking. "We remember the past in order to dream the future, in order to dream or imagine the future into existence, just as the Spider Woman thought the world into existence in the act of creation."[45] Tribal theology, in like manner, must reclaim their past for shaping and building a better future they want.

The third main concern of a tribal theology is that it be equipped to recognize the "differentiated complexities" that go beyond the simplistic binary of colonizer/colonized. An indigenous theology that is influenced by postcolonial thinking and discourse must be amenable to the fluidity and hybridity which

[43] *Ibid.*

[44] George E. Tinker, *Spirit and Resistance: Political Theology and American Indian Liberation* (Minneapolis: Fortress Press, 2004), 4.

[45] Tinker is here referring to the creation story of the Southwestern Indian peoples, especially of the Laguna Pueblo Indians. *Ibid.*

characterize tribal existence. In other words, it must reject the West's worldview which is organized according to, "discreet and mutually exclusive categories,"[46] such as: same/other, spirit/matter, subject/object, civilized/primitive, pure/impure, and rational/chaotic. Modern history is replete with evidence of how such binary thought pattern were manifested in the ways that the colonizer work continuously to delineate and reinforce a clear differentiation between himself and the colonized. Fortunately for projects such as tribal theology postcolonial theory recognizes that things are never organized in such exclusive, rigid, and hierarchical terms. Indeed, there are nuances, in-between spaces, intersections, and psychological manipulations at work in relationships. Spivak suggests that postcolonial theory turns its "critical glance not specifically at the putative identity of the two poles of a binary opposition, but at the hidden ethico-political agenda that drives the differentiation between the two."[47]

Some of the most common metaphors of postcolonial identity are the borderlands, crossroads, and frontiers and which are clearly indicative of the "interstitial" nature of identity.[48] Identity as viewed through a postcolonial lens is not a "fixed set of traits, but rather evolves through a continuing process of interrelation, identification and differentiation. A person's identity is formed as she or he negotiates a sense of belonging to some groups and being distanced from others."[49] For over seventy years now Nagas have been struggling to negotiate their identity as a people over against that which is imposed on them by India. Their search for their own identity is conducted in the midst of their struggle for political sovereignty on the one hand, and religious and cultural selfhood on the other.

Still postcolonial theorists continue to employ terms that constitute collective identity for a group of people, a race or an ethnicity. There are numerous examples such as Latin American, Asian, African, Feminists, American, the poor which continue to be used in spite of the fact that there are clearly few if any "pure" ethnic/racial groups or cultures any where anymore. In reference to Asia, Kwok Pui-lan argues that the use of "Asian" does not necessarily mean an essentialized notion of Asia since Asia is constitutive of multiracial and multicultural groups.[50] There are some who would argue there is no such thing as "Asia." In this sense "Asian" serves heuristic and discursive role to group together all aspects of Asian people and their cultures. It signifies

---

[46] Keller, Nausner, and Rivera, "Introduction," in Keller, Nausner, Rivera, ed., *Postcolonial Theologies*, 11.

[47] Gayatri Chakravorty Spivak, *Critique of Postcolonial Reasons: Toward a History of the Vanishing Present* (Cambridge: Harvard University Press, 1999), 332.

[48] Homi Bhabha calls such perception of identity as an "interstitial perspective" which challenges the conventional understanding of identity.

[49] Catherine Keller, et al, "Introduction," 11-12.

[50] Pui-lan, *Postcolonial Imagination*, 40

that there is some sort of collective consciousness of the Asian people. Further more, Asian culture is not monolithic, it is multifaceted and stratified and hence the use of "Asian" must be seen as a discursive and political construct.

Sugirtharajah makes the following observation regarding the task of theological reflection: "In the postcolonial context Christian theological reflection needs to take on board not an imagined homogeneity but a plurality of identities and coalescing of cultures."[51] In a similar manner and in order to be relevant, tribal theology in the Northeast India must take into serious consideration the plurality of identities and coalescing of cultures within the broad spectrum of tribal peoples. Rather than resorting to painting all the indigenous peoples with one broad stroke, tribal theology should be able to accommodate and affirm the diverse and variable identities that exist within the tribal people themselves in the Northeast India.

Cosmic Interrelatedness and Interdependence: Contextual Theological Reference Point

Space, creation and land are integral to the holistic worldview of indigenous people. Space, creation, and land together serve as the foundation of indigenous people's concept of life, relationship and interdependence. Indigenous worldview is creation-centered and is characterized by understanding the interdependence and the inter-relatedness of *all* creation, including human beings. Therefore, indigenous peoples believe that the whole of creation are our relatives. The Lakota nation of American Indians has an expression which describes beautifully all that concerns the indigenous worldview, "We are all related." According to Standing Rock Sioux scholar Vine Deloria, Jr, the similar phrase, "All my relatives" is not merely a religious sentiment which many people have supposed, but it also "describes the epistemology of the Indian worldview, providing the methodological basis for the gathering of the information about the world."[52] Deloria goes on to explain the implication of this worldview when he states:

> "We are all relatives" when taken as a methodological tool for obtaining knowledge means that we observe the natural world by looking for relationships between various things in it. That is to say, everything in the natural world has relationship with every other thing and the total set of relationships makes up the natural world as we experience it. This concept is simply the relativity concept as applied to a universe that people experience as alive and not as dead or inert.[53]

---

[51] Sugirtharajah, *Postcolonial Reconfigurations*, 7.

[52] Vine Deloria, Jr, *Spirit & Reason: The Vine Deloria, Jr., Reader*, Eds. Barbara Deloria, et al (Golden: Fulcrum Publishing, 1999), 52.

[53] *Ibid.*, 34.

The many concepts expressed by "All our relations" articulates succinctly that humans along with other creations are part of this integrated whole. Space, creation and land are representative of relationship, reciprocity, inter-dependence and wholeness.

Given this reality, indigenous theologians have argued convincingly that an indigenous theology must begin with space and creation, and not with humans. Tinker explains:

> That all American Indian spiritual insights and hence Indian theology must begin with creation is reflected already in the basic liturgical posture of Indians in many North American tribes. Prayers are most often said with the community assembled into some form of circle – a key symbol for self-understanding in these tribes because it represents the whole of the universe and our place and role within it. All see themselves as coequal participants in the circle, standing neither above nor below anything else in creation.[54]

Likewise, Wati Longchar, a Naga theologian, affirms spatiality as the primary datum for doing tribal theology. He brings out a clear distinction between dominant Christian theology and tribal theology in the following argument.

> The dominant Christian theology looks at space from the point of view of humanity. Humanity is the point of reference and the norm. In this case, the primary datum of doing theology is humanity and their liberation. However, for the tribals, the point of departure is space. Space is the point of reference and the key to understanding human selfhood, God and spirit. The space is the foundation for liberation.[55]

Placing space and creation as theology's starting point is crucial because it affirms the relatedness of all beings and all that is created. Consequently, we are all destined to be together as one universal family in which everyone is a coequal participant. Space and creation centered theology provides an orientation to life which is, again, centered on relationship, reciprocity and wholeness. It conveys the imperative recognition of cosmic oneness. And this idea of space is further rooted in the understanding of land; land is a space and a place.

Theologically, this spatial understanding has a far reaching significance. As Nirmal Minz points out, "Space means that everything is integrally related to one another and therefore, they must treat each other with justice, required and demanded of each other."[56] Additionally, it is land that provides identity and

---

[54] Tinker, *Spirit and Resistance*, 91.

[55] Wati Longchar, *An Emerging Asian Theology: Tribal Theology: Issue, Method and Perspective*, Tribal Study Series no. 8 (Jorhat: Tribal Study Centre, 2000), 68.

[56] Nirmal Minz, "Tribal Perspective on Ecology," in Wati Longchar and Yangkahao Vashum, ed., *The Tribal Worldview and Ecology*, Tribal Study Series no. 2. (Jorhat: Tribal Study

security to the people a part from being the Mother to the people. To this day, the tribal people identify themselves with their village rather than their names.[57] A stranger on being enquired would tell his or her village name first, followed by his or her name. Land not only holds them together as a community but also it provides them their status as a people in the world. As Tinker explains, "... Indigenous peoples experience their very personhood in terms of their relationship to the land."[58]

This space/creation centered theology enables us to re-evaluate and reconsider the traditional views of God, Christ, Spirit and salvation including our human place in creation. From a spatial perspective, Longchar argues that God is also organically related to the whole of creation. He explains further:

> This understanding of God leads us to conceive Christ in a new way. Christ is no longer conceived as the one who works only in the hearts of the believers. But, we are challenged to see Christ as the incarnate one who is organically related to the total eco-system. Jesus shares His Being with the whole created order. Since Jesus Chris is an integral part of creation, all parts of creation are now reconciled to Christ. It rejects a Christ of personalism. The incarnation of God in Jesus represents God's entry into finite space.[59]

In like manner, the space-creation centered theology enables us to conceive of human, creation, and church as organically related to one another and to God. From a tribal point of view, therefore, a space-creation centered theology provides a corrective to the human-centered theology of the dominant Christian tradition.

Conclusion

Land and space theology brings in the necessary corrective to the one sided approach of the traditional Christian theology which is anthropocentric in nature.

A living and meaningful theology does not arise in a vacuum; it must always emerge out of a peoples' historical experience. A theology which is empowering and meaningful must, however, not only be grounded in the socio-economic and political realities of the people, it must also incorporate the best of the peoples' values and traditions. Accordingly, Indigenous theology will be this sort of empowering theology and will likewise be informed and guided by indigenous peoples' values and traditions. A significant component of a postcolonial-indigenous theological methodology is the reclamation of the past stories and

---

Center, 1998), 4.

[57] Yangkahao Vashum, "Theology of Land: A Naga Perspective," in Wati Longchar and Yangkahao Vashum, ed., *The Tribal Worldview and Ecology*, Tribal Study Series 2 (Jorhat: Tribal Study Center, 1998), 75f.

[58] Tinker, *Spirit and Resistance*, 102.

[59] Longchar, *An Emerging Asian Theology*, 89.

traditions which sustained the people for tens of generations. When these traditional resources are incorporated with the people's contemporary experience, it becomes possible to construct a relevant and meaningful theology of culture and liberation. Additionally, a postcolonial theological methodology provides a niche for a theology that recognizes not only the plurality of identities and coalescing of cultures but also the "differentiated complexities" which are the consequence of the hybridity that is contemporary indigenous peoples' reality. Indigenous theology must be able to not only affirm but also accommodate the diverse and viable identities that exist within themselves.

Chapter 4

Sources for Studying Tribal Theology

Introduction

Doing theology can be understood as reflections on the faith of' our fathers and mothers. However, more often than not, one refers to the Christian traditions (Bible and traditions) in its strict sense. But this claim can no longer hold true if a relevant theology has to be developed in a given context taking into account the living traditions of that particular people. With the emergence of contextual-liberation theologies, there has been, and more so today, a growing upsurge for taking seriously the traditions of our respective fathers and mothers for doing a theology that is relevant and meaningful to the people. Contextual theologies have come to stay in the world of theology, opening up new vistas for doing theology.[1] Tribal theology as a contextual theology has been on the reckoning for

[1] For a detail discussion on contextual theology, consult Stephen B. Bevans, *Models of Contextual Theology*. Revised and Expanded Edition. Faith and Culture Series (Maryknoll: Orbis Books, 2002); Felix Wilfred, *Margins: Site of Asian Theologies* (Delhi: ISPCK, 2008); Wati Longchar, comp., *Contextual Theologies: Method and Perspectives* (Kolkatta: SCEPTRE, 2013); Robert J. Schreiter, *Constructing Local Theologies* (Maryknoll: Orbis Books, 1989); Clemens Sedmak, *Doing Local Theology: A Guide for Artisans of a New Humanity* (Maryknoll: Orbis Books, 2002); K. Thanzauva, *Theology of Community: Tribal Theology in the Making* (Bangalore: Asian trading Corporation, 2004); Wati Longchar, *An Emerging Asian Theology: Tribal Theology: Issue, Method and Perspective*. Tribal Study Series, no. 8 (Jorhat: Tribal Study Centre, 2000); Yangkahao Vashum, Peter Haokip and Melvil Pereira, eds., *Search for a New Society: Tribal Theology for North East India* (Guwahati: North Eastern Social Research Centre, 2012); Razouselie Lasetso and Yangkahao Vashum, eds., *Tribal Christian Theology: Methods and Sources for Constructing a Relevant Theology for the Indigenous People of North East India*. Tribal Study Series no. 15 (Jorhat: Tribal Study Centre,

quite sometime now. Efforts to develop relevant tribal theology using the available traditional resources is slowly paying its dividend, although we still have to go a long way.

This chapter attempts to identify and discuss some of the important sources for doing tribal theology. By sources we mean the resources or the raw materials necessary for shaping theology. John Macquarrie calls them the formative factors.[2] These formative factors or sources determine the character of a given theology. According to James Cone, "The sources are the relevant data for the theological task..."[3] A word about the sequence of the given sources. The sequence of the discussion is not necessarily in order of importance. This is because it is difficult to know which source is more important. They are all interdependent. One cannot really make a sharp distinction one from the other. Hence, it is important to look at it as one composite whole in which each is indispensably related.

1. Tribal Traditional Heritages

Tribals are well known for their rich traditional heritages. The traditional heritages include the past and the present, socio-cultural tradition, customs, religious beliefs and practices. They include myths and legend, folktales and stories, wisdom and proverbs, mores and morals, songs and so on. These cultural traditions existed and are transmitted orally from generation to generation. Renthy Keitzar describes the oral tradition of the tribal people as the unwritten 'Prime Bible." He writes that

> These may be called as the unwritten 'Prime Bible' of the tribal/ indigenous people. One can find in these oral traditions their beliefs, norms, and practices; hence a great and rich treasure of theological value is hidden with this 'Prime Bible' of the people.[4]

a) Tribal Religion

Tribals are said to be deeply religious in their own way. Tribals have a holistic view of religion in which they have a holistic view of realities. Their religious life does not make distinctions between sacred and secular, spiritual and physical, heavenly and earthly, all these together constitute wholeness of life. In this sense, for the tribal people, religion would simply mean living in the spontaneous awareness of,

---

2007); Shimreingam Shimray, ed., *Tribal Theology: A Reader*. Tribal Study Series no. 12 (Jorhat: Tribal Study Centre, 2003).

[2] John Macquarrie, *Principles of Christian Theology* (London: SCM Press, 1996), 4.

[3] James H. Cone, *A Black Theology of Liberation*. Second Edition (New York: Obris Book, 1986), 21.

[4] Renthy Kietzar, *In Search of a Relevant Gospel Message* (Guwahati: CLC, 1995), 85.

an encounter with, acknowledgement of, and obedience to the active reality of the presence of God.[5]

Tribals believe in the Supreme Being/High God, who is the Creator and Sustainer of the Universe. They believe in the God who is loving and merciful, just and compassionate. Most tribals have a masculine name for the Supreme God. But, there are some tribes who have both the masculine and feminine names for God. The feminine term for God thus indicates the feminine nature of God as the mother. Some of these tribal conceptions of God as male and female can be very well used in formulating an inclusive theology of God.[6]

In like manner, the tribal belief in the Spirit, especially the benevolent spirits can be used for interpreting the understanding of the Holy Spirit from a tribal perspective. The spirit pervades and controls the whole universe.[7]

Tribal religion does not have a written scripture like other religions do. But, they have myths and legends, folktales and stories in which the whole of their religious ethos are embodied. Myths, especially, unravel and teach how the Supreme Being works and reveals his/her mysteries through creation, the place of the animal kingdom in this universe and so on. Thus, myths are our scripture and creed.[8]

What is myth then? Mercea Eliade defines myth as "a 'true story' and, beyond that, a story that is most precious possession because it is sacred, exemplary, significant."[9] In a similar way, David Scott says,

> A myth is a story that is sacred to and shared by a group of people who find their most important meaning in it; it is a story ... about the sorts of questions that religions ask, stories about such things as life after death, supernatural/divine intervention in their lives, transformations, the creation of the world and human nature and culture and basically about meaning itself.[10]

Myths thus convey profound theological meanings and the religious truth of a particular group of people. They tell us about God, spirits and their relations

---

[5] Wati Longchar, "The Traditional Ao-Naga Worldview and Its Contribution Towards a Christian Understanding of Creation" (Unpublished Doctoral Dissertation, SATHRI, Bangalore, 1996), 110.

[6] For detail discussion consult Eyingbeni Hümtsoe-Nienu, *God of the Tribes: Christian perspective on the Naga ancestral idea of the supreme Being* (Mokokchung: Clark Theological College, 2014).

[7] Wati Longchar, "The Myths: A Resource for Doing Tribal Theology", a paper presented at the Clark '95, November 13-15, 1995.

[8] Qouted by Longchar, *Ibid*, 2.

[9] Quoted by Wati Longchar, *Traditional Worldview and Modernity*, 2-9.

[10] Samuel Rayan, "Reconceiving Theology in the Asian Context," *Doing Theology in a divided world*. eds., F. Virginia and Torres, 124.

with human beings and creation. They tell us how human beings understand themselves, their life realities, and their relationship with god and creation. Tribals have a number of myths and folktales that explain unity of nature and religion, nature and culture, and the God-human-world relationship These myths understood within the right perspective can become an invaluable source for theologizing in the context of the tribal people.

b) Socio-cultural Traditions

Tribals have a set of social and cultural principles based on social justice and kinship relations. Tribal life is characterized by communitarianism, the principle of selfless love and concern for the welfare of community basically characterizing the social and cultural life of the tribal community. This governing principle of the tribal society is known as *sobaliba*[11] in Ao-Naga and *tlawmngaihna*[12] in Mizo. It is a social-ethical principle of the tribal community, which provides the basis for a communitarian society to exist and function effectively. This spirit of altruism may very well be described as the philosophical and ethical foundation of a communitarian society. This is clearly seen in the way tribal people live out their life in the community. They lead a life of sharing and caring, justice and honesty, simplicity and truthfulness. The welfare of the community, takes precedence over all other things. Thus the tribals live in community, work with community, and die for the community's sake. As R. R. Shimray rightly says, "They work in groups, eat in groups and sleep in groups. There is no individual cultivation nor harvest, no individual house making.... All things were done in the full presence of the entire community."[13]

Another cultural practice of the tribal people that is of paramount importance is the system of 'bachelors dormitory', which is widely known among the Nagas as *morung* and as *zawlbuk* among the Mizos. It may be rightly described as the cultural institution of the tribal community. This *morung* system has multiple functions. It is the cultural training centre where the youngsters are taught and trained in all kinds of skills. It is the custodian of culture, traditions and values of tribal community. It is the sign of communitarian integrity and harmony. It is an institution where people learn to maintain a high ethical principle and strict disciplines. Because of all these, K. Thanzauva describes *zawlbuk* as an institution where the principle of *tlawmngaihna* is put into practice.[14]

The tribal traditional values such as the principle of *sobaliba/tlawmngaihna* and cultural practices such as the *morung/zawlbuk* systems have a great deal of

---

[11] *Ibid.*

[12] K. Thanzauva, "A Theological Basis for Social Transformation: Methodological Implications of Third World Liberation Theology in the Context of Mizoram," North East India (an unpublished Doctoral Dissertation, 1993), 236.

[13] R. R. Shimray, *Origin and Cultures of Nagas* (New Delhi: Pamlei Shimray, 1985), 120.

[14] Thanzauva, "A Theological Basis...," 279.

theological insights to offer for formulating tribal theology. There is a need for 'rediscovery' of some of these important traditional/cultural values for developing a theology that is contextually relevant and authentic. Thanzauva calls for such a rediscovery of cultural values for theology. In his attempt for rediscovery of the concept of *tlawmngaihna,* Thanzauva calls for reinterpretation of the concept in the changing situation of today. Accordingly, this is what he says,

> The universal concern of Christian theology, the biblical teaching of love and justice, must be incorporated into *tlawmngaihna* to meet the challenges of today. Thus, *tlawmngaihna* in the modem situation is love in action to protect and uphold the marginalised, and a commitment to create a just, harmonious, progressive, participatory and self-reliant society.... It requires involvement in the struggle against exploiting systems and structures, which spoil the harmony of community.[15]

This is how one can develop a tribal theology of social ethics using some of the traditional resources.

Similarly, one can also make an attempt for rediscovery of *morung/zawlbuk* for constructing tribal ecclesiology in the context of the modem society. Here again, Thanzauva has made an attempt along the same line. He concludes, saying, "A *zawlbuk* ecclesiology suggests that the local church should be an instrument for the well-being, harmony and development of the local community where it exists, without losing its universal nature."[16]

2. Tribal Experience

Experience is one of the most important sources for doing theology. C. S. Song, one of the leading Asian theologians, categorically states the significance of experience for theology as follows:

> The totality of life is the raw material of theology. Theology deals with concrete issues that affects life in its totality and not just with abstract concepts that engage theological brains. No human problem is too humble or too insignificant for theology. Theology has to wrestle with the earth, not with heaven.

[17]Any theology that is divorced from the concrete life experience of the people can hardly be called a living theology. Contextual theology begins by raising existential issues of the people. Tribal theology, for that matter, has to be done by raising existential questions in the context of the people's suffering and

---

[15] *Ibid.*, 272.

[16] *Ibid.*, 288.

[17] C.S. Song. *Tell Us Our Names: Stoiy Theology from an Asian Perspective* (Indore: Satorakashan Sanchai Kendra, 1.986), 6.

pain; by taking into serious consideration peoples' emotional feelings, aspirations and hopes.

Today, the life story of the tribals of North East India is marked by violence, ethnic crises, division, underdevelopment, land alienation, and poverty. The whole of North East India is burning with the problem of insurgency, militarization, foreigners issue, state sponsored terrorism, human rights violations, etc. There is an increase in peoples unrest and uprising movements manifested in the form of rallies, bandhs, and strikes where people go into a frenzy leading to the virtual paralysis of normal life. And the sum product of all these problems is the suffering of the innocent masses.

It is a plain fact that the Northeast tribals are the most neglected and alienated people in India. There is total negligence of the people in all fronts: economic, social, political and in all areas of development works. Commenting on the poverty stricken situation of the North East India, Raveena says, "The mother cause of any upheaval is underdevelopment, unemployment, backwardness and the feeling of being left out ... earlier by the British government ... subsequently by India itself..."[18] Thanzauva also speaks along the same lines on the problems of the North East tribals. Analysing the tribal situation of the North East from the sociological point of view, he comes out with the findings that suppression, assimilation, isolation policy, faulty developmental policy of the government, etc, are the major causes of the tribals' unfortunate condition. He goes on to say that these are theological agenda. All these represent and reflect the life context of the tribals.

These life realities of the tribals challenge us to reflect upon the faith experience of the community; to raise theological questions such as what is God for us? What is Christ for us, the tribals of North East India? In this connection, what James Cone describes about the black people's experience in the United States of America is significant. Cone asserts,

> The Black experience is a source of black theology because this theology seeks to relate biblical revelation to the situation of Blacks in America.... Black theology cannot speak of God and God's involvement in contemporary American without identifying God's presence with the events of liberation in the Black community.[19]

Tribal peoples experience is also a source of tribal theology because it seeks to experience and discern God's presence in the midst of the tribals' struggle for liberation. Tribal people's experience of pain and suffering therefore, serves as a primary source for doing tribal theology.

---

[18] Raveena, "Anatomy of Insurgency," *North East Sun*, (July 29, 1.995), vol. i, no. l, 6.

[19] James Cone, *A Black Theology of Liberation*, 25

3. Tribal History

History is important for all human communities because it is in history that people's identity is shaped. People's history in a way stands for the identity of the people. People without history of their own are therefore considered to be people without identity. To lose one's identity is to lose one's meaning of life's existence. Theologically speaking, history is important because it is in human history that God acts. Song puts it this way, "The frontiers of our theology must move from the history of Israel and the history of Christianity in the West to the history in which we are involved in Asia. With this expansion of our historical horizon, we gain broader and deeper insights into the mystery of God's ways with the nations."[20] God acts in history. The areas of God's activity include, human experience in history, current events and culture.[21]

Tribals of North East India too have their own history. But, their history, for most part of it, has been characterized by suffering and restiveness. Thanzauva describes that the history of tribals is a history of suffering, danger of genocide, exploitation, discrimination, displacement and alienation.[22] It is a history where the tribals have been at the receiving end. It is a history in which the very survival of the tribals has been threatened. The history and experience of the tribal people today is further complicated by the onslaught of booming tourism,[23] issues of illegal migrants/immigrants and refugees coming in to our land. While people from outside of the region are welcomed and treated as guests, there is genuine underlying fear that the local people will be outnumbered by the others.[24] Today, in fact the whole of Northeast Indian people comprising 8 states are living in fear and trembling, because the Indian government has been treating the region as a dumping ground for the refugees and migrants/immigrants. The latest and the most controversial issue relates to the present government's attempt to introduce and pass the Citizenship Amendment Bill (CAB) which will allow Indians (barring Muslims) settled outside of India (Pakistan, Bangladesh, and Afghanistan) who had fled religious persecution before December 2014 to be eligible for Indian citizenship and settle down anywhere they like and desire in the country. Of

---

[20] C.S. Song, *Tell Us Our Names*, 8.

[21] S.B. Bevans, *Models of Contextual Theology* (New York: Orbis Books, 1994), 17.

[22] K. Thanzauva, "Theological Basis," 114.

[23] In recent years the governments of the day have been promoting the Northeast Indian regions as tourism destination to the world through hosting and organizing annual festivals such as Hornbill festivals in Nagaland, Sangai and Shirui Lily festivals in Manipur, etc. which have impacted negatively to the local people – prostitution and trafficking of women and children, promotion of drugs, alcohol and other intoxicant substances, threat to cultural identity of local and indigenous people, environmental and ecological degradation, human rights abuse, etc.

[24] The classic example is that the indigenous people in the state of Tripura have been reduced to minority in their own land by the outsiders; the tribal population is 31.8% according to 2011census.

course, the main target no doubt, is the Northeastern states. The whole of North East India witnessed protests, rallies and bandhs against the bill; in fact, the whole region came to a grinding halt for a considerably long period due to the violent protests and demonstrations against the bill. The bill was eventually passed in December 2019 as Citizenship Amendment Act, 2019.[25] The people of the region fiercely opposed the bill/Act because it is unconstitutional (discrimination on the basis of religion – Muslims excluded) and it will result in the loss of their political rights, culture, and land rights.[26] And the indigenous people will be reduced to minority in their own land.

Of course, surely, tribal history is more than all these. It is also more importantly tribals saying no to all forms of exploitation and discrimination. It is more importantly the history of the tribal people's struggle for liberation. It is the history in which tribals of North East India are fighting for their rights and freedom.

The tribals' involvement in history in the struggle for liberation is a source of tribal theology. Kosuke Koyama, out of his involvement with the farmers of Northern Thailand, asserts that "involvement is the only 'soil' from which theology germinates."[27] It is in their history that tribals have to find their interpretation of God's work in the world because divine activity is inseparable from their history.

4. Christian Heritages

Under Christian heritages, revelation, scripture, tradition and reason will be discussed as sources tor theology. Each of them will be briefly discussed because they have been regarded as primary sources for Christian theology all through the years.

a) Revelation: Revelation is the primary source of theology and is also a basic category of theological thinking. The basic truth is that unless God reveals himself to us through His creation, and especially through Jesus Christ, we cannot formulate theology. For Christian faith, revelation takes place in human history. It is an event. For James Cone, "It is God's self revelation to the human race through a historical act of human liberation."[28] The exodus event in the Old Testament is God's revelatory act. In the New Testament, God's revelatory event

---

[25] The bill eventually passed in the parliaments as Citizenship Amendment Act, 2019 (CAA). Although, the CAA exempts tribal areas of North East India covered under Sixth Schedule and "Inner Line" provision, the people of the region are highly skeptical about the overall Act because people fear that those provisions could eventually be revoked. For detail consult "The Citizenship (Amendment) Act, 2019," http://egazette.nic.in/WriteReadData/2019/214646.pdf (12/04/2020).

[26] https://m.economictimes.com/news/et-explains/citizenship-amendment-bill-what-does-it-do-and-why-is-it-seen-as-a-problem/articleshow/72436995.cms (12/04/2020). Assam will be the most affected of all the states since the state already has innumerable Hindu migrants from Bangladesh and the people genuinely fear the Act will threaten their cultural and linguistic identities.

[27] Kosuke Koyama, *Waterbuffalo Theology* (New York: Orbis Books, 1989), viii.

[28] James Cone, *A Black Theology of Liberation*, 29.

happens in the person of Jesus. Therefore, "In Christian thinking the man Jesus must be the decisive interpretive factor in everything we say about God because he is the plenary revelation of God," affirms James Cone.[29] He goes on to say that revelation is not just a past event, it is also a present event in which we can encounter with God now in history.

b) Scripture: The Bible is primarily the word of God. The Bible is the original document about the events on which Christianity is based. It is the record of God's revelatory acts in the life of the people. "Scripture is not itself revelation" writes John Macquarrie, "but it is one important way ... by which the community of faith keeps open its access to that primordial revelation on which the community' has been founded."[30] It is true that revelation comes in a person not in a book. However, the Bible is an indispensable witness to God's revelation, therefore, it is one of the primary sources of Christian theology. Tribal theology is biblical theology only when it takes seriously the importance of the Bible in its theological discourse.

c) Tradition: Tradition is another important source of theology. "Tradition refers to the theological reflection of the church upon the nature of Christianity from the time of the early church to the present day. It is impossible for any student of Christianity to ignore tradition; the New Testament itself is a result of it," writes James Cone.[31] In fact, tradition contributes a great deal toward the formulation of Christian doctrines or creeds. The Christian tradition is not simply a rival to scripture, but in many ways it is complementary to Christian scripture. Having acknowledged the importance of tradition for theology one has to be also careful in using tradition for theological discourse. This is because not all the so-called traditions of the church are relevant for a given context. Some could be very oppressive in its meaning and content, formulated at the behest of the rich and powerful.

d) Reason: Another important source of theology is reason. By reason we mean two things: the first is the faculty to think and reason, the ability to know what is right and what is wrong. It refers to the discerning capacity of a person. The second usage refers to philosophy - the philosophical thoughts and traditions. It also refers to the rational character of theology. It is in this sense that reason becomes an important source of theology. A number of theologians have relied on philosophies for their theological formulations. For example Thomas Aquinas's theology was greatly influenced by Aristotle and his philosophy, and Paul Tillich, Rudolf Bultmann and many others by Heideggerian existentialists philosophy.

The role of reason cannot be denied if theology is to be reasonable and systematic. No doubt, some times reason can play an exaggerated role in theology

---

[29] *Ibid.*, 30.

[30] John Macquarrie, *Principles of Christian Theology*, 8.

[31] James Cone, *A Black Theology of Liberation*, 33.

and it can even subordinate revelation and experience as the debate between reason and revelation indicate in the history of Christian theology. Aquinas put too much emphasis on reason which made Christian theology appear like an intellectual law and philosophical discipline. Owen C. Thomas offers two aspects of reason in theology. First, "Human reason is active in the receiving of God's self-disclosure…." Secondly, "Reason is active in the work of theology, in analyzing and reflecting on the testimony to and interpretation of revelation in the Bible and the history of Christian theology."[32]

Conclusion

What I have done so far is a modest attempt to identify and discuss some of the important sources for doing tribal theology. They are all indispensable sources. Relevant tribal theology, or any contextual theology for that matter, arises at a particular point of history, in the dynamic interaction of the gospel, life experience and culture. Tribal theology has to emerge out of the interaction of the text (Bible) and the tribal experiences of actual life and faith in their own context to express their relationship with God who is concerned with their total salvation. A creative interaction of gospel and culture is therefore necessary for developing a holistic theology of life. I would like to conclude by quoting Samuel Rayan, one of the most distinguished Roman Catholic theologians of India. He says that

> We want theology to be a service to life and to human wholeness. It should be service to life at all levels - from the tiny blade of grass to the singing birds to the growing baby.... Our theology will be at the service of those who work, suffer, and hope, those who struggle for justice and human dignity for all women and men.[33]

---

[32] Owen C. Thomas, *Introduction to Theology.* Revised Edition. (Serampore: Indian Theological Library/Senate of Serampore, 1989), 7.

[33] Samuel Rayan, "Reconceiving Theology in the Asian Context," *Doing Theology in a divided world.* eds., F. Virginia and Torres, 124.

Chapter 5

Theology of Land
A Naga Tribal-Indigenous Perspective

"The earth is the Lord's and all that is in it,
the world, and those who live in it."
(Ps. 24:1 NRSV).

Introduction

The chapter begins with the assertion of the holistic worldview of the Nagas, around which revolves the total being of the people – their personality, thinking and outlook. Their spirituality is intrinsically connected to it. Then a research into the Naga tribal/indigenous concept of land follows. This is followed by a brief study of the biblical understanding of land. Finally, with the resources drawn from tribal traditions and the Bible, an attempt is made to develop a theology of land.

A word may also be said about the materials used for the paper. Although, the subject is with special reference to the Nagas, the use of materials related to other non Nagas is also inevitable, since they are expressive of the commonalities found in all the tribes. In spite of the fact that every tribe in the world has its own distinctiveness, and yet, the general features that run through all the tribes is visibly undeniable. Hence, the reference to other non-Naga tribes as well.

Naga Tribal Worldview

The Naga-tribal worldview is aptly described as the holistic vision of life. This idea of the holistic view of reality transcends the idea of dualism or duality of the western world. For the Nagas there is no distinction between sacred and secular, physical and spiritual, earthly and heavenly.[1] All these together constitute wholeness of life. This holistic vision or the primal vision can be called, "Undifferentiated Unity." M. M. Thomas describes the primal vision as follows: "In it there is the vision of the spiritual continuum with which the dead and the living, natural objects, spirits and gods, the individual, clan and tribe, animals, plants minerals and humans form an unbroken hierarchical unity of spiritual forces; and the human self is not an individual self but an extended universal self present and actively participating in an all parts of the totality"[2] M. M. Thomas' use of the term 'hierarchical' may be found to be a deviation from the Naga-tribal understanding of the organismic unity of human and creation. The term 'hierarchical' connotes coercion and dominion. Whereas the Naga tribal holistic vision of life moves beyond hierarchy, overcomes dualism and establishes equality and community. According to this vision, life of all forms are inter-related to one another and they all together constitute an organic unity. In this sense, human, nature and spirit do not stand apart from each other as opposing factors. Rather they "continue as a basic texture of existence, is what makes man truly human. Balance and harmony of man-nature-spirit are essential for man to continue to remain human."[3] In the same vein K. Thanzauva talks about "a community model of God-self-world relationship."[4] In this cosmic community, Thanzauva says, "God is seen as the originator and ground of community. Thus, the act of creation is regarded not as the potter or the artist does, but as 'bodying forth' as the mother does. This means that the universe including our earth with all its creatures lives and moves and has its being in God."[5] This then explains the inter-connectedness or the unity of all the entities. Hence, to the Nagas, the land is not an unattached entity of the universe but very much a subject of theological concern. This tribal holistic view of reality is theological concern. This tribal holistic view of reality is therefore important for our deeper understanding of the Naga-tribal concept of land. It is this holistic vision of life that has shaped the Naga concept of land.

---

[1] Yangkahao Vashum, *Tangkhul Naga – Christian Theology of Human Rights* (unpublished M.Th Thesis, Gurukul, 1994), 75. Cf. Renthy Keitzar, "Tribal Cultural Ethos and Christianity in North East India", ETC Journal, Vol. 1, No. 2 (Jan – May, 1998), 49.

[2] M.M. Thomas, "Primal Vision and modernization", a paper presented in the National Seminar on Theological Implications of the Primal Vision Sponsored by BTESSC/GLTC, September 9-12, 1993 at GLT College, Madras, 2.

[3] Nirmal Minz, Primal Religious Perspectives on ecology", Daniel D. Chetti, ed. *Ecology and Development: Theological Perspective*, GLTC, 1991

[4] K. Thanzauva, *Theological Basis for Social Transformation: Methodological Implications of Third World Liberation Theology in the Context of Mizoram, North East India* (unpublished DTh Dissertation, Melbourne, 1993), 300.

[5] *Ibid.*, 301.

Naga Tribal Concept of Land

The Naga-tribal concept of land is basically based on the wholeness of life. It is based on the tribal view of 'God-self-world relationship.' For the Nagas, land is associated with their life. Land is the source of their life and it is part of their lives itself. To the Nagas, land is sacred. They have no other temple than the land. Land is a gift of God. Hence, in the Naga concept there is no room for treating land as an object to be used as a commodity for sale. Humans are not the real owners of the land. God is the ultimate owner. Humans are placed as custodians of God's creations. Further, it is the land that owns the community and gives their identity. As Thanzauva points out, land is integral to their concept of history. "It is by land that they count their time, measure distance and understand their lives. It cannot be owned by legal means except by living in it."[6] In the words of Wati Longchar, "The land not only sustains the individuals, village, clans and tribe, but it also unites the Creator, spirits, ancestors and living beings as one family. The land is the symbol of unity for all life."[7] The importance of land to the tribals may be further illustrated by the following atatements:

(a) *Speech delivered by the Chief of Seatle in 1854 (N. America)*:

> The Great Chief of Washington sends word that he wishes to buy our land... how can you buy and sell the sky, the warmth of the land? The idea is strange to us... Every part of this earth is sacred to my people...
>
> We know that the white man does not understand our ways... he treats his mother, the earth and his brother, the sky as things...
>
> I do not know. Our ways are different from your ways...
>
> One thing we know, our God is the same God. This earth is precious to Him. Even the white man cannot be exempted from the common destiny.
>
> This we know: the earth does not belong to man; man belongs to the earth... whatever befalls the earth befalls the sons of the earth.[8]

(b) *Letter from Black to White*:

> The land is my backbone. I only stand straight, happy, proud and not ashamed about my colour because I still have land. The land is the art. I can paint, dance, create and sing as my ancestors did before me. I think of land as the history of my nation... we will be the lowest people in the world, because you have broken my backbone, took away my arts,

---

[6] *Ibid.*, 316.

[7] Wati Longchar, *Returning to Mother Earth: Theology, Christian Witness and Theological Education: An Indigenous Perspective.* PTCA Series no. 4 (Tainan: PTCA, 2012), 29.

[8] Quoted from Nirmal Minz, *op.cit.*, 45.

history and foundation. You have left with nothing. Without land, I am nothing.[9]

Indigenous people's voice from India[10]

(c) The land is our mother, how can we leave her, where will we go? What will we eat? The mother earth provides us with crops and food. We won't give her up so easily.

(d) We will give our blood, our life; we are the people of this land since the time of our great fore-parents. They were buried here and their spirits live here. Our village land is sacred. Our religion, culture and identity are rooted in this land. How can we sell our life sustaining mother?

The above statements are expressive of how the indigenous-tribals from different parts of the world, irrespective of the geographical differences, look at, perceive, understand and relate themselves to the land. What the land means to them. They all share the same affinity to the land. They reflect the people's experience of exploitations, alienations, and their struggles and cries for their lands at the backdrop of the onslaughts of powerful global market economic forces and the state collaborators. The states in cahoots with powerful corporations usurp and exploit land and natural resources of the indigenous people. Without land, tribals are no people. Land is everything for the tribals. It is their backbone. Landlessness is equal to people without roots and history. Most of all, the tribals have filial relations with the land.

Land is a Gift of God

For the Nagas, land is primarily a gift of God. For them land, forest, rivers, mountains, etc, are primarily not the means of production but are means of livelihood created and given by God. The Nagas believe in the Supreme Being who is the Creator and Sustainer of heaven and earth. Since the land is a means of livelihood they have their fixed time and mode of cultivation. They would cultivate for only certain months. And after that everything takes a break - fields are left fallow, animals are left free and people too go visiting their relatives. For the Nagas making an effort at greater production beyond their needs will be a sign of greed and a sign of pride. The God given land is therefore used for their sustenance only and not for profit making. Land being God's gift is shared by all. It should not be commercialized.

---

[9] Quoted in K. Thanzauva, *op.cit.*, 316.

[10] Wati Longchar, *Returning to Mother Earth: Theology, Christian Witness and Theological Education: An Indigenous Perspective*. PTCA Series no. 4 (Tainan: PTCA, 2012). 8-10.

Land is Sacred

Since land is a gift of God, it is sacred. Secondly, land is the dwelling place of the gods/spirits. God is believed to be in all the things of the earth. Thirdly, land is sacred to the Nagas because, the ancestors have lived and worked on the same land; their bones are lying in their land and are finally taking rest there.[11] Hence, land is a "sacred place of communion with their ancestors and spirits. Their past history is enshrined in the lives of the ancestors."[12] It is precisely for this reason that the Nagas do not till the ground, plough the fields without permission from the gods/spirits of land. Before they start digging the ground for building their houses, the will of God is sought. There is also what is known as the practice of ordeal involving eating of earth in order to settle land disputes whenever there is lack of evidence to know who is wrong and who is right. The contenders will eat the soil invoking the name of the Supreme Being. Within the specific time limit whoever dies is considered to be the guilty person. It is believed that the supernatural being has restored justice in the land by punishing the guilty. Hence, much respect and honor is paid to the land.

Land is the Mother Earth

The Nagas hold that land is the mother earth. Basically, there are two reasons: most of the Nagas have their myths/folktales which say that they are children of the earth. The Ao tradition holds that the Aos came out of six stones, called *Longtrok*.[13] The Chang Naga legend says that human existence on earth started when man emerged from a big hole of earth.[14] The Tangkhuls have a folk tale which tells that they originated from the bowel of the earth called *Miwurlung*.[15] According to this folk tale, they came upon the earth led by a person called Phungshoka (the one who led) and came to settle down in their present country. This event is considered as the mother earth giving birth to them. Secondly, land is considered as the generous mother not only for giving birth to them but also because she nurtures and sustains them by the produce of the land: The earth with her natural bounty is the source of their life and sustenance. Hence, the mother earth is deeply respected and honoured. The Nagas attach much of their relational

---

[11] M. Horam, *Nagas Old Ways New Trends*, (Delhi: Cosmos Publications, 1988), 15f.

[12] Johnson Vada Kumchery, "The Earth Mother and the Indigenous People of India", in *Journal of Dharma*, Vol. XXVIII, No. 1 (Jan – March, 1993), 89.

[13] Panger Imchen, *Ancient Ao-Naga Religion and Culture* (New Delhi: Haranad and Publications, 1993), 20

[14] *Folk Tales from Nagaland Part I & II*, (Kohima: Directorate of Art and Culture, Nagaland), 1989, 151.

[15] Yangkahao Vashum, *Op.cit.*, 55. Cf. R. Brown, "The Tangkhul Nagas: Statistical Account of the Nature, State of Manipur, 1983" in Verrier Elvin, ed., *The Nagas in the Ninteenth Century*, (Calcutta: Oxford University Press, 1969, 481.

feelings with the land. The feeling of the mother-child relations with the earth pervades the hearts of the Nagas.

Land is a Space and a Place

For the Nagas, land is both a space and a place. Land for the tribals is a 'space' because unlike the Euro-American/Western thinking which gives first priority to temporal awareness or time, the tribals give priority to the awareness of space as a basic category of life orientation. Space here signifies relationships and connectedness. Theologically, this has a far-reaching consequence. Nirmal Minz comments, "Space meant that everything is integrally related to one another and therefore, they must treat each other with justice, required and demanded of each other."[16] In this sense, felling a tree without reciprocity of supplementing its loss is wrong. Such reciprocity keeps the balance between humans and nature. It holds life in balance and in harmony.

Land is a place because it is the land that gives identity to the people. Walter Brueggemann says that 'place' connotes 'home' and is bound up with a sense of belonging, a story which conveys an identity, a basis for participating in history.[17] The Nagas until recently identified themselves with their village rather than their names. A stranger on being asked would tell his or her village name rather than his or her name. This is so because the land holds the community together and hence, the land gives them security and their identity. Land further gives them their status - their place in the world.

For the Nagas, mountains and vales, rivers and rolling hills, and gorges and ranges signify life, story and history of the people as opposed to the Euro-western idea of wilderness fit to be exploited. It is through the mountains and valleys, hills and rivers that their stories and histories are embedded. R. R. Shimray poignantly states, "Every mountain, every range, and every ridge has a legend and every peak a tale to tell."[18] Most of the mountains, valleys, hills, rivers, gorges and ranges are known and identified by the stories/incidence associated with them. Therefore, every place has stories to tell. Some of them are regarded as sacred places. Further, they serve as the boundary lines between and among the neighboring villages and tribes. In this way, land is regarded and connected to the people.

Land Ownership

In the tribal society, land is owned by the community in general. Land tenure in Naga society is well reflected in the report that follows:

---

[16] Nirmal Minz, "The Adivasi Perspective on Ecology" in *Ecology: A Theological Response,* ed. Andreas Nehring. (Madras: GLTC, 1994), 69.

[17] Quoted by K. Thanzauva. *Op.cit.*, p. 326.

[18] R. R. Shimray, *Origin and Culture of Nagas* (New Delhi: Mrs. Pamleiphy Shimray, Privately published, 1985), 6.

> In Nagaland, each tribe had a well demarcated history within the villages inhabited by that tribe were located, with well-defined boundaries. Though the practice of each tribe differed, the village land was generally classified as (a) common village land, (b) clan land, (c) individual land and (d) *morung* land. The village council was responsible for the management. Clan land was mostly jhum land owned by a particular clan certain areas, usually terraced land, were owned by individuals. Some portion of the village land was designed for *morung* where the young boys slept there.[19]

The stated report is expressive of the land system among the Nagas in general, though each tribe has different systems. In most cases, it is the community or the village that owns the land. The village chief holds the nominal ownership of the land. The village chief is assisted by the village council, the people's representatives. However, the ultimate power rests in the hands of the people as a whole, who empower the chief and the council to carry out the tasks on behalf of the village. However, there are some tribes like the Sumis and Chang Nagas, in their case, the village chief seems to be all in all. The land tenure is in the chief's hand.[20]

To the Naga, the idea of commercialization or privatization is a recent development, which was never heard of before. The tribals in North East India, are confronted with the problem of privatization through which now land is being owned by a few privileged/rich people, resulting in the landlessness of many in their own land. Further, there are cases of abuse of land and desacralisation by the outsiders in close collaboration with few self-vested insiders. A much more serious case is the forceful occupation of the Naga lands by the alien forces which has virtually threatened the very existence of the Nagas in their own mother land. The age-old community ethos and the very fabric of the community life which is the hallmark of the Naga society is virtually reduced to a horrendous state.

The Nagas in the past went to war when there was the case of land encroachment. They gave their lives for the sake of the land. The Nagas are staunch protectors of their land. They know that without land they are no people. Hence, whenever there is sign of external coercion the Nagas would oppose tooth and nail. This attitude is reflected in the ongoing conflicts between the Naga National forces and the Indian armed forces. As R. R. Shimray rightly observes, "The Naga homeland which the forefathers selected... Every mountain, every range, and every ridge has a legend and every peak a tale to tell,"[21] is so dear and mysterious to be parted with. To part an inch of land is equivalent to giving away a portion of the self (person).

---

[19] Planning Commission, *The Report of the Working Group on the Land System Among Tribals in the North Eastern India*, May 1984.

[20] J. H. Hutton, *The Sema Nagas* (London: Oxford University Press, 1968), 144 f.

[21] R.R. Shimray, *Origin and Culture of the Nagas* (New Delhi: Mrs. Pamleiphy, 1985), 6.

Land in the Bible

This section will examine the biblical understanding of land. Walter Brueggmann observes that land in the Bible stands for hope, blessing and security.[22] Hence, land in the Bible is one of the most important theological themes. The first account about land is written by the Yahwist, the first theologians in the Bible. It is the promise of land by Yahweh to Abraham (Gen. 12:1:15:7).

Land is a Gift of God

Land in the Bible is primarily God's gift to the Israelites. It is the fulfillment of God's promise to the people of Israel. All the three sources – Yahwist, Priestly and Deuteronomist – talked about the concept of land. All the writers reflect the idea that land is a gift of God – a promise fulfillment. However, it is the Deuteronomist who has made the land as the central theme of his theology (Deut. 8:7-10). God's promise of land to the Israelites is amply found in the Bible. Abraham and his descendants are promised land (Gen. 13:15). Issac and his descendants are promised land (Gen. 26:3). Also Jacob and his descendants are promised land (Gen. 28:13). Quoting Gen. 12:1-3 in which Abraham is promised land by Yahweh, Raphel Jospe says that "the promised land is thus not incidental to Israel's covenant with God, but lies, as an essential component, at its very foundation."[23] According to Raphel and others, the biblical account of God's covenant with Abraham and his descendants begins with a territorial imperative. In this sense, land is the primary content on which God entered into covenantal relationship with Israel. This is why Martin Buber speaks of land as a "primary datum" for Israel.

Besides the promise of land to the patriarchs, there is also another promise given to Moses. Here the context is the promise of Exodus. "I have seen the misery of my people in Egypt. I have heard their outcry against their oppressors... I have come down to rescue them from the hand of the Egyptians, and to bring them up out of that country into a fine, broad land, a land flowing with milk and honey" (Exodus 3:7-8). Land, therefore, is a gift of God, who delivered Israel from captivity and gave them freedom from their oppressors. Hence, land in the Bible is a sign of freedom and identity.

Land as the Inheritance of Israel

The Bible speaks of land as inheritance of the people of Israel. There are two terms used: *nahala*[24] (inheritance) and *ahuzza* (property/possession). Friedrich Horst opines that the two *nahala* and *ahuzza* are essentially the same. According to him,

[22] Quoted in Ruide Menzes, "The Pentateuchal Theology of Land" in *Bible Bhashyam: An Indian Biblical Quaterly*, Vol. XII, No. 1, March, 1986, 5.

[23] Raphel Jospe, "Jerusalem's Significance to World Jewry", in *Journal of Dharma*, Vol. XVIII, No.1, (Jan-March, 1993), 18.

[24] Quoted in Rui de Menzes, *Op.cit.*, 21.

ahuzza is an abstract juridical term compared to the more general term *nahala.* In fact, in most cases, the two terms are used together (cf. Number 32:32, 35:2). It is widely accepted that it is the Deuteronomist who is responsible for the theology of land in the Bible, and the identification of this land as Israel's inheritance (*nahala*). The land is a pure gift of Yahweh to her. The promised land is a result of the promise sworn on oath by Yahweh to the patriarchs. The land is promised "to your fathers" to Abraham, Issac, and Jacob (Deut. 1:8; cf. 31:7; Deut. 26:4;6:18, etc). Secondly, it is also found that land has been promised on oath by Yahweh to the Israelites directly. As Yahweh says to Joshua, "You shall bring the children of Israel into the land I swore to give them" (Deut. 31:32).

Nahala is the ownership of land as passed down from father to son. Yahweh being seen as Israel's father Deut. 14:1; 8:5). He too has left a patrimony (heritage) for Israel.[25] Leviticus 27:16-25, deals with the differences between land bought by commercial transaction and land acquired through inheritance. The land possessed through inheritance is inalienable and retains the right for its redemption or repurchase in the year of jubilee. In most cases, land possessed as inheritance, ancestral property, is never given out for sale (cf. I Kings 21:3f). Commercialization of land (real estate profiteering) is vehemently protested by the prophets in their time (Isaiah 5:8; Micah 2:1 ff, etc).

Israel's Conditional Ownership of Land

Although, Israel is gifted with the land as their inheritance, Yahweh is presented as the ultimate owner of the land. Israel is spoken of as a stranger on Yahweh's land. A section in the Holiness Code dealing with the Jubilee Year (Lev. 25:23,24) deals with this unique relationship of Israel to the land. For it says, "The land belongs to me," "You are only strangers," etc. Both Gerhard Von Rad and F. Horst believe that this new understanding of land as belonging to Yahweh seems to point to Canaanite theology where the Baals are the owners and the bestowers of fertility of the land.[26]

However, there are ample evidences in the Bible which related the giving of land with the Israelites' abiding of God's law in return. Moses in Deut. 6:17-19 has warned that their entry into Canaan (promised land) and the permanence of their stay on it is conditioned by their obedience to Yahweh and His law. Prosperity and long life on the land depend greatly on their keeping of His laws and commandments (Deut. 4:40). Though, Yahweh is giving this land forever ("... for an everlasting possession" Gen. 17:8; 35:3-4), the Deuteronomist is aware that Israel can lose this precious gift in case of infidelity and disloyalty. Further Yahweh's blessing upon the land in terms of the produce of fields is conditioned

[25] *Ibid.*

[26] *Ibid.*, 18.

upon obedience.[27] This is evident in the concluding part of the Holiness Code (Leviticus) and Deuteronomy. The famous prayer of the farmer (Historical Credo) in Deuteronomy 26:5-10 expresses the gratitude and thanks offering to Yahweh for the bounteous harvest he received from the God-given land. However, Israel's disobedience could result in the withdrawal of all these blessings (Deut. 28, cf. Lev. 26:3 ff). Here again the blessing of fertility is solely the gift of Yahweh. The prophets are therefore critical against those who are ungrateful to Him and admonish them to be grateful to Yahweh. "Let us fear Yahweh our God, who brings us the rains of autumn, and spring showers in their turn, who brings us unfailingly fixed seasons of harvest" (Jer. 5:24; cf. Hosea 2:10 ff).

Ownership of Land

Land in the Bible is not given to various individuals but to Israel, that is to the people of Israel. Hence, Israel as a community is the owner of the land. Joshua 13 -19 records that all the tribes are assigned land by lot by Joshua. The meaning of the allotment according to Norman K. Gottwald is this: "All the tribes found a home in the land and settle down to a life of autonomous economic self-development based on their land-holding."[28] The rights to land-holding have always been Israel. Then the allotment of land to the clans and families follows. Even when individual family is allotted land for settlement, the entitlement comes through the community/tribe. Even in the account of the second allotment of the land according to Ezekiel 48, it is the tribe that is apportioned the land. Alongside the portions of the twelve tribes, a portion is designated for a "holy reserve." Upon it the temple is to be built. This is again a reassertion of Yahweh's ownership of the entire land – that the entire land belongs to Yahweh. Hence, Yahweh is the ultimate owner of the entire land, the earth and everything in it.

A Naga-Tribal Theology of Land

There is no one theology in the world that can claim to be universally binding to all. Doing theology is never the monopoly of a section of people in the world. It is the privilege and concern of everybody/anybody. This is because "truth" is not a fixed proposition. Rather truth is always relational. Truth is contextual. So, is theology. Christian theology has never been a "once-for-all given faith proposition." "Theology" as K. C. Abraham defines, "is a reflection on the articulation of the faith experience in a given context."[29] Therefore, theology can be said to be always situational and contextual. So is the faith experience of the

---

[27] Walter Zimmerli, *Old Testament Theology Outline*, trans. David E. Green, (Edinburgh: T&T Clark, 1994 reprint), 68.

[28] Norman K. Gottwaald, *The Tribes of Yahweh: A Sociology of the Religion of Liberated Israel*, 1250-1050 B.C.E. (London: SCM Press Ltd), 183.

[29] K. C. Abraham, "Paradigm Shift in Contemporary Theological Thinking", a paper presented in the Gurukul Summer Institute, Madras, 1995), 6.

people in a given context. The following is an attempt to develop a theology of land using the resources drawn from the Naga traditions and Christian traditions (Bible).

Community Ownership of Land

Both the Naga tradition and the Bible affirm that land is a gift of God. That God is the Creator and Sustainer of heaven and earth. And God in His wisdom has provided human beings with the land and her natural bounty, for their sustenance. Above all, to use and keep them for God's glory. Human beings are placed with the responsibility to look after and care for God's creation. God has placed them as His custodians who are in return accountable to God. Hence, in a true sense of Naga tradition and the Bible, God is the ultimate owner of the universe.[30] The Bible and the Naga tradition advocate community ownership of land. The land being a pure gift of God, it cannot be the monopoly of the few. It has to be shared by all the people. In a community based ownership, sharing and equality become the basis of their life and existence. The piece of land which an Israelite family owns is understood as a share of the given land. Bastiaan Wielenga thus rightly points out: "It was the material basis for equality and freedom in Israel."[31] To it the impoverished who lost their land, the sojourners and slaves should return in the Jubilee year (Lev. 25:10,41). The "share" is not the same as private property with its exclusive character and absolute right of use and abuse… It is a share, it is the material basis for equality and freedom with others. It cannot be sold according to one's own wishes (I Kings 21). According to Naga traditional belief, to sell out the ancestral land/property is equivalent to invoking a curse upon the family.

In both the Naga tradition and the Bible, there is no substantial material that supports a theory of private property or capitalistic value. It is always the nation. Community is the recipient of rights and never the individual. Land is given to the people, to the community as such. In the Bible, amassing of wealth or property by individuals to the detriment of other began during the early capitalism of the Monarchy and this was vehemently resisted by the prophets.[32] Commercialization and privatization of land is against the will of the Naga people and above all it is against the will of God. Hence, there is a great need for reclaiming and restoring the biblical and the Naga community ownership of land today for tomorrow's sake. The Naga-tribal theology of land considers community as the only legitimate custodians of land because the land is the gift of God. "The land is the Lord's and the fullness thereof, the world and those who dwell therein." (Ps. 24:1).

---

[30] O. Alem, *Tsungremology: Ao Naga Christian Theology* (Mokokchung: CTC, 1994), 99.

[31] Bastian Wielenga, *It's a Long Road to Freedom: Perspectives of Biblical Theology* (Madurai: TTS, 1981), 148.

[32] Rui de Menzes, *Op.cit.*, 27.

God-human-land Relationship

Both the Naga tradition and the Bible affirm that humans are children of the earth.[33] The Creation account affirms that God created human being out of *adama* (earth/soil). The Naga tradition affirms that God let the earth give birth to human beings. This is why the land is called the mother earth. Hence, to the Nagas, there is a strong sense of relationship between the land and the people. There is an organic unity among God and human and the land. This feeling of oneness or the symbiotic relations among God and human and land makes it unique in the theological understanding of the Nagas. Hence, the Nagas and other tribals understand creation not in terms of the potter or the artist but in terms of "bodying forth" as the mother does.[34] Even in the teachings of the prophets that look forward to an age of salvation following God's judgment, the land retains an important place (Hos. 2:17; Jer.32:15; Ezek. 36:28 ff; 37:25).

This symbiotic relation between the land and the people according to Naga tradition makes all the difference with the Euro-western concept of land as objects of human use – utility concept. This symbiotic or organismic relationship between human beings and the land (the whole creation) does not end with the life here on earth itself. But, the same relationship continues to exist even in the land of the dead (*Kazeiram* in Tangkhul Naga). Most of the Nagas do not believe in heaven or hell. What they believe is the extension of the present life to the life after death in the land of the dead. According to the Naga belief, in the land of the dead, the dead continue to sustain their life by tilling the ground/land. Even the domestic animals continue to survive with the dead in the land of the dead as it does on the earthly life. Here again, land retains an important place as it does in the Bible. In this sense, the relationship between human beings and the earth (creation) seems to find its meaning in the messianic vision of the new heaven and new earth (Isaiah 11:9; 65:17-25; cf. Rev. 21:1-14).

Land is the Symbol of Freedom and Identity

In both the Naga tradition and the Bible, land stands for freedom and identity of the people. In the Bible, the promised land stands for freedom and identity of Israel as a sovereign nation. It is to be the basis of a new society, of fellowship in freedom and equality of the people of Israel. Land gives roots and security to human beings. In Genesis, when Cain is expelled from paradise, he becomes rootless and Godless! Cain is a man without security and identity. When the

[33] "Earth" and "land" are both legitimate translation of the Hebrew *eretz*, but each is used in different context with different connotations. "Earth" is particularly used in the context of the creation narratives, while "land" is the home in the historical narratives of Israel's struggle for national and religious identity. If "earth" points to the physical basis and environment for life, "land" points to territory that is possessed, struggled over, used and perhaps exploited. Geoffery R. Liburne, *A Sense of Place: A Christian Theology of Land* (Nashville: Abington Press, 1989), 31.

[34] K. Thanzauva, *Op.cit.*, 301.

Israelites are taken as captives to the foreign land they become rootless, and their identity as a free nation is shattered. This is true with the Nagas also. Land gives security and identity to them. Land means freedom. Take for example, the case of incest. According to Naga tradition, incest is considered to be a serious crime. Hence, the offenders are dissociated from the village and they remain as persons without identity and security.

Land for the Nagas, is therefore, both a space and a place. A space represents the nature of reciprocity among the people and between human beings and the rest of creation. Whereas, place represents belongingness and identity of the people. The Nagas affirm that human beings belong to the land and not vice versa. There is an old saying among the Tangkhul Nagas: "Do not cheat the land, the land is much older than human beings." Let us recall the cry of the Chief of Seattle: "This we know: the earth does not belong to man; man belongs to the earth ... Whatever befalls the earth befalls the sons of the earth..And the cry of the Black: "The land is my backbone... Without land I am nothing." To the Naga, landlessness is equal to being without roots and history. Hence, for the Naga, the land is the symbol of freedom and identity.

Land is Life

The Nagas, along with the rest of the indigenous people all over the world affirm that land is life. Land for the Nagas is central to their lives. Their whole life activity revolves around the land and its surroundings. It is central to their identity, spiritual, economy and to their very survival.[35] Land is life because land has her own distinct life and power in herself. Land is never a dead object. Land is life for the Nagas because, "it is a living entity endowed with spirits." Thanzauva further asserts, "In a non-literate society the land is their scripture through which they read about the spirits and God and create myths and songs."[36] In this sense, their concept of land shapes their spiritual life too. Their spirituality finds its expression through their relatedness with the living land.

Land Rights are Human Rights

Thanzauva rightly observes when he says, "Struggle for land rights in the context of the tribals means the tribal rights to land as well as the intrinsic rights of the land and all its creatures."[37] There is a biblical tradition which speaks of a community based on laws which goes beyond the human community of law - a community of the earth and human beings rooted in the special rights of God, the Creator, to what He has created. We find this in enactments about the Sabbath and the

---

[35] J. H. Thumra, "The Primal Religious Traditions" In P.S. Daniel, et.al. ed. *Religious Traditions of India* (Kotttayam: ITL & SSC, 1988), 72. Cf. also A. Wati Longchar, *The Tribal Religious Traditions in North East India: An Introduction* (Jorhat: The author, 1991), 93 f.

[36] K. Thanzauva, *Op. cit.*, 326.

[37] *Ibid.*, 327.

Jubilee Year (Ex. 23 & Lev. 25). According to these laws the weekly Sabbath and the regular sabbatical year are meant for all human beings, animals and earth for rest and rejuvenation. This is the inalienable rights of the whole of creation including human beings.

A similar faith tradition can also be found in the Naga society particularly in the observance of agricultural *genna* or taboo. During the observance of *genna* no action of any sort that would bring damage to the land is allowed. Whoever violates this observance is considered to have insulted the mother earth and hence a severe action is taken against the culprit. This observance of *genna* is considered with the welfare of the fertility of the land, concerned with the welfare of the animals and their fields. In both the observances of the Jubilee Year and the *genna*, there is an underlined fear that repercussions would befall upon the community if they disregard them. Hence, the intrinsic rights of the land and all its creatures are honored.

Secondly, in the tribal context of alienation of land, land rights is a concrete term more conceivable than human rights. Unlike the western concept of human rights which is characterized by political and individual rights, human rights to the Nagas is primarily a community right, part of what it means to exist authentically. Hence, the tribal's struggle for the land rights is a struggle for community rights of land. It denounces the exploitative utilitarian approach to land which alienated them from their land. Most of all, it is an affirmation that land is the gift of God to all. In this connection, John D. Arcy May rightly suggests that rights to land needs to be supplemented by rights of the land, extending to the earth as a home of the one human community and nature as the matrix of all life.[38] In this sense, selling out of lands, forests, rivers, mountains, etc., is a religious crime for the Nagas. It is nothing but desacralization of the sacred temple. Further, the forceful domination of Naga or tribal lands by the alien forces has rendered many people landless or homeless in their own motherland. They have become foreigners in their own land. In the Bible "foreign land" is a place of injustice and death and has lost its meaning as a gift of God. "Foreign land" represents in the Bible all forms of exploitation and discrimination. In such a situation of land alienation, the Nagas are struggling for their rights, to retain their God-given land which is their rightful claim. "This struggle for their rights," says Gustavo Gutierrez, "is located within a quest for the Kingdom of God and its justice - in other words, the struggle is part of the journey to a meeting with God of the Kingdom."[39] True to what Gutierrez says, it is a collective undertaking of liberation – the claim for the land rights are claims for human rights for the Nagas. It is a claim for the wholeness of life.

---

[38] Quoted in K. Thanzauva, *Ibid.*, 328.

[39] Gustavo Gutierrez, *We Drink From Our Own Wells: The Spiritual Journey of a People* (Quezon City: Claretian Publications, 1984), 11.

Conclusion

The Naga tribal theology of land affirms that land is a gift of God to all human beings for their life and sustenance. Land is the place where God and the spirits interact with human beings. Land is therefore, sacred. Land being the gift of God, ultimately, it is God Himself who is the owner. Human beings are custodians of God's creation. They are stewards placed by God with the responsibility to take care of His creation. Hence, the Nagas affirm the community ownership of land which is characterized by sharing and equality. The land thus stands for freedom and identity. No land means no identity and freedom. Land stands for hope, security and blessing. The Nagas' relation with the land is unique. They have a filial relationship of intimacy with the land and to its creation. Hence, reckless abuse of land, mountain, river, etc. is a crime. It is a desacralization of the sacred temple. Therefore, the Nagas struggle for their land rights is a struggle for the wholeness of life. It is a struggle for the restoration of the broken relationship between human beings and the land with all its creation, being perpetuated by the wanton abuse of land and forceful alienation by the human forces.

The struggle for rights is a struggle for identity. It is also a struggle for justice and participation. The Nagas in the past rejected any kind of relationship that fails to ensure justice, as contrary to God's will. This focus on justice in our struggle for the land rights gives us a concrete direction as well as a new theological meaning for it. And most of all, land is life to the Nagas and they are intrinsically related to the land and to all its creation.

Chapter 6

Space, Creation and Land
An Indigenous-Tribal Eco-Theology of the North East India

Introduction

Ecological crisis is a serious problem confronting contemporary world. This crisis has never before been as acute as it is today. In fact, it has undeniably become a contemporary reality that affects the very survival of the earth and its children. Ecological thinking is therefore no longer the concern only of the environmental activists but everyone who is concerned with life. This is a serious threat that concerns not only human beings but the whole of creation. The human greed and desire for more is the main factor behind the ecological crisis. Of course, the people most affected are the tribal/indigenous people all over the world. In the name of development, big factories and industries have been set up in the fertile lands of the indigenous people. Land for the tribal and indigenous people is their life. Land and natural resources of the indigenous people have been forcibly taken away; many indigenous and tribal people have been displaced from their lands. In most of the cases, the promises to pay them compensations in return have remained hollow and unfulfilled. As a result people are left dry and high not knowing where to go and whom to look for help. For the indigenous/tribal people, it is a question of life and death; it is a question of survival.

This research examines the impact of ecological crisis on the tribal/indigenous people of the Northeast India and subsequently proposes to articulate an eco-theology using cultural resources of the tribal people of the region. For this I intend to examine the socio-cultural and religious traditions, worldviews, creation myths, and rituals and rites of the tribal people. The tribals are known to be close with the nature and their worldview is highly creation centered. The tribals view everything to be in relations. Everything including God-human-world is believed to be inter-related. Therefore, examining and understanding tribal worldview is critical for articulating a relevant and meaningful eco-theology. Further, their traditions of agricultural taboos (rituals) and other related practices offer rich resources for developing such an important theology.

The Judeo-Christian Tradition/Theology

Christian theology has for centuries taught a high anthropology placing human beings over all the other created beings. Human beings have been considered as the center as well as the apex of the whole creation.[1] Thus, the relation between humans and nature has been understood in terms of "humans above nature." Underlying this claim has been the inalienable dignity which inheres in every human being, believed to have derived from the biblical assertion that "human beings are created in the image of God" (Gen. 1:26a, 27). And this inherent dignity of human person has been identified as the source of human rights.[2] This together with the command to "have dominion" (Gen. 1:28b) has been taken as the theological basis for the claim that humans are superior to other creatures. Non-human created beings are considered inferior and fit for human use and dominion. This inherent anthropocentrism and the domineering attitude of humans have done much violence against the whole of creation. Lynn White, Jr has squarely accused Judeo-Christian tradition as responsible for the environmental crisis due to its emphasis on human "dominion" over nature. White argues that as far as the ecological crisis is concerned "Christianity bears a huge burden of guilt."[3] In like manner a Roman Catholic priest Thomas Berry observes that "traditional Western spiritualities have not enabled their followers to mitigate or even to understand or protest the terrifying assault of American society on the natural world."[4]

In the hierarchical perception of creation, humans are at the helm of hierarchy ruling over the rest of God's created beings. Humans are next to the angels according to this hierarchical structure of creation. God is at the top followed by angels, humans, and the rest of creation respectively.

Then there is the dualistic view which makes a sharp distinction between matter and spirit, physical and spiritual, earthly and heavenly, etc. Anything to

---

[1] Gerhard von Rad, *Old Testament Theolog y* (London: SCM Press, 1975), 144.

[2] Jürgen Moltmann, *On Humanity: Political Theology and Ethics* (London: SCM Press, 1984), 9f; John W. Montgomery, *Human Rights and Human Dignity* (Grand Rapids: Zondervan Publishing House, 1986), 63f.

[3] Quoted in Clifford Chalmers Cain, *An Ecotheology: Reunderstanding Our Relation to Nature*, Toronto Studies in Theology, vol. 98 (Lewiston: The Edwin Mellen Press, 2009), 64.

[4] Thomas Berry, *The Dream of the Earth* (San Francisco: Sierra Club Books, 1990), 113.

do with matter or material is regarded as evil and good only as long as it is useful to humans.

Additionally, the concept of heaven and hell has further widened people's negative attitude towards the worldly material things. After all what is important is saving the "soul" to enter into eternal life in heaven. The physical body will perish anyway with the world. "This world is not our home, we are just passing through" and so why should we care for the world?

Such understanding has for most part predominated the thinking and attitude of Christians towards nature and the rest of creation.

Ecological Crisis in North East India

The Northeast region is known for its rich biodiversity and dramatic scenery.

The following figures highlight the biodiversity significance of the region:[5]

1. 51 Forest types are found in the region broadly classified into six major forest types viz., tropical moist deciduous forests, tropical semi evergreen forests, tropical wet evergreen forests, subtropical forests, temperate forests and alpine forests.
2. Out of the 9 important vegetation types of India, 6 are found in the North Eastern region.
3. These forests harbor 80,000 out of 15,000 species of flowering plants. These include:
   - 40 out of 54 species of gymnosperms
   - 500 out of 1012 species of Pteridophytes
   - 825 out of 1145 species of orchids
   - 80 out of 90 species of rhododendrons
   - 60 out of 110 species of bamboo
   - 25 out of 56 species of canes.

Having said this, the Northeast India is no exception to the problem of ecological crisis. In fact, the onslaught of the economic globalization and industrialization has heavily affected the region. The culture of consumerism has pervasively invaded the people of the region.

Today in the name of development several industries and factories have been set up. As a result, a number of farmers and poor villagers have been displaced from their own lands; their fertile lands and natural resources have been blatantly destroyed.

The North East India is a part of the Indo Burma biodiversity "Hotspot." Global biodiversity "hotspots" is identified and defined as "areas of high biological diversity and high endemism but under severe anthropogenic threats."[6] Initially,

[5] Forest Survey of India (FSI), 2003.

[6] "Biodiversity Significance of the Northeast India WWF India" mdoner.gov.in/writereaddata/.../13biodiversity9583338441/pdf. (retrieved 23/06/2011), 7.

the Himalaya "hotspot" consists of Arunachal Pradesh, Sikkim and Darjeeling district of West Bengal, parts of Nepal, China and Bhutan. However, in 2000 it was modified to the "'Indo Burma hotspot' covering central Nepal to the whole of North East India, Andaman and Nicobar Islands, Hainan island in southern China, Myanmar, Thailand and on to Indochina, then south to Isthmus of Kra in the Malaysian peninsula."[7] It is said that the hotspot is, the second largest and next only to the Mediterranean basin with an area of 2,20,60,000 sq km among the 25 identified globally.

> All the global hotspots are based on two criteria: species endemism and degree of threat. To qualify as a hotspot an area must contain at least 0.5% or 1500 of the world's 300,000 plant species as endemic. It might be pertinent to mention here that all the global hotspots have a minimum of 2500 endemics. The other criteria are number of vertebrate species (excluding fish) and degree of threat through habitat loss. To qualify as a hotspot, the region should have lost 70% or more of its primary vegetation.[8]

Some facts and figues on the Indo Burma hotspot (Myers, 2000):[9]

Original extent of primary vegetation	2,060,000 sq km
Remaining primary vegetation (% of original extent)	100,000 sq km (4.9)
Plant species	13,500
Endemic plants (% global plants)	7000 (2.3%)
Vertebrate species	2185
Endemic vertebrates (% of global vertebrates)	528 (1.9%)

Today the reality is that "the primary vegetation in extensive areas of the Northeast India has been disturbed and modified and in some places destroyed by seismic activities, frequent landslides and resultant soil erosion."[10] While these natural causes have contributed only marginally to the change in vegetation type, human induced activities have led to irreversible transformation in the landscapes and resulted in colossal loss of biodiversity in the entire region. The region has witnessed excessive logging since the colonial days for revenue generation. The practice continued until the Supreme Court ban on logging in 1995, however clandestinely it is done in most of the Northeast states.

Agriculture is the main stay of the people in the region. A considerable number of people practice slash and burn (also known as jhum/shifting cultivation)

---

[7] *Ibid.*

[8] *Ibid.*, 8.

[9] *Ibid.*, 8.

[10] *Ibid.*

which also contribute to the deforestation. However, it is by far the logging business which is causing much destruction to the environment. In the process, rich and beautiful flora and fauna are destroyed and the bio-diversity of the region is severely affected. Animals and birds of all types are found in the region but their numbers are rapidly decreasing due to poaching, and deforestation. The beautiful landscape of the region is rapidly changing; land slide, soil erosion and flooding have been occurring frequently. Climatic change is another visible effect of all this.

It is noted that the Northeast India has 64% of the total geographical area under forest cover and it is often quoted that it continues to be a forest surplus region. However, the forest cover is rapidly disappearing from the entire region. Four of the eight states, Arunachal, Assam, Mizoram and Sikkim, lost dense forests as shown in the following table:

Forest Assessment Figure

State	2001 Assessment			2003 Assessment			Change		
	Dense	Open	Total	Dense	Open	Total	Dense	Open	Total
Arunachal P	55,932	14,113	68,045	53,511	14,508	68,019	-421	395	-26
Assam	15,830	11,884	27,714	13,042	14,784	27,826	-2,788	2900	112
Manipur	5,710	11,216	16,926	6,538	10,681	17,219	828	-535	293
Meghalaya	5,681	9,903	15,584	6,481	10,348	16,839	810	445	1,255
Miroram	8,936	8,558	17,494	7,488	10,942	18,430	-1,448	2384	936
Nagaland	5,393	7,952	13,345	5,707	7,902	13,609	314	-50	264
Sikkim	2,391	802	3,193	2,396	900	3,262	-29	98	69
Tripura	3,463	3,602	7,065	5,046	3,047	8,093	1,583	-555	1,028

Another major factor to be considered is the construction of mega dam projects in the region. It is said that altogether 168 dam projects sites have been identified in the whole of the Northeast region. The region is being projected as the future powerhouse of the nation. Already projects such as Loktak hydroelectric project in Manipur, Doyang in Nagaland, Gumti dam in Tripura, and Ranganadi hydroelectric project in Arunachal Pradesh have adversely impacted the lives of the people and the eco-biodiversity of the region.[11] Several indigenous people's traditional homelands have been submerged and the wetland ecology has been severely impacted. Two major Dam Projects that will have serious ecological impact and life threatening consequences in the region are the 2000 MW Lower Subansiri Hydroelectric Project and 1500 MW Tipaimukh Dam Project which are located in Assam-Arunachal and Manipur-Mizoram borders respectively. While the former is located in the Subansiri, a tributary

[11] Neeraj Vagholikar & Partha J. Das " Damming Northeast India: Juggernaut of Hydroelectric Power Projects Threatens Social and Environmental Security of the Region," http://chimalaya.files.wordpress.com/2010/12/damning-northeast-india-final.pdf (Retrieved 7/7/211), 1.

of the mighty Brahmaputra, the latter is being built at the confluence of Barak and Tuivai rivers. On completion the Lower Subansiri will be the largest dam in India.

The tragedy is that the whole of Northeast India falls under the earthquake prone zone areas. Both the dams are located in highly seismic zones – zone V. The constructions have been going on without the consent of the people and in the face of people's strong protests and oppositions. In June 2011 the expert committee on Lower Subansiri dam recommended that the height of the dam be reduced, the safety be improved, and environmental flows be increased.[12] The constructions of these dams will submerge a number of villages in and around the areas and destroy several vegetations and plants, animals and bio-diversity. They will adversely affect the downstream flows of water leading to severe disruptions on eco-systems. These dams will also affect a great deal on the neighboring Bangladesh, especially in the northeastern part of the country. The main impacts of mega dams include loss of land and heritage, population influx and cultural displacement, threat of life and properties, ecological disasters and imbalance in water resource distribution, weapon for mass destruction, and above all, methane gas emission and global warming.[13]

Other industrial activities that are contributing to the environmental crises in the region include coal mining operation, crude oil exploration, petroleum refinery, fertilizer industries, paper industries, cement industries, etc. The hazardous wastes of the industries are dumped into the flowing rivers and polluting the waters besides destroying fish and other living organisms in the water.

Cultural Resources from the Tribals of North East India

Theological reflection based on tribal life experiences and traditional heritage is an essential task of indigenous theology. The indigenous peoples are endowed with rich cultural and religious resources and, rather than condemning them as evil and demonic, every effort should be made to reclaim these resources for the purpose of theological reflection. In this search for an articulation of meaningful theology we must retrieve the cultural values that are known to be life affirming and liberating. This search will involve processes of recollection, remembering and sharing with a view to formulating a theology that will ultimately be inclusive, dialogical, liberating, and above all empowering.

Traditional heritages include past and present socio-cultural traditions, customs, religious beliefs, and practices. This includes, but is not limited to, myths and legends, folktales and stories, wisdom and proverbs, mores and songs

---

[12] *Ibid.*, 6.

[13] Quoted in Vagholikar & Das "Damming Northeast India," 7.

which were mostly transmitted orally from generation to generation and serve as the text of what Renthy Keitzar calls the unwritten "Prime Bible."[14]

Tribal Worldview: Holistic Vision of Life

Tribal worldview is characterized by a holistic vision of life. They perceive reality in wholeness. There is no idea of dualism or duality of things. There is no distinction between sacred and the secular, physical and spiritual, earthly and heavenly. All these together constitute the wholeness of life. If one is affected, all are affected. According to this vision, life of all forms is interrelated to one another and they all together constitute an organic unity. In this sense, human, nature, and spirit do not stand apart from each other as opposing factors.

Tribal Cosmology: God-Human-World Relationship

The fact that indigenous people see themselves as interrelated in all their life totality to the whole creation can be seen from the creation myth and other practices and beliefs. I have identified three tribal traditions of the Northeast India for our purpose.

The first one is a Tangkhul Naga creation myth which tells the story of the great assembly of all the creatures. It goes like this.

> *The great assembly of all creatures was convened by Kasa Akhava (God) to determine the duration of day and night. Kasa Akhava invited the opinions of the creatures. After a spell of silence the mole came out with a suggestion that day and night should each be one year in length. This suggestion was rejected by all due to its impracticality. The discussion continued but no acceptable proposal was forthcoming. The rooster was then left with the responsibility to determine the length of day and night. The rooster should crow when he is exhausted and needed rest. This would signal the end of the day. Again the rooster should crow after he had sufficiently rested by night, heralding the dawning of the day. The rooster, hence became the timekeeper for the world.*
>
> *Soon a scene was created by a hungry flying fox who disturbed the peaceful sleep of his fellow creatures at night. He was seated on a tree enjoying a walnut. By mistake the walnut fell from his hands and hit the crab lying below. The crab, filled with fury, destroyed the nest of the giant ants, who in turn stung a sleeping wild boar. The agonized bear went wild and destroyed a banana tree. This disturbed the tiny bat sleeping peacefully on*

[14] Renthy Keitzar, *In Search of a Relevant Gospel Message* (Guwahati: Christian Literature Center, 1995), 21. According to Jan Vansina, oral traditions are documents of the present since they are told in the present. They are also of the past since the stories told belonged to the past. Therefore, oral traditions have both the past and present dimensions simultaneously. Jan Vansina, *Oral Tradition as History* (Madison: University of Wisconsin Press, 1985), xii.

> *a banana leaf. The angry bat sped about wildly and landed in the nostrils of a sleeping elephant. The agitated elephant then went wild resulting in the death of a man.*
>
> *Kasa Akhava called all the creatures for an explanation and found that the flying fox was responsible for the unruly scene which ended in the death of a man. The flying fox was punished by having one of his legs amputated and given to the magpie, who was considered to be the eldest among the creatures.*[15]

The second story comes from the Khasis of Meghalaya. The Khasis believed that their ancestors descended from heaven/sky world. According to the Khasi origin story, God created sixteen families in heaven and allowed them to live with Him in heaven.[16] God also gave them the freedom to move between heaven and earth through a golden ladder. On one such occasion, seven families decided to settle down on earth leaving behind the nine families in heaven. "These seven families came to be known as *Ki Hynniew Ha Tbin* (The Seven Below) and those who remained in heaven as *Ki Khyndai Ha jrong* (The Nine Above)."[17] The Khasis claim they are the descendents of these seven families.

Then there is the log-drum of the Wanchos of Tirap district of Arunachal Pradesh. Log-drum constitutes as one of the finest symbols of the Wancho people's culture. It is a drum curved out of a huge tree. In the past, log-drum is used for a number of purposes and occasions ranging from organizing defense mechanism, announcing natural calamities to heralding the beginning of community festivities and celebrations. A number of different beats symbolized different meanings to the villagers.

> Construction of such huge drums involves series of sacred and secular activities. But, when this is dragged to the village from the distant forest the Wanchos sang songs through which they beg pardon from each and every creature of the forest expressing how inevitable that tree was to them for which they had to cut and disturb their habitat.[18]

---

[15] R. Luikham, *Folktales and Tales of the Nagas* (Delhi: Immanuel publishers, 1983), 77ff; Cf. Yangkahao Vashum, "A Tangkhul Creation Myth: Implication for a Holistic View of Human Rights," in *The Tribal Worldview and Ecology*, Tribal Study Series no. 2, eds. A. Wati Longchar and Yangkahao Vashum (Jorhat: Tribal Study Centre, 1998), 34-40.

[16] R. Tokin Roy Rymbai, "Evolution of Modern Khasi Society (Babu Jeebon Roy)," in J. N. Chowdhury, ed. *The Khasi Canvas: A Cultural and Political History* (Shillong: Srimati Jaya Chowdhury, 1978), 415.

[17] *Ibid.*

[18] Sarit K. Chauduri, "Folk Belief and Resource Conservations: Reflections from Arunachal Pradesh," in *Indian Folklife: A Quarterly Newsletter from National Folklore Support Centre*, Serial no. 28, January 2008, 5. Of course, log-drum is not unique to the Wanchos alone; it is a cultural symbol of most the tribals in the region.

All these stories speak for themselves. The creation myth explicitly brings out all that is concerned with our lives, our human relationship with *Kasa Akhava* and with non-human creation. *Kasa Akhava* is in the profoundest way asserted as the creator and sustainer of the universe. The *Kasa Akhava* is seen as respecting the creations and their roles in shaping and caring the created world. The whole creation is depicted as a family with *Kasa Akhava* as its head. In tribal society one most prominent practice is that important decisions are taken by the family sitting around the hearth-fire. This is indicative of the universal family which requires the participation and cooperation of all family members in decision making and carrying out the given responsibilities. The whole creation is depicted as co-workers - responsible partners – in caring for *Kasa Akhava's* created world.

While the second story unravels how from the very beginning God and human family are connected to each other, the third story brings out how human and nature maintain their interdependent living relationship, especially humans towards the nature.

The tribals have a sober view of anthropology. There is no myth, legend or belief which teaches that human beings are superior to other created beings. Human beings are seen as co-workers with other creatures. Hence, the human relationship with the whole creation is characterized by mutual respect and mutual dependence. Further, their relationship is accentuated by the common responsibility they share in caring for God's created world.

The Interrelatedness of All: Rites and Rituals

The creation myths are also about interrelatedness and connectedness of all beings. That we are all intrinsically related to one another and what one does affects each other, for good or bad. The underlying assumption is the peaceful co-existence of the whole creation and human kind. Because of the organic relationship that humans maintain with other creatures, what one does good or ill affects non-human creatures too. This interrelatedness between humanity and all of creation is reflected further in the performances of rites and rituals. Rites and rituals for the indigenous people are an integral part of life. They are performed for maintaining balance and harmony in the community. They convey the message of wholeness and unity. It is basically for this that, although the rituals are performed by an individual, it is done for and on behalf of the whole community.

> For instance at the time of sowing the [rice] paddy, the village chief offered sacrifices and performed the paddy sowing rites a day ahead of the people. If in some rare cases, an individual by mistake [or willfully] did the sowing ahead of the village chief the entire village suffered from failure of crops that particular year and had to face famine.[19]

[19] R. R. Shimray, *Origin and Culture of the Nagas* (New Delhi: Privately published by Mrs. Pamleiphi Shimray, 1985), 22f.

In the tribal perception, neither humanity nor creation is unique in itself. In this sense, there is a distinction but no separation between humanity and creatures, the being and beings and all other entities. A distinction is made only at the existential level. K. Thanzauva, a Mizo theologian, points out that the apparent hierarchy in the relationship of beings is not a social order or the idea of degradation. [20] He goes on to say that, though there are functional differences, God, human and world form a community in which they are interrelated and hence it is appropriate to describe this relationship as a "community model of relationship."

Tribals and the Land

For the tribal people, land is life. Land is central to their lives. Their whole life activity revolves around the land and its surroundings. It is central to their identity, history, spirituality, economy and their very survival. Land is life because the land has her own distinct life; the land is never a dead object. It is a living entity endowed with spirits. "In a non-literate society the land is their scripture through which they read about the spirits and God and create myths and songs."[21]

Secondly, the importance of land to the indigenous people lies in the fact that even the Supreme Being is understood in relation to the land. A number of the Northeast Indian tribes including the Aos, Sangtams and Chang Nagas call their Supreme Being, *Lijaba. Li* means "soil" and *Jaba* means "enter," meaning "the one who enters" or "indwells in the soil."[22] It is the belief of the people that *Lijaba* enters into the earth with the seeds and rises up again along with the crops. Hence for the people, the blooming flowers, trees bearing fruits and rice signify the presence of the Creator.

Thirdly, the tribal people's notion of time and history are related to the land. Their yearly calendar and agricultural activities are based on the cycle of the earth. All the festivals, dances and songs of the people are connected with land. Moreover, their religious activities are all centered on the land. R. R. Shimray poignantly puts it, "Every mountain, every range, and every ridge has a legend and every peak a tale to tell."[23]

---

[20] K. Thanzauva, *Theology of Community: Tribal Theology in the Making* (Aizawl: Mizo Theological Conference, 1997), 157.

[21] Thanzauva, *Theology of Community*, 130. For a detail discussion on tribal concept of land refer to Yangkahao Vashum, "Theology of Land: A Naga Perspective," in *The Tribal Worldview and Ecology*, Tribal Study Series no. 2, eds. A. Wati Longchar and Yangkahao Vashum (Jorhat: Tribal Study Centre, 1998), 69-94.

[22] A. Wati Longchar, "A Creation-Poem of the Ao Nagas: A Theological Exploration," in *The Tribal Worldview and Ecology*, Tribal Study Series no. 2, eds. A. Wati Longchar and Yangkahao Vashum (Jorhat: Tribal Study Centre, 1998), 16.

[23] Shimray, *Origin and Culture of the Nagas*, 6.

Fourthly, tribals believe that it is the land that owns the people and not the other way round. The people know that it is the land that gives them their identity. Land is therefore highly respected.

Fifthly, people's ethical life is again closely related and based on the land. As long as one lives on this earth, one is expected to live an honest and truthful life. Honesty, truthfulness, sincerity and faithfulness are highly valued virtues among the tribal people. First, they believe the Supreme Being is everywhere and knows everything. And so they live in the constant awareness of the presence of the Supreme Being. Secondly, they also believe that land is older than human beings and therefore the land is wiser than the humans. One of the tribal wisdoms says: "The land never lies; do not lie to the land." Swearing in the name of the Supreme Being and the land is like an anathema. Only for resolving serious cases such as land or boundary disputes, when every possible effort fails, people resort to swearing in the name of the Supreme Being by eating a lump of soil. Normally, the one who gets sick or dies prematurely is declared the guilty one.

The Land Tenure System and the Tradition of Conservation

In the tribal society, the land is owned by the community in general. For example the land tenure in Naga society is well reflected in the report that follows:

> In Nagaland, each tribe had a well demarcated territory within the villages inhabited by that tribe were located, with well-defined boundaries. Though the practice of each tribe differed, the village land was generally classified as (a) common village land, (b) clan land, (c) individual land, and (d) *morung* land. The village council was responsible for the management. Clan land was mostly jhum land owned by a particular clan certain areas, usually terraced land were owned by individuals. Some portion of the village land was designated for *morung* where the young boys slept there.[24]

Similar system is also found among the Khasi-Jaintias of Meghalaya. The land is classified into *Ri Kynti* (clan land) and *Ri Raij* (community land).[25] The principle behind this land system is to ensure that no one in the village is made landless and poor. In the past, landlessness and beggars were unknown to the tribal society.

The cited report is expressive of the land system among the tribals in the Northeast India in general. In most cases, it is the community or the village that

---

[24] Planning Commission, *The Report of the Working Group on the Land System Among Tribals in the North Eastern India*, May 1984.

[25] R. T. Rymbai, "The Traditional Ecological Concepts of the Khasi-Pnars," in *The Tribal Worldview and Ecology*, Tribal Study Series no. 2, ed. A. Wati Longchar and Yangkahao Vashum (Jorhat: Tribal Study Centre, 1998), 16.

owns the land. The village chief holds the nominal ownership of the land.[26] The village chief is normally assisted by the village council, the people's representatives. However, the ultimate power rests in the hands of the people as a whole, who empower the chief and the council to carry out the tasks on behalf of the village.

There are a number of ways by which the tribal people conserved and preserved their lands.

a) Terrace cultivation method which is widely practiced in the region protects the land from erosion and landslides.
b) Shifting/Jhum cultivation which takes place after 6-8 years; leaves the land fallowed in between the period of the cycle year for rejuvenation and rest of the land. Of course, it needs to be pointed out that in recent years the length of cycle years has drastically shortened due to a number of factors including increase in populations, logging business, etc.

The Ethics of Conservation: Genna, Taboo and Totem

The terms *Genna* and taboo simply mean prohibition. While the former is used to mean rest or holiday, the latter is used more in the sense of prohibition, something that is not to be done or touched. Sometimes they are interchangeably used meaning the same thing. Observance of *genna* or rest is an integral part of the tribal people. There are a number of *gennas* including the observance of the "Mother Earth's Day," *gennas* before the seed sowing and harvest, *gennas* connected with purification ceremonies, hunting, festivals and others. Normally, the observance of the *gennas* lasts from 3 – 7 days depending upon the nature of the ceremony. During the *genna* observance complete rest is observed and the people are tabooed from working or carrying out their daily activities.

The Earth is regarded as the Mother because many tribes believed they emerged from the cave or hole of the earth.[27] Mother Earth's Day is observed for 3-6 days to mark their respect and care for the mother earth. During these days no action of any sort that would bring damage to the land is allowed. Nobody should dig or break the ground or even collect the mud out of it. Whoever violates this observance is considered to have insulted the mother earth, and hence a severe action is taken against the culprit.

The practice of taboo encompasses the whole activity of the indigenous society. For our purpose, I would like to mention some of the taboo observances in relation to conservation of land and nature. Killings of animals at certain stages of their life are prohibited. Hunting and trappings are tabooed during the breeding seasons; pregnant animals cannot be killed. Fishing and the use of certain

[26] There are tribes like the Kukis of Manipur and the Sumis of Nagaland where land holding is in the hands of the village chiefs.

[27] The Ao Nagas believed they emerged from the legendary six stones called *Longtrok*; similarly the Changs, Marings, Anals and Tangkhul Nagas believed that they emerged from the cave or hole of the earth.

poisonous roots or leaves which kill fish during the spawning season is tabooed. Whenever animals give birth to a new one such as a calf is born or a pig is littered or chickens are hatched, the whole family would observe taboo for protection and preservation of the young ones.

Wanton felling of trees and plants are strictly prohibited. Whenever, trees are felled, they would first pray and ask their forgiveness. Before clearing the jungle for cultivation and farming, ceremonies are conducted to get the approval of the land. Only then would they begin their work.

Closely connected with the observance of *genna* and taboo, is the practice of totem.[28] A totem is usually "a species of an animal or of a plant or insect or bird and very rarely a class of inanimate objects, very closely related to a group in that the group of people is believed to descent from the animal or any of the species."[29] There are a number of clans in the Northeast who trace their origin to the totem animal or plant. They have a great deal of respect and hence they would not eat their totem animal or plant. To do so would be tantamount to destroying their ancestors. Hence, the totem animals are accorded a status that ensures protection. The other way of maintaining their close relationship is by conferring religious significance to the totem animal or plant. In this case, the totem animal is eaten sacramentally on certain ceremonial feast (and otherwise tabooed) by all who belong to that totem animal. "This symbolized the establishment of mystic kinship or blood relationship between the totem animal and the clan," claims J. H. Thumra.[30]

All these – *genna,* taboo and totem – practices are part of the tribal people's prudent ways of relating and conserving the land, nature and creation.

Space, Creation, and Land: An Indigenous Eco-theology

Ecology is about the art of relations; it is about relationships. Eco-theology is therefore about theology of the art of relations or relationships. It is concerned with how God-human-world are related to each other.

Space, creation and land are integral to the holistic worldview of indigenous people in the Northeast India. Space, creation, and land together serve as the foundation of indigenous people's concept of life, relationship and interdependence. Indigenous worldview is creation-centered and is characterized by understanding the interdependence and the inter-relatedness of all creation, including human beings. Therefore, indigenous peoples in the Northeast India and some of the American Indians that I know believe that the whole of creation are our relatives. The Lakota nation of American Indians has an expression which

[28] The term "totem" is derived from the language of the Ojibway tribe of the North America which simply means "brother-sister kin."

[29] J. H. Thumra, "The Primal Religious Traditions," in *Religious Traditions of India*, ed. P. S. Daniel, et al, (Serampore: Indian Theological Library, Senate of Serampore College, 1988), 51.

[30] *Ibid.*, 59.

describes beautifully all that concerns the indigenous worldview, "We are all related." According to Standing Rock Sioux scholar Vine Deloria, Jr, the similar phrase, "All my relatives" is not merely a religious sentiment which many people have supposed, but it also "describes the epistemology of the Indian worldview, providing the methodological basis for the gathering of the information about the world."[31] Deloria goes on to explain the implication of this worldview when he states:

> "We are all relatives" when taken as a methodological tool for obtaining knowledge means that we observe the natural world by looking for relationships between various things in it. That is to say, everything in the natural world has relationship with every other thing and the total set of relationships makes up the natural world as we experience it. This concept is simply the relativity concept as applied to a universe that people experience as alive and not as dead or inert.[32]

The many concepts expressed by "All our relations" articulates succinctly that humans along with other creations are part of this integrated whole. Space, creation and land are representative of relationship, reciprocity, inter-dependence and wholeness.

Given this reality, indigenous theologians have argued convincingly that an indigenous theology must begin with space and creation, and not with humans. In the light of this, George E. Tinker is highly critical of the World Council of Churches program on Justice, Peace, and the Integrity of Creation (JPIC). He argues that theology of creation is not merely a justice issue to be set along other justice and peace concerns. Rather it is the foundational theology for the self understanding out of which justice, and then peace will flow naturally and necessarily.[33] Likewise, Wati Longchar, a Naga theologian, affirms spatiality as the primary datum for doing tribal theology.[34]

Placing space and creation as theology's starting point is crucial because it affirms the relatedness of all beings and all that is created. Consequently, we are all destined to be together as one universal family in which everyone is a coequal participant. Space and creation centered theology provides an orientation to life which is, again, centered on relationship, reciprocity and wholeness. It conveys the imperative recognition of cosmic oneness. Our destiny is the same. The Bible

---

[31] Vine Deloria, Jr, *Spirit & Reason: The Vine Deloria, Jr., Reader*, Eds. Barbara Deloria, et al (Golden: Fulcrum Publishing, 1999), 52.

[32] *Ibid.*, 34.

[33] George E. Tinker, "Spirituality and Nature of American Personhood: Sovereignty an Solidarity'" in *Spirituality of the Third World*, ed. K. C. Abraham & Berndetta Mbuy-Beya (Maryknol: Orbis Books, 1994), 127-128.

[34] A. Wati Longchar, *An Emerging Asian Theology: Tribal Theology Issue, Method and Perspective.* Tribal Study Series, no. 8 (Jorhat: Tribal Study Center, 2000) , 68.

speaks likewise. "In Christ all things, visible or invisible will be reconciled" (Col. 15-20; Eph. 1:10). "The creation waits for... liberation and glorious freedom" (Rom. 8:19-21). It seems we are all eternally bound together!

Theologically, this spatial understanding has a far reaching significance. As Nirmal Minz points out, "Space means that everything is integrally related to one another and therefore, they must treat each other with justice, required and demanded of each other."[35] Additionally, it is land that provides identity and security to the people a part from being the Mother to the people. To this day, the tribal people identify themselves with their village rather than their names.[36] A stranger on being enquired would tell his or her village name first, followed by his or her name. Land not only holds them together as a community but also it provides them their status as a people in the world.

This space/creation centered theology enables us to re-evaluate and reconsider the traditional views of God, Christ, Spirit and salvation including our human place in creation. From a spatial perspective, Longchar argues that God is also organically related to the whole of creation.[37] In like manner, the space-creation centered theology enables us to conceive of human, creation, and church as organically related to one another and to God.

This worldview of spatiality essentially accentuates and locates the all important life qualities of relationships among and between human beings and the whole of creation. This understanding extends and embraces the way indigenous peoples view the world and relate themselves to the spirits and God. For the indigenous thinkers, the traditional linear thinking of temporality that is fundamental to the Western intellectual tradition is quite alien to indigenous peoples and is in fact destructive to their livelihood.

From the indigenous people's point of view, therefore, a space-creation centered theology provides a corrective to the human-centered theology of the dominant Christian tradition. Indigenous theology affirms that the world is our home; it is the home where God, spirit, human and the whole creation live together as a universal family.

Conclusion

One might ask what does this space-creation centered theology anything to do with all that is happening in the world? Wouldn't this be another theological construct that will simply remain in the confines of such academic seminar or

---

[35] Nirmal Minz, "Tribal Perspective on Ecology," in Wati Longchar and Yangkahao Vashum, eds., *The Tribal Worldview and Ecology*, Tribal Study Series no. 2. (Jorhat: Tribal Study Center, 1998), 4.

[36] Yangkahao Vashum, "Theology of Land: A Naga Perspective," in Wati Longchar and Yangkahao Vashum, ed., *The Tribal Worldview and Ecology*, Tribal Study Series 2 (Jorhat: Tribal Study Center, 1998), 75f.

[37] Longchar, *An Emerging Asian Theology*, 89.

consultation? What impacts would it bring to bear in the day today living reality of the people, and especially, in the context of the ecological crisis in which we live today? Simply put it, can it bring about positive change in the lives of the people?

First of all, revolutions and changes in human history are brought about by and through ideologies and philosophies. It might be helpful for many of us to be reminded that we are where we are considerably because of the influence of modern philosophical-ideologies and scientific teachings.

Space-creation centered theology calls for critical reevaluation of our ways of life, our Christian spirituality and our attitude towards all God's creation. The ecological crisis which we are confronted today is primarily a spiritual crisis. Looking from the indigenous people's holistic view of life, there is no separation between what is physical and spiritual, matter and spirit and everything including human, spirits and the rest of creation are interrelated and interconnected. For the indigenous people spirituality is therefore a way of life; our living style, habit and the way we conduct and relate with other fellow human beings and creation are all integral part of their spirituality.

In the contemporary world, many people are disenchanted with the way things are. I believe that even those who profess to die a capitalist and gung-ho about the globalized way of life are looking for meanings of their life. On the other hand, people everywhere are crying for justice and peace. What is happening in India and many other parts of the world, such as movements against corruption and injustices against the poor and the marginalized, against the environmental crisis and so on are manifestations of their dissatisfactions of the way things are being run and done. They are looking for change; they are looking for alternative ways of life.

Space-creation centered theology of the indigenous people can serve as one possible alternative to the modern world of globalization and its lifestyle. Space-creation centered theology can also serve as a source of inspiration towards building a community where all forms of life could flourish and live together in harmony.

Chapter 7

Tribal Theology of Eco-Human Rights
Resources from the Tangkhul Tradition

With the emergence of contextual theologies, tribal people in India have also been attempting to do theology using tribal resources. The aim is to develop a theology that is contextually relevant and meaningful to the tribals in India. In this chapter, an attempt is made to develop a tribal theology of eco-human rights based on the resources drawn from the traditions of the Tangkhul Nagas and Christian traditions as well. The Tangkhuls are one of the Naga tribes in North East India. Racially, they belong to the Mongoloid racial group, and they maintain their own distinct culture. They are geographically located within the state of Manipur in North East India.

The Tangkhuls, like many other tribes, practiced tribal religion in the past. The main characteristics of this religion were the worship of a Supreme Being and their loyalty towards the spirits. There were many other practices, too. In fact, the ethos of the Tangkhuls is strongly influenced by the worldview of their ancestors. However, with the advent of Christianity the practice of tribal religion is almost a bygone story. It all began in 1896, when Reverend William Pettigrew arrived in Tangkhul land preaching the good news of the Kingdom of God.[1] The Tangkhul Christians celebrated their centenary in 1996. Today, the Tangkhuls, with a population of 183, 998 (2011 census) have practically all become Christians.

---

[1] Jonah M. Solo and K. Mahangthci, eds. *Forty Years in Manipur Assam: An Account of the Work of Rev. & Mrs. William Pettigrew* (Imphal, Manipur: Privately published by Mrs. M. Asenath and Mrs. K. Ruth, 1986), 3.

The chapter is broadly divided into two sections. The first section deals with human rights in relation to the rights of the whole creation. The second deals with human rights in the context of human relationships.

Traditional Tangkhul practices and beliefs contain a number of values that protect and promote human rights and the rights of the whole creation. Basic to their understanding is the all-important eco-worldview. The Tangkhuls claim their identity as deeply rooted in nature. The land is their life and identity. They live and grow up with nature. They feel one with the whole creation. Their closeness with nature and the whole of creation is central to the understanding of their existence. The meaning and uniqueness of being a human can be found only in relation to the rest of creation.

1. Limitation of Traditional Christian Theology

Christian theology has for centuries taught a high anthropology, placing human being over all the other created beings. The human being has been considered as the crown or the apex of the whole creation.[2] Thus the relation between humans and nature has been understood in terms of "human above nature." Underlying this claim has been the inalienable dignity which inheres in every human being, believed to have derived from the biblical assertion that "human kind is created in the image of God" (Gen 1:26a, 27). And this inherent dignity of human person has been identified as the source of human rights.[3] This together with the command to "have dominion" (Gen 1:28b) has been taken as the theological basis for the claim that the human being is superior to other creatures. Non-human created beings are considered inferior and fit for human use and dominion. Descartes said that "man is the Lord and owner of nature." This inherent anthropocentrism and the domineering attitude of humans has done much violence against the whole of creation.

However, today, even among Christians, many have grown disenchanted with the use of the specific emphasis on the "image of God" to assert the dignity of human beings and the accompanying belief that the other creatures are lesser beings whose value lies only in their usefulness to people. Brevard S. Childs, after considering various views on the two creation stories in the book of Genesis, concluded that the stories upheld "... the priority of creation"[4] and not dominion as traditionally understood. This means creation has an integrity of its own which is not derived from human beings but God, the Creator.

---

[2] Gerhard von Rad, *Old Testament Theology (London:* SCM Press, 1975), 144.

[3] Jürgen Moltmann, *On Humanity: Political 7'heology and Ethics (London:* SCM Press, 1984), 9 f, John Warwick Montgomery, *Human Rights and Human Dignity* (Grand Rapids: Zondcrvan Publishing House, 1986), 63 f.

[4] Brevard S. Childs, *Introduction to the Old Testament as Scripture* (Philadelphia: Fortress, 1979), 155.

This is not to maintain that the dimension of creation or space is absent from the Christian tradition. Nor is it to argue that the tribals in general and the Tangkhuls in particular do not have a sense of time. But, as A. Wati Longchar asserts, it is a question of priority or emphasis. The dominant Christian theology looks at creation from the point of view of humanity. Humanity is the point of reference and the norm. In this case, the primary datum of doing theology is humanity and the liberation of humans. However, for the tribals the point of departure is creation. Creation is the point of reference and the key to understanding human selfhood, God, and spirit.[5] Tribal traditions speak of the interrelatedness of all: God, human and world. There is an Ao-Naga tradition which says that *Lijaba,* the Supreme Being, enters into the earth with the seeds and rises again along with the crops. Hence, for the Aos, the blooming flowers and rice signify the presence of the Supreme Being. In this sense, creation is the exegesis of God.[6] Even the scientific creation myth speaks of the interrelatedness of all beings in the universe. Paul F. Knitter approvingly quotes the physicist Brain Swimme:

> Though scientific knowledge has put lethal weapons in our hands, it has also provided the earth with the first common story of our origins and development. The scientific enterprise has eventuated in a creation myth that offers humanity deeper realization of our bondedness, or profound communion not only within our species, but throughout the living and non-living universe.[7]

Dorothee Soelle reminds us of the fact that human beings are part of the earth. She rightly states, "We (humans) are created in God's image, and yet, we are made from dust."[8] "Made from dust" affirms our frailty earthliness, and mortality. This points to the fact that human beings can never claim their dignity or worth apart from the earth. This is a reminder of the fact that human beings are closely interrelated to nature, and their existence becomes meaningful only when this relationship with the earth is acknowledged. Otherwise, in a way, we deny our very humanity. It is in this context that we turn to the traditions of the Tangkhul Nagas for holistic view of humans rights.

---

[5] A. Wati Longchar, "A Creation-Poem of the Ao-Naga: A Theological Exploration," in *The Tribal Worldview and Ecology,* ed. by A. Wati Longchar & Yangkahao Vashum (Jorhat, Assam: Tribal Study Centre, 1998), 62.

[6] *Ibid.,* 58.

[7] Paul F. Knitter, *One Earth, Many Religions: Multifaith Dialogue and Global Responsibility* (Maryknoll: Orbis Books, 1995), 120.

[8] Dorothee Soelle and Shirly A.Cloys, *To Work and Love: A Theology of Creation* (Philadelphia: Fortress Press, 1984), 29.

2. Resources from the Tangkhul Traditions: A Holitic View of Eco-Human Rights

Unlike the Christian tradition which teaches "High" anthropology, the Tangkhuls have a sober view of anthropology. There is no myth, legend or belief which teaches that the human being is superior to other created beings. The only teaching one finds in Tangkhul traditions is the equality of human beings with other creatures. The human being is seen as a coworker with other creatures. Thus, the co-creatureliness of all beings is what makes the difference in the perception of the Tangkhuls. Hence, the human relationship with the whole creation is characterized by mutual respect and mutual dependence. Inter-dependence is the hallmark of their relationship. Further, their relationship is accentuated by the common responsibility they share in caring for God's created world.

a) Holistic View of Life: The Tangkhuls' worldview is characterized by a holistic vision of life. The Tangkhuls, like other tribals, perceive reality in wholeness. There is no idea of dualism or duality of things, There is no distinction between sacred and the secular, physical and spiritual, earthly and heavenly. All these together constitute the wholeness of life. If one is affected, all are affected. This holistic vision, or the primal vision, can be called "undifferentiated unity," M. M. Thomas describes the primal vision as follows: "In it there is a vision of a spiritual continuum within which the dead and the living, natural objects, spirits, gods, the individual, clan and tribe, animals, plants, minerals and humans form an unbroken hierarchical unity of spiritual forces; and the human self is not an individual self but an extended universal self present and actively participating in all parts of the totality."[9] According to this vision, life of all forms are interrelated to one another and they all together constitute an organic unity. In this sense, human, nature, and spirit do not stand apart from each other as opposing factors. Rather, they "continue as the basic texture of existence, is what makes man [sic] truly human. Balance and harmony of man-nature-spirit are essential for man [sic] to continue to remain human."[10] It is basically against this backdrop that we have to understand the claim that human rights in Tangkhul society cannot be understood apart from the rights of the whole creation, even including the rights of the dead. So, also the dignity of a person cannot be understood apart from the dignity of the whole creation.

Leonardo Boff states that the dominant ethics of present-day society is utilitarian and anthropocentric. According to this human beings regard themselves

---

[9] M. M. Thomas, "Primal Vision and Modernization." National Seminar on Theological Implications of the Primal Vision Sponsored by the Board of Theological Education Senate of Serampore College and the Gurukul Lutheran College and Research Institute. Madras, 9-12 September, 1993, 2.

[10] Nirmal Minz, "Primal Religious Perspective on Ecology",in *Ecology and Development Theological Perspective,* cd. Daniel D. Chetti (Madras: Gurukul Lutheran Theological College and Research Institute, 1991), 49.

as lords and masters of a nature that exists to satisfy their needs and to realize their desires. This ethical stance has led to the denial of the intrinsic value of the living creatures in nature. Boff writes,

> It does not understand that rights do not belong only to humankind and to nations, but also to other beings in creation. There is a human and social right, but there is also an ecological and cosmic right. We do not have the right to what we have not created.[11]

Boff calls for a new ethical order that is eco-centric or centered around ecology. In the same way, Jürgen Moltmann himself confesses that the dignity of human beings can never be understood in isolation from the dignity of the whole creation. As a result, to base human rights on human dignity alone also shows the limitations and perils of the inherent anthropocentrism. Moltmann thus says,

> Human rights have to be harmonized with the rights of nature ... human dignity is not something that separates human beings from all other living things. It is merely a special example of the dignity of all the living .... Unless human rights can be integrated into the foundational rights of nature these rights cannot claim universality.[12]

What Moltmann and other theologians are saying today had already long .been present in Tangkhul tradition. They are not a new thing for the Tangkhuls. The only thing is that they have not been utilized for our faith articulation until recently.

b) The God-Human-World Relationship: The fact that the Tangkhuls see themselves as interrelated in all their life totality to the whole creation can be seen from the creation myth and other practices and beliefs.

There is a Tangkhul creation myth which tells the story of the great assembly of all the creatures.[13] The creation myth explicitly brings out all that is concerned with our lives, relationship with God and with non-human creation. God is in the profoundest way asserted as the creator and sustainer of the universe, and whose way of dealing with the whole creation and human beings is characterized by equality, justice, freedom to life, to responsibility, to participation, and so forth. The whole of creation is depicted as a family with God as its head. In Tangkhul society one prominent practice is that important decisions are taken by

---

[11] Leonardo Boff, *Ecology and Liberation:* A *New Paradigm* (Maryknoll: Orbis Books, 1995), 29.

[12] Jürgen Moltmann, "Human Rights, the Rights of Humanity and the Rights of Nature," ed. Hans Kung and Jürgcn Moltmann (Philadelphia: Trinity Press International, 1990), 122.

[13] R. Luikham, *Folklores and Tales of the Nagas* (Delhi: Immanuel Publishers, 1983), 77 ff. Cf. Khayaipam Khamrang. "Towards an Eco-Theology: Resources in the Primal Religion of the Tangkhul Nagas," M.Th Thesis (Madras: Gurukul Lutheran Theological College & Research Institute. 1992), 57 ff.

the family sitting around the hearth-fire. "In the creation myth, the picture of all the creatures discussing together animatedly, consultation and consensus, words of wisdom from *Kasa Akhava,* search for order, tracing the eldest and giving him his due, etc., remind one of a family image."[14] This is indicative of the universal family which requires the participation and cooperation of all family members in decision making and in carrying out given responsibilities. The whole creation is depicted as co-workers-responsible partners- in caring for God's created world. These are all nothing but the constituents of rights. It is in this God-given relationship among all creatures and humankind that the rights of all creation are founded. In other words, the basis of the fundamental rights of the whole creation is God s right to - that is, claim on - the whole creation. This means that rights in their true sense are gifts of God and never a privilege granted by the state or society. Hence, the ultimate court of appeal for justice is always God.

c) The Interrelatedness of All: The underlying assumption is the peaceful co-existence of the whole creation and human kind. Because of the organic relationship that humans maintain with other creatures, what one does for good or ill affects non-human creatures too. This interrelatedness between humanity and all of creation is reflected further in the performance of rites and rituals. Rites and rituals for the Tangkhuls are an integral part of life. They are exercises performed for the welfare and peaceful existence of the community. They convey the message of wholeness and unity. It is basically for this that, although the rituals are performed by an individual, it is done for the sake of or on behalf of the whole community. "For instance at the time of sowing the [rice] paddy, the village chief offered sacrifices and performed the paddy sowing rites one day ahead of his subjects. If in some rare cases, an individual by mistake did the sowing ahead of the village chief the entire village suffered from failure of crops that particular year and had to face famine."[15] The consequences of an individual violating the observance of rites and rituals is borne not only by the individual but. by the whole community.

In addition to this, rites and rituals are essential for the sake of the whole creation and humanity's co-existence in peace and harmony. Negligence in observance or breaking the prescribed rites and rituals would not only affect the human social order but the whole cosmic order. It was told in the past, in a Tangkhul village called Torah, that all the pigs in the village suffered from a peculiar disease and they all died. It was found out that a person in the village had not observed the intended rites and rituals after a sow was littered.[16] As Khamrang rightly points out, "Rites and rituals for the Tangkhuls are the signs that the whole

[14] Khamrang, "Towards an Eco-Theology," 62.

[15] R. R. Shimray. *Origin and Culture of the Nagas* (New Delhi: Privately published by Mrs. Pamleiphi Shimray, 1985), 22 f.

[16] *Ibid.*

world is interrelated and inter-connected. When one part is subjected to gross misuse the whole order is adversely affected."[17]

This sense of cosmic oneness in Tangkhul tradition stresses the equality of all creatures, including humans. What John V. Taylor says about African traditional religion holds true also for the Tangkhuls. Taylor argues that an essential feature of primal religion is the sense of cosmic oneness:

> Not only is there less separation between subject and object, between self and non-self, but fundamentally all things share the same nature and the same interaction one upon another - rocks and forest trees, beasts and serpents, the power of the wind and waves upon a ship, the power of a drum over a dancer's body, the power in the mysterious cave of the *kokola,* the living, the dead and the first ancestors, from the stone to divinities of hierarchies of power but not of being, for they are all one, all are now.[18]

In the tribal perception, neither humanity nor creation is unique in itself. In this sense, there is a distinction but no separation between humanity and creatures, the being and beings and all other entities. A distinction is made only at the existential level. K. Thanzauva points out that the apparent hierarchy in the relationship of beings is sacred order *(heiros)* rather than a social idea or the idea of gradation. Thanzauva thus writes:

> The spirits, humans and animals are differentiated at the existential level, but there is no real distinction in the tribal cosmology that may convey the ontological separateness between the Supreme Being, spirits and human beings. Perhaps the best way to grasp the differentiation is to think of the functional aspects of interrelatedness of all existing things and beings in the larger context of the cosmic process.[19]

Thanzauva goes on to say that, though there are functional differences, God, human and world form a community in which they are interrelated and hence it is appropriate to describe this relationship as a "community model of relationship."

d) The Kinship-family Relationship with Creation: The Tangkhuls have a folktale which tells that they originated from the bowels of the earth, called *Miwurlung.*[20] According to this they came upon the earth led by a person called

---

[17] Khamrang, "Towards an Eco-Theology," 67.

[18] John V. Taylor, *The Primal Vision Christian Presence Amid African Religion* (London: SCM Press, 1977), 54.

[19] K. Thanzauva, *Theology of Community: Tribal Theology in the Making* (Aizwal, Mizoram: Mizo Theological Conference, 1997), 157.

[20] R. Brown, *The Tangkhul Nagas: Statistical Accounts of the Nature State of Manipur,* 1973, in *The Tangkhul Nagas in the Nineteenth Century,* ed. Elwin Verrier (Oxford: Oxford University Press,

Phungshoka (the one who led) and came to settle down in their present country. This event was seen as the earth giving birth to the Tangkhuls. Hence, the earth is considered to be a generous mother who not only gave birth to them but also nurtures and sustains them by the produce of the land. Mr. Kashung, 85 years old, of Grihang village, recalled how their ancestors would observe (*gennas*)'[21] for three days to mark their respect and care for the mother earth.[22] During these days no action of any sort that would bring damage to the land is allowed. Nobody should dig or break the ground or even collect the mud out of it. Whoever violates this observance is considered to have insulted the mother earth, and hence a severe action is taken against the culprit. It was considered tantamount to violating the rights of the earth.

The closeness of the Tangkhuls with nature or other created beings is further seen in the practices of totemism. There are some clans among the Tangkhuls who trace their origin to the totem animal or plant. The Keishing clan of the Bungba village claim their affinity to the buffalo. They have a great deal of respect and hence they would not eat their totem animal. To do so would be tantamount to destroying their ancestors. Hence, even today the animal is accorded a status that ensures protection. In this way, the clan tries to establish solidarity and oneness with the totem animal or plant. The other way of maintaining their close relationship is by conferring religious significance to the totem animal or plant. In this case the totem animal is eaten sacramentally on certain ceremonial feast occasions (and otherwise tabooed) by all who belong to that totem animal. This symbolized the establishment of mystic kinship or blood relationship between it and the clan," claims J. H. Thumra.[23] It is here that we find a fundamental value that the Tangkhuls attach to the creation. This is in fundamental contrast to traditional Western understandings of creatures as mere commodities for human use. The Tangkhuls would see the creatures or nature as having personalities which emanate the warmth of fellowship through such mystic kinship they maintain with them.

In this context what Khamrang says is true. "The Tangkhuls also revitalize nature by assigning will to the forces of nature. Only a living person can have a will and it is a will that seeks meaning in life."[24] It is therefore, not possible for human beings to think of themselves as apart from nature, but they are a part of the whole. These kinds of practices or beliefs bring to life the long

---

1969), 481.

[21] The term *genna* means 'prohibition." It is used in two ways: (1) It means a rest or a holiday, or (2) it means anything forbidden or prohibited. Observance of *genna* or taboo is a significant practice of the Tangkhuls.

[22] Khamrang, "Towards an Eco-Theology," 69.

[23] J. H. Thumra, "The Primal Religious Tradition" in *Religious Traditions of India,* ed. P. S. Daniel (Serampore: Indian Theological Library, Senate of Serampore College, 1988), 59.

[24] Khamrang, "Towards an Eco-Theology," 113.

cherished bonds of relationship between humans, plants, and'animals. Hence, the protection accorded to these animals or plants are entitled to rights of protection as much as human beings are. Their protection in turn is the protection of human rights, because they are inseparably related to one another as they together form a universal family.

3. Theological Validation

There is a biblical tradition which speaks of God entering into a "personal pact" with the whole creation. The Bible speaks of a covenantal family of the whole creation (Gen 9:8-17; cf. Hosea 2:20). God establishes a covenant not only with Noah and his family but with every living creature - birds, cattle, and every wild animal, every living thing on earth and the earth itself. "This covenant of God with the bird and beast," says Samuel Rayan, "is a corrective the Bible administers to human pretensions to superiority and to domination without responsibility. The imperative of this covenant is an equal and functional earth, a family of God in which humans and non-humans have to be respected."[25] In this sense to speak of human rights apart from the rights of the whole creation is untenable. In the midst of such an "organismic" relationship in which God has already established a "personal pact" with the whole creation one can no longer speak of human identity apart from the identity of the whole creation.

There is also a biblical tradition which speaks of a community based on law which goes beyond the human community of law - a community of the earth and human beings rooted in the special rights of God, the creator to what he has created. We find this in the enactments about the Sabbath and the Jubilee year (Exod. 23 and Lev. 25). According to this, the weekly Sabbaths and the regular Sabbatical year are meant for all human beings, animals, and earth for rest and rejuvenation. This is an example of the rights of the whole creation including human beings. It is concerned with the restoration of fertility for the land, concerned with the welfare of the farm animals, and of their fields. It is thus concerned with the benefit of the whole creation. The observance of the "Sabbath of the earth" is necessary so that the people and the whole creation can live in peace. Whoever disregards it will be visited by drought and thunder for having destroyed the earth's fertility.

A similar faith tradition can also be found in the Tangkhul society, particularly in the observance of agricultural *genna* or taboo. The duration and intensity of the observance varies according to the purpose and kind of *germa.* However, the purpose of the *genna* related to agriculture is for the restoration of fertility for the land, and the welfare of the animals. It is observed for the holistic benefit of the whole creation. In both the Old Testament observance of the Sabbath or Jubilee

[25] Samuel Rayan, *Ecological Dimensions of Our Eaith: To Care for the Earth-Towards a Theology of Nature,* Kunchala Rajaratnam Endowment Lectures. Series 1 (Madras: Gurukul Lutheran Theological College and Research Institute, 1991), 9.

year and the Tangkhuls' observance of *genna*. there is an underlying fear that repercussions will be visited upon the community if it disregards them. Otherwise they are meant for the good and benefit of both creation and humankind. The peaceful coexistence of the whole creation in dignity and responsibility is the right of all created beings. This aim, and not just the welfare of humanity alone, should be the concern of human beings.[26]

This organic or symbiotic relationship between human beings and the whole creation does not end with the life here on this earth itself. But, the same relationship continues to exist in the land of the dead *(Kazeiram* in Tangkhul).[27] The Tangkhul did not believe in hell or heaven. What they believed was the extension of the present life to the life after death. In *Kazeiram* all the animals, fowl and other creatures continue to live together with human beings as they were in the earthly life. This seems to suggest that human beings and the rest of the creatures have the same destiny. In this sense their relationship is eternally bound.

In the Bible this co-creatureliness and these relationships are clearly seen in the messianic vision of the new heaven and the new earth (Isa. 11.9,65.17-25, Rev. 21:1 -4). The messianic kingdom will be characterized by the peaceful coexistence between domestic animals and wild beasts, and of humans with all of nature.

David G. Hallman thus affirms, "The vision of the shalom kingdom, the one community of all God's creatures living in harmony and justice, is grounded in God's unfailing love."[28] In both the Tangkhul tradition and the biblical tradition human beings and creation as a whole look for the same destiny - *Kazeiram* and "New Heaven and New Earth" respectively.

Human Rights in the Context of Inter-Human Relationships

We have seen that human rights in the Tangkhul tradition cannot be understood apart from the rights of the whole creation. In this sense, humanity together with the whole of creation is understood as a universal family or community. Basically, this is so because of their vision of "undifferentiated unity." In this section our focus will be on the understanding of human rights as community or social rights. In other words, human rights as understood in relation to the community or social life.

1. Sociological Context

The Tangkhuls, like most other tribes, understand humanity sociologically as "expressed in the traditional pattern of societal life in community: a village,

[26] C. Dean Freandenberger, *Global Dust Howl: Can* We *Stop the Destruction of the Land Hefore It's Too Late?* (Philadelphia: Ausburg Fortress Press, 1990), 32.

[27] Thumra, *op. cit,* 72.

[28] David G. Hallman, ed. *Ecotheology: Voices from South and North* (MaryKnoll: Orbis Books, 1994), 8.

where people, animals and gods live together as coexistent in a kind of messianic kingdom."[29] The village is the center of the community, around which the corporate life revolves. In a socio-political sense, the village is the kingdom and state of the Tangkhul people. Interestingly, the identity of one's existence is defined in relation to one's attachment to one's native village.

Furthermore, their social life is characterized by a network of intra-kinship relationships instituted as family, clan, village and tribe. It is within this socio-organic body, a corporate organization, that people relate to one another. Accordingly all political institutions and social institutions are based on kinship. Even the maintenance of social order is based on and carried out through the system of kinship.[30] This is evidenced in the way they settle disputes. First the clans or the families of involved parties will try to settle the matter among themselves amicably. Only when they cannot do so would they refer the matter to the village council. Here again the village council is made up of representatives of various clans or family units. It is therefore, in the context of the intrinsic nature of their society or corporate life that human rights have to be understood.

2. Human Rights as Essentially Rooted in Relationship

As stated, individual existence has to be seen as an inseparable part of the whole community. And this has been so in the traditional life. Hence, human rights have to be defined in terms of the peaceful and harmonious existence of the whole community within the fabric of relationships. Disruption of this peaceful existence of the people in any form is nothing but violation of rights. For the Tangkhuls, "rights" are not merely an integral part of human nature, but are essentially rooted in relationship. What Zvobgo has said about the third world view on rights is quite true in the case of the Tangkhuls. He says, "Rights from a third world view do not exist as an integral part of human nature. They arise from a person's destiny of living in a relationship with family, friends, ethnos-linguistic groups, and nation.... No rights can be exercised apart from one's relationship with another."[31] Rights are therefore, in essence relationships and service and responsibility at once. The tribal view of humanity is always relational and never as a separate entity. The Tangkhuls understand the human as being whose essence of life is relation.

---

[29] Renthy Keitzar, "Developing Tribal Theology," A Paper Presented at the Theological Consultation for Northeast India (Council of Baptist Churches in North East India, Guwahati. Assam, November 5-8, 1988). 20.

[30] M. Horam, *Naga Insurgency: The Last Thirty Years* (New Delhi: Cosmos Publications, 1988), 18.

[31] Eddison J. M. Zvobgo, "A Third World View," in *Human Rights in American Policy,* ed. Donald P. Kommers and Gilburt D. Loescher (Notre Dame: University of Notre Dame Press, 1979), 93.

The biblical understanding of human being has always been relational. The creation of male and female in the "image of God" essentially reflects the relational nature of human being (Gen 1:27). Hence, Jürgen Moltmann rightly asserts that "the Image of God is human beings in all their relationships in life; the image of God in human beings together with others."[32] He goes on to say that only in human fellowship with other people is the human person truly in the image of God. Human dignity, which is believed to have derived from the "image of God" and is subsequently seen as the source of human rights, is then relational in its essence.

The relational nature of the image of God is further affirmed in the incarnation of Jesus Christ. "The incarnation is ... an affirmation of people's dignity. The *Imago Dei* of creation is reinterpreted and is placed within the grasp of all people as they share in a new covenantal relationship with Christ."[33] In the Bible rights of humans as separate entities are non-existent. So, is the case in Tangkhul society. They are always seen in relationship. Rights in the Bible are never born in solitude. Their existence and their exercise assumes community.

3. Individual Rights vis-a-vis Community Rights

In a community like the Tangkhuls, where there is a well founded network of relationships and where the community feeling is so deeply rooted, the idea of individual rights seems inconceivable apart from the rights of the whole community. As stated in the preceding discussion, because of one's reckless deeds the whole village or community suffers repercussions. The Old Testament also sees the community as a corporate whole in which the behavior of the individual affects the whole and vice versa (Josh. 7:16-21; Lev. 26:34-46).

This is not to undermine the dignity or value of the individual person. For the Tangkhuls, the inherent dignity of a person is always assumed in the belief that God created the universe and the creatures in it, including human beings. And this worth or dignity which is basically a relationship in essence can be seen only in relation to other human beings. In other words, the dignity of a person can be recognized and realized only in community. This is so because the human person is not only sacred but social. In this sense inhuman treatment, torture, or murder of persons is not merely a violation of the individual's right. Much more than that, it is a violation of the community's right to live in peace together. It is a violation of collective rights. For the Tangkhuls, any form of human rights abuse goes against the interest of the whole community. It brings about a great deal of chaos and confusion in community life. Family life is shattered, disintegrated. It shatters the living relationship of the community which is the binding factor of their existence together.

---

[32] Moltmann, *On Humanity,* 23-25.

[33] Ron, O. Grady, *Bread and Freedom: Understanding and Acting on Human Rights* (Geneva: World Council of Churches. 1979), 73.

The basis of communal solidarity in Tangkhul society has been kinship. This kinship solidarity is the strength of the community. This sense of solidarity provides security to the people. The sense of belonging to one's community is acknowledged in every bit of work that is done. Thus, in a community set up there is no individual existence apart from the community.

The village, as noted before, is in a socio-political sense, the kingdom-state of the Tangkhul people. According to this, the village is an independent political unit which is free from any external coercion or rule. Hence, whenever there was (or is) a sign of external coercion the Tangkhuls would oppose it vigorously. This attitude is reflected in the ongoing conflict between the nationalist Nagas and the Indian armed forces. The Nagas have been struggling for independence for a number of decades now. The Tangkhuls (Nagas) find it difficult to live under foreign powers to which they had not been accustomed. The Nagas feel their right to self-determination, the freedom they uphold so dearly, is usurped by the foreign powers.

This is also a case of land encroachment on the part of India and Mayanmar, which is a serious threat to traditional Naga society. In the past such boundary encroachment, if not withdrawn immediately, led to war, because this act amounts to the denial of basic justice which is very dear to the people.

4. Human Rights and the Concern for Justice

The question of justice is inseparably linked with the question of human rights in the community life of the Tangkhuls, They cannot be separated in any way. They are like two sides of the same coin. In fact, on the principle of justice rests all the customary laws of the Tangkhuls. The seriousness of this was marked by the practice of war in the ancient life of the Tangkhuls. People would go to war when the rights of the individual or community were threatened or denied. As cited already, encroachment of the village boundary, divorce of a woman without valid cause, and breaking of the observance of the community *genna* led to war. These are all issues of justice and at the same time questions of human rights. Justice is operational and takes the shape of its role in the context of the community life. And hence for the Tangkhuls their social and community life is founded on the principle of justice.

Justice is taken into cognizance in all aspects of life activities in political, economic, religious, and social life. Also in the Bible, rights and justice are inseparably related. Rights are implied in particular statements of the demands of justice (Exod. 22:20-26; Jer. 22:16). Justice in the Bible is associated with God's community-building and protecting power.[34] Both the biblical and Tangkhul

[34] Ulrich Duchrow and Gerhard Liedke, *Shalom: Biblical Perspective on Creation, Justice and Peace* (Geneva: WCC, 1989), 78. Cf. Jose Miguez Bonino, *Towards a Christian Political Ethics* (London: SCM Press, 1983), 84.

traditions understand justice as a relational concept which is operational and takes its role in the context of community life.

5. Human Rights and Social Relations

Another very significant aspect of human rights is in the area of social relations. It may not be wrong to describe that Tangkhul society is "egalitarian."[35] Of course, this does not mean that the Tangkhuls treat everyone as equal in every aspects of their life and with everybody.

First, the Tangkhuls are patriarchal society. By tradition men are regarded as the heads of the family; they inherit the family properties and it is in their names that family descent and identity is preserved. Major decision making processes are taken by men both in the family as well as in the society. Other than certain exceptional cases, women generally are not given leadership roles. This is where we have to seriously reconsider women's place and their rights in the society today. Having said this, women hold a respectable status in the society when compared with other societies. They can freely mingle and interact with their men counterparts; they can freely participate in the social activities. There are special provisions in the customary laws for the protection of women, thereby recognizing the important status of women. In this way, the rights of women in Tangkhul society are protected and promoted.[36] One of the unique rights that women enjoyed in the past has been that of peacemaker.[37] Writing about the Naga woman, Haimendorf said, "Many women in more civilized parts of India may well envy the women of the Naga hills, their high status and their free and happy life; and if you measure the cultural level of a people by the social position and

---

[35] I use the term "egalitarian" with some reservation given the fact that tribal society including Tangkhul society is not egalitarian in the sense of being equal in all aspects of their life, and especially in relation to women and their place in tribal society. However, the egalitarian principles and values are, at the same time, found in tribal society. For example, tribal community follow consensus decision/view. For a useful and detail discussion on this, consult Lovely Awomi James, *Tribal Theology: Reviewing the Naga Traditional Worldview*. Christian Heritage Rediscovered – 48 (New Delhi: Christian World Imprints, 2017).

[36] However, as noted above, in spite of the respectable status they enjoy, women play a very limited leadership role in the society. Normally it is the male members who sit in the village council. There were, however, exceptional cases like the case of the famed Harkhonla of Marem Khullen village who in her days was a wise and powerful council member of the village. See Marem Baptist Church, *The Marem Baptist Church History-cum-Ciolden Jubilee Programme* (Marem, Manipur: Marem Baptist Church History Committee and Golden Jubilee Committee, 1992), 4. In the case of rights to inheritance, here again, the Tangkhul customary law allows only males to inherit property. Smith is right when he says, "Though a woman can possess property she cannot inherit it." Cited in M. Horam, *Social and Cultural Life of the Nagas: The* Tangkhul *Nagas* (Delhi: B.R. Publishing Corp., 1977), 83. This of course refers to the handed down family property. Otherwise, women too can possess and inherit properties.

[37] The role of *Phukreila*, a woman married to a man from a different village, as peacemaker is a highly respectable role and status among the Tangkhul society.

personal freedom of its women, you will think twice before looking down on the Nagas as 'savages.'"[38]

The second area is in their economic life. Generally, the land and the forests are owned in common. Natural resources are shared by the community.[39] This is the reason why no begging is found in Tangkhul society. While there exist economically rich and poor families, strictly speaking, there is no social stratification among the Tangkhuls. In general the people are self-sufficient. The community as a whole is engaged in the economic production. Here, again, women play an important role. Women are equally productive as men and hence there is a great sense of dignity attached to their place in the economic life. Biological difference cannot be the bar?[40]

In the Bible this egalitarian concern is brought out in the story where the Israelites were fed with manna in the wilderness (Exod. 16:13- 21). This is an expression of the prophetic understanding of how God's resources are to be shared for the benefit of all. In the New Testament, this egalitarian concern is expressly seen in the life of the early Christian community. All believers sold their properties and possessions and distributed to everyone according to one's need (Acts 2:44-45).

The third area is in relation to their political life. The Tangkhuls like other tribals follow a democratic principle where equality of privileges and rights are given to everyone. The village council under the leadership of the headmen or village chief shoulders the administrative role.[41] They are the people's representatives (representatives of each clan). In this way all the sections of the people in the village are represented in the decision making process. Participation is also ensured to all during the public business sessions. As stated above, however, women are not given place to participate in the public business sessions and their

---

[38] C. vnon Fure-Haimendorf, *The Naked Nagas* (Calcutta: Thacker, Sprink & Co., 1993), 32.

[39] In recent years, things are unfortunately changing rapidly towards privatization and commercialization of properties and resources. Few rich and powerful people have taken control of land and natural resources thereby widening the gaps between the rich and the poor.

[40] One of the striking practices of the Tangkhul society is that every' village has a common pool of grain collected from each household after the harvest. Every family would make a voluntary contribution of one-tenth of its paddy and keep them in the village granary. The families who may not have sufficient food due to crop failure in a particular year are provided food-grains out of this common pool. The village council looks after this responsibility. "This is a very good practice and an effective check against beggary," comments M. Horam (Horam, *Tangkhul Nagas,* 80).

[41] *Ibid.,* 77. In contemporary Tangkhul society, there are broadly three different administrative systems followed and adopted by villages according to their conveniences: 1) Traditional village council system headed by the village chief/headman and the council members constituted by all clan representatives. 2) Village Administrative Council (VAC): under this system the leaders are democratically elected headed by the village President or Chairman. 3) Village administration is under the traditional village council system headed by the village chief/headman, while development projects are in the hands of the Village Development Council (VDC).

leadership role is very limited. Normally each village would hold two public business sessions in a year in which all the adult males are expected to participate in the deliberation. All the major or key decisions which the village council could not handle would be taken during this business session. Everybody has a say on any issue related to the welfare of the community.

One of the marks of this social equality or egalitarian principle is sharing, the antidote of greed. The land of the village is owned and shared in common. Resources vital to the community life, like water, forests, and other resources are owned and shared in common. The administrative power of the village is shared through the council of elders. The burdens of the poor and needy are shared by the village. These are all basic values upholding and promoting human dignity and in turn human rights. A sense of equality commands respect for all people.

6. Human Rights and the Judicial System

The Tangkhuls have had the distinction of running a clean judicial system, treating everyone equally, irrespective of sex or status. The village council, which shoulders the judicial responsibility, would render prompt and impartial judgment. Hence, instant and inexpensive justice is available for all.[42] The life affirming concern of the Tangkhuls is thus expressly displayed through their judicial practices and the customary laws they observe for the protection and promotion of human rights. Although they did not have written laws in the past their awareness and concern for human rights were enmeshed in the culture of the people. They had far-reaching unwritten laws which were very elaborate. This is like what St. Paul says of the laws written on the hearts of the people. (Rom 2:14-16). The Tangkhuls came to have proper written customary laws only as late as 1988, compiled and prepared by the Tangkhul Naga Long, which is the apex body of the whole Tangkhul political system. The present customary laws are written down only after consulting the various laws practiced by the Tangkhul villages for the common appeal of justice for all the Tangkhul villages.[43] These are meant basically for maintenance of social order in community life, and are necessary requisites for the protection of human

---

[42] In so far as any dispute or matter which could not be decided by the village council due to lack of evidences or witnesses, the matter was most likely settled by oath. The oath is taken usually by biting or eating a small piece of earth. It was believed that the person swearing falsely would run the risk of either dying before reaping a harvest during the year or of swelling up and dying. Horam, *Tangkhul Nagas,* 87; A. Wati Longchar, *The Tribal Religious Traditions in North East Mia* (Jorhat: Assam, ETC, 1991). 66. Horam points out here that before the annexation of the Tangkhul territory by the British, there was no question of appealing to any court other than the village court. He thus comments, "But even after courts were set up by British, most villagers were loathe to override the authority of their village court. The same holds true even today.... The British, however, must be given their due in preserving among the Nagas this deep regard for their traditional laws and thus for their village court." (*Tangkhul Nagas.*, 86).

[43] *The Tangkhul Naga Shiyan-Yanza,* compiled and prepared by the Tangkhul Naga Long (Ukhrul, Manipur, 1988).

rights. The laws cover the whole gamut of life, from birth to death. There are laws on marriage, divorce, rape, theft, murder, defamation, settlement of disputes, war and peace, and many other related laws. And all these laws are strictly observed. As Champhang Jajo says, "The laws laid down and practiced by the village courts constitute the core that cements the tribal community's life."[44] The laws are thus laid down on the basis that every person in the society should enjoy his or her maximum life here on earth and thereby live out their live meaningfully within the fabric of community-relationship. They are based on the responsible freedom one enjoys and the duty one has towards fellow human beings and the whole creation.

The Tangkhul society can be very well correlated with the Israelites in the Old Testament, whose mode of life was also communitarian. Their life as the covenantal people of Yahweh was also regulated by the commandments God gave them through Moses and the series of laws they proposed and laid down. James A. Bergquest rightly points out, "The commandments stand as the essential - but not the exclusive - summary of law God wants his people to live in both their individual and their community relationships."[45] Further, the laws prescribed in the Deuteronomic Code were meant to safeguard every person's right to life, to food, clothing, housing, to work and leisure. They also wanted the members of the society to be sensitive to and respectful of the feelings and dignity of others (Cf. Deut. 24:10-12).

7. Human Rights in All Their Totality

Understanding human rights in all their totality has been the traditional mark of the Tangkhul Nagas. This understanding goes well with the biblical notion of rights which encompasses all aspects of human life. Rights are thus indivisible. They are all interrelated, whether it be rights concerned with life protection, socio-economic life, or freedom or self-determination. They are all inseparably interrelated. This is the biblical and also the traditional understanding of Tangkhul Nagas. It is rooted in the wholeness of the person.

The Tangkhuls are basically an inclusive society. It is inclusive in the sense that all the people in the community experience a sense of belonging together and no one is made to feel that he or she does not belong. It is also inclusive in the sense that there is a sense of oneness not only with the living but also the dead - the ancestors. The ancestors are believed to be part and parcel of the family or community. They are believed to be participating in all the activities of the family or community. This inclusive attitude which is always receiving, accepting and

---

[44] Champhang Jajo, *Christian Life in Tribal Context in Manipur* (Ukhrul: Published by the author, 1990), 12.

[45] James A. Bergquest. *The Ten Commandments and Responsible Freedom* (Delhi: ISPCK, 1971), 16.

respecting, is the hallmark of the Tangkhul society and indicative of the concern they have for human rights.

In the Bible (Isa. 56:1-7) the prophet speaks of his vision of an inclusive society in which all experience a sense of belonging together and no one is made to feel that he or she does not belong. This sense of belonging together provides no room for the people to discriminate against or exploit others.

This inclusive society is further characterized by the sense of being needed or expected. It is in this sense of being needed or expected that the Tangkhuls would see the worth or dignity of a person. In this connection what Dorothee Soelle says is helpful: "We need to understand ourselves as having been expected and cherished before we came into the world.... Our sense of self-worth and dignity is rooted in our being needed, if not by our parents then by someone else, who values who we are."[46] The human being is therefore, essentially a relational being whose dignity or worth can be seen and realized only in community life where one's presence is needed and cherished at all times.

Conclusion

A human being, according to the Tangkhul worldview, is never in isolation. He or she is always part of a community. A human being is always part of the universal community which includes all of creation, the earth itself and also the spirit world. At the same time, the individual belongs to the larger human community. A human being is thus essentially a relational being. A human being is inseparably related to nature and the whole of creation and to his or her follow beings at the same time.

This is the basic reason why human rights violations can never be understood apart from the rights of the whole creation. This is why the dignity of a human person can never be understood apart from the dignity of the whole creation. This interrelatedness, or the symbiotic relationship that human beings maintain with the whole creation is what makes human beings human. In the nature of this relationship there is always the interconnection between cause and effect. One's action or deeds will affect the rest of the members of creation whether for good or ill. If one is adversely affected, the whole cosmic relationship is disturbed or disrupted. Human rights violations in this sense are nothing but disruptions or distortions of the peaceful coexistence of human beings and the whole creation as a universal community. The whole creation is also adversely affected in such situations. This is tantamount to the violation of the rights of the whole creation. Any violation committed against the earth and nature will also adversely affect the human community.

Human rights exist in the context of inter-human relationships. Here again human rights are understood in terms of the collective rights of the whole community of which the individuals is a part. Human rights, according

---

[46] Soellc and Cloyes, *To Work and Love,* 29.

to Tangkhul traditions and the biblical tradition, assume community. Further, the question of human rights is inseparably linked with the question of justice. Rights to protection of life, social equality, economic justice, political freedom, rights to participation in the overall decision making process - all these together constitute human rights for the Tangkhuls. Rights are therefore indivisible. They are all interrelated. This is the affirmation of the Tangkhuls and the biblical faith. In this final analysis human dignity can be found only in relationship with fellow human beings and the whole creation.

Chapter 8

Religion's Ambience for Peace in Contemporary Tribal and Adivasi Communities[1]

Introduction

We are meeting at a time when India as a nation is going through one of the most testing times in her history. We know that the length and breadth of India is embroiled with violence of all kinds – violence stemming from racial, ethnic, caste, religious, gender, social, economic, and political. Explosions of bombs, gun-fires, and killings are taking place on daily basis. We hear and witness innocent lives being blown up for no crime of their own; their only crime is that they happen to be on the streets or at work places. Their only crime is that they happen to belong to a certain racial/ethnic group, caste, religion, etc. In recent years, terrorism related violence is high on India's agenda. The memories of 26/11 terror attack in Mumbai where many civilians and law enforcement personnel were killed are still fresh in most of our minds. Streets, shopping centers, market and work places which used to be relatively peaceful are no longer safe. These days when people step out of their homes, they feel something amiss; they do not feel safe anymore. While economically the rich are becoming richer and richer, the poor are becoming poorer and poorer. The number of starvation and poverty related death is increasing every year; the number of poor farmers committing suicide is increasing at an alarming rate. These seem to be the reality of contemporary India.

[1] This essay is a revised version of the Keynote Address delivered in the 3rd Dalit-Tribal-Adivasi Theological Interface held during November 24-26, 2009 at CNI Program Center, Nagpur.

While we recognize the challenging time of our nation, such general overview of the Indian situation should not be allowed to hijack the issues of the people who are most affected – the Dalits, the Tribals and Adivasis and other minorities. These are the people who have been at the receiving end of the society for centuries and they continue to be the most oppressed and discriminated in India. Perhaps the plights and conditions of these people are worsening day by day. The recent violence meted out against the poor tribals and adivasis including the 2008 Kandhamal incident in Orissa, the Nandigram incident in West Bengal and others are some of the grim reminders the tribal people go through in their lives. Then we have today the tribals and adivasis being caught up in the crossfire between the Naxalites and Indian armed forces. The ongoing Operation Green Hunt against the Naxalites in Lalgarh, West Bengal, and neighboring states is causing untold suffering and misery to the people. "Maoists attack at will, forces are on the backfoot and frail widows are the enemy," writes Tusha Mittal.[2] This captures well the irony of the ongoing operation. The tribals are caught in a spiral of random violence in this offensive. At the same time, the ongoing operation has brought to the fore the extreme neglect and deprivation of the tribal people for decades; the miserable living conditions of the people are brought to the full view of the entire world. These tribals have never heard the word "development" in their lives nor have they seen any developmental work in their areas.

Tribal/Adivasi/Indigenous people in India[3]

In India these groups of peoples are not properly defined. Rather they are simply specified as "Scheduled Tribes" for the administrative and political purposes. Generally, they are referred to variously as "tribal," "tribal groups," "Scheduled Tribes" "native," "indigenous ethnic minorities," "aboriginals," "hill tribes," "indigenous cultural minorities," or "indigenous peoples." They identify themselves as indigenous peoples because they claim they are the descendents of

---

[2] *Tehelka,* 7 November 2009, vol. 6, Issue 44, 27. On October 23, 14 adivasi women were released from Midnapore jail. These women were swapped for OC Atindranath Dutta. The Media compared it with a "Kandahal" swap.

[3] Total Scheduled Tribes Population is 10, 42, 81, 034 (104 millions) according to 2011 census, that is 8.6% against the total Indian population. And there are 705 number of individual ethnic groups, etc. notified as Scheduled tribes in 30 states/UTs.

Sharing of Resources

15% of country's total Resources is shared by the Scheduled Tribes in India. 8.6% of total population belongs to ST.

Their Locations in India (6 Regions)

Central region with 46.6% (Jharkhand, Chhatisgarh, Bihar, MP, Orissa, West Bengal);

Western region with 27.6% (Maharastra, Dadra & Nagar Haveli, Daman Diu, Gujarat, Rajasthan); Northeastern region with 12.4% (AP, Assam, Manipur, Meghalaya, Mizoram, Nagaland, Tripura, Sikkim); Southern region with 11.3% (Andhra Pradesh, Tamilnadu, Karnataka, Kerala);

North-Western region with 2% (UP, Uttaranchal, HP, J&K); Island region with 0.1% (Andaman & Nicobar, Lakshadweep).

the populations which inhabited the country or geographical region, at the time of conquest or colonization, or at the time of inroads of non-indigenous religions and cultures, or the establishment of present state boundaries; and are recognized as well by other groups, or by state Authorities, as a distinct collectivity. These people retain some or all of their own social, economic, cultural and political institutions. While some continue to settle in their ancestral homelands, many may have been displaced from their traditional domains or may have resettled outside their ancestral domains. The tribals/adivasis suffer encroachment on and dispossession of their lands by settlers, companies or state agencies from within the country. In terms of religious beliefs, while tribes such as in Northeast India have embraced Christianity, many others have either been Hinduized or embraced other religions. Of course, there are still many tribals who continue to practice their traditional religions such as in Arunachal Pradesh and elsewhere.

The tribals/adivasis are one of the most oppressed and exploited peoples in India. They are one of the least developed groups. Socially and economically speaking, they are considered by the mainstream society as "less advanced." Perhaps the following statistics are indicators of the plights and conditions of the tribals/adivasis in India.

> The percentage of household in living conditions reveal that only 40.6 are in good condition, other 53 percent are in unliveable condition whereas the rest 6.4 percent are in dilapidated situation. The 39.2 percent of tribes use hand pump for drinking water, 24.4 of Tribals depend on tap water for drinking, well water is used by 21.1 percent, 7.8 use tube well water, the rest of the (7.5) tribal use any other source of water for drinking purposes. The 46.7 percent tribes go to the nearby premises to collect water, 33.6 percent of them go to faraway places to fetch drinking water whereas only 19.7 have water within the premises. Electricity as the main source of lighting is used by only 52 percent of the Tribal households. Kerosene is used by 46 percent of them. Bathing facility is enjoyed by only 31percent households and latrine facility is utilized by 23 percent of the Tribals. For cooking, 87 percent households use firewood/crop residue, cow-dung cake and a small population (9 percent) use cooking gas. While coming to usage of television there are 21.9 percent users, radio/ transistor is used by – 14.2 percent and only 5.2 percent have computer/laptop. Availing of banking services is done by 45percent of the Tribes. The enrolment ratio in schools, for classes I – V for the boys is 137.2 percent and for the girls 136.7 percent for classes I – XII is 96.8 for boys and 92.8 percent for girls. With regard to health-Infant mortality is 62.1 percent, while 68.5 percent women suffer from anaemia. In rural areas 47.3 percent Scheduled Tribes and in urban area 33.3 percent Scheduled Tribes live in below poverty line. All this data present the grim situation in which

Tribes of our land are living in. While comparing their share with the rest of the groups, Tribes lag behind all other social groups in every aspect.[4]

Tribals of North East India

Ethnologically the Tribals in Northeast India belong to the Australoid, Caucasoid, and Indo-Mongoloid (Tibetan-Burman speaking) racial groups.. In general the tribes can be categorized as comprising two broad divisions – the hills tribes and the plains tribes. The hills tribes consist of various groups of the Mizo-Kuki-Chin family, Nagas, Khasis, Garos and Arunachalis and reside in the states of Mizoram, Tripura, Nagaland, Manipur, Meghalaya and Arunachal Pradesh respectively. Most of the hills tribals have been heavily Christianized with the exception of Arunachalis who have been isolated and protected from the influence of Christian missionaries by the Indian Government. Prior to the conversion to Christianity, the Tribals practiced what might be called a primal religion, which is very often incorrectly classified as animism. In contrast, the plains tribals are concentrated primarily in the Brahmaputra and Barak Valleys of Assam, Manipur Valley and plains in Tripura. Most of these tribals have been Hinduized[5] and assimilated into Hindu culture, but some have been more strongly influenced by Islam, and there are others follow Buddhism and traditional religions. Three quarters of the region are covered by hills and a quarter by plains (the Brahmaputra valley and Barak valley of Assam, the Tripura plains, and Manipur plains).

There is another tribal group known as the *adivasis* who were either brought to the region by the British, or they migrated to Northeast to work as laborers on tea plantations. Having come from Orissa, Bihar, Andhra Pradesh especially, most of them either belong to Munda speaking family or Dravidian speaking family. They form a substantial presence in the region, especially in the plains of Assam where tea gardens are concentrated.

Conflict Situations of North East India

Northeast is the hotbed of ethno-political movements for identity of the indigenous-tribal peoples of the region. The oldest insurgency group in Asia is also found in the region – the Naga insurgency movement. The whole of Northeast states, with the exception of Sikkim, is caught up with either movements for independence or separate homeland or state or autonomous status within the states. Broadly speaking, there are two kinds of movements: One seeking for political sovereignty/independence such as the Naga national movements for

[4] "Tribal Situation in India," https://shodhganga.inflibnet.ac.in/bitstream/10603/190674/3/chapter%201.pdf. This is a summarization of the tribal situation in India following the 2011 census report of the government of India (22/04/2020).

[5] The Meiteis of Manipur and the Ahoms of Assam are the most highly Hinduized groups in the region.

independence; and the other for greater autonomy or autonomous status/ regionalism or statehood. Of course, both the movements can be described as movements for identity. In the following, a brief overview of the various movements operating in the Northeast states will be given.

Nagaland

Inhabited by predominantly Nagas – consists of 16 major tribes and a number of sub-tribes – is known for decades of struggles for Naga sovereignty in the region. Perhaps the very fact that the Naga insurgency movement is known as the oldest insurgency group in Asia, speaks volumes about the Naga people and their struggles. The Naga national movements for independence has come along way entailing decades of violence and human rights abuses, and intermittently punctuated by ceasefires and peace talks. However, till date, solution to the long standing issue remains elusive.

Naga national movement spearheaded by Naga National Council (NNC), formed in February 1947, under A. Z. Phizo's leadership declared independence of Nagaland on 14th August 1947 a day ahead of India's independence; boycotted 15th August 1947 independence day of India. The signing of Shillong Accord in 1975 resulted in the division of NNC and subsequently the formation of National Socialist Council of Nagaland (NSCN) in 1980 headed by Th. Muivah and Isak Swu. In 1988, NSCN split into two factions: NSCN-IM and NSCN-K; the former group led by Isak and Muivah and the latter by Khaplang. Today, besides the two NSCN factions, there are also NNC (A) and NNC (P) operating in Nagaland. NSCN-IM continues to remain as the dominant group among them. For the first time in Naga history, the Nagas became Member of the Unrepresented Nations and Peoples' Organization (UNPO) in January 23, 1993. This is followed by a number of representations at the United Nations (UN) for the cause of the Naga struggles. Then in July 25, 1997, NSCN – IM entered into Ceasefire and Peace Agreement with Government of India (GOI) which came into effect from August 1, 1997 followed by the NSCN-K group in 2001. The Ceasefire and Peace process started under three conditions: a) That there be total ceasefire between the two sides; b) That talks must be held at the highest level, i.e., at Prime Minister's level; and c) That it must be held at the neutral country. One positive outcome of this peace talk is the GOI's recognition of the unique history of the Naga people. Whereas, several rounds of talks have been held and till date no tangible solution has emerged. Meanwhile, blame games between the parties, abuses of human rights, factional clashes between and among the various factions resulting in the loss of many innocent lives, have characterized the contemporary Naga society.

However, in recent times, the Nagas are beginning to experience relatively a more peaceful life with many civil societies and organizations including peace loving individuals working for peace and harmony in the region. The Forum for

National Reconciliation (FNR) under the leadership of Rev. Dr. Wati Aier and many other well known Naga personalities with him, is making all efforts to bring together all the various Naga insurgency groups and the Nagas as a whole. The Forum is making tremendous progress and is being supported by all the Nagas including the various Naga insurgency groups.[6] Additionally, the recent resumption of talks between NSCN–IM and GOI has brightened people's hope for peace in the region. Th. Muivah, IM's powerful General Secretary, himself is leading in the talk. While the political sovereignty of the Nagas remains to be the ultimate dream, integration of all the contiguous Naga areas comprising Nagaland, Manipur, Assam, and Arunachal Pradesh has become the critical component of the ongoing peace process. It must also be pointed out that the unity of the Naga national groups further deteriorated when more factions emerged in the recent years. NSCN (Unification) was formed by few cadres and ranks from NSCN (K) and NSCN (IM) who signed an inter-factional "truce agreement" in November 23, 2007. NSCN (K) further split with the emergence of NSCN (Reformation) under Y. Wangtin and P. Tikhak in April 6, 2015.

Peace Agreement 2015 and Aftermath: Naga peace talk entered into a critical phase with the signing of Peace Agreement between the GoI and the NSCN I-M in August 3, 2015 in New Delhi in the presence of honorable Prime Minister Narendra Modi and Th. Muivah, the General Secretary and a host of high dignitaries from both sides.[7] Interlocutor for Naga Peace Talks, Shri R. N. Ravi, signed the Agreement on behalf of the Government of India. Shri Isak Chishi Swu, Chairman and Shri Th. Muivah, General Secretary were the signatories on behalf of the NSCN. The agreement turns out to be the Framework Agreement for final solution. This hard earned agreement took place after over 80 rounds of peace negotiations between the two sides and it gave a glimpse of hope to the people. However, the talks has further dragged on.

Many things have happened between the signing of the framework agreement in 2015 and 2020. Isak Chishi Swu, the Yaruiwo (Chairman) of the NSCN (IM) passed away in June 28, 2016 and his death was a setback to the ongoing peace talks. In 2016 another historical development took place with the coming together of six factional groups to form a Naga National Political Groups (NNPGs) comprising of the following groups: GPRN/NSCN, FGN, NNC (Parent Body), NPGN/NNC (NA), NSCN (R) and the NNC/GDRN (NA).[8]

---

[6] There are many other civil society groups including Naga Hoho, Naga Students' Federation, Naga Mother's Association, United Naga Forum, etc., who are also actively involved in bringing about peace and supporting the peace process.

[7] The high dignitaries from the GoI include hon'ble Home Minister, Shri Rajnath Singh, National Security Adviser, Shri Ajit Doval and others. The NSCN was represented by its entire collective leadership and senior leaders of various Naga tribes. https://pib.gov.in/newsite/PrintRelease.aspx?relid=124221.

[8] https://morungexpress.com/6-naga-political-groups-form-working-group/(21/04/2020).

NSCN (IM) elected Q. Tuccu as its Yaruiwo/Chairman and Tongmeth Wangnao as Vice Chairman respectively in February 2019. Meanwhile, the GOI appointed R. N. Ravi, the government's interlocutor for Naga talks as the Governor of Nagaland state in July 20, 2019 which was vehemently opposed by the people, especially the NSCN (IM). The GOI entered into peace parleys with the Working Committee of the NNPGs even when the peace talks with the NSCN I-M on the other hand continued. The GOI set October 31, 2019 as the last date to wrap up the Naga peace talks against the will of the Naga people. NSCN (IM) and many others opposed this move. However, the GOI stood by the decision. The pressure was mounting on NSCN (IM) and the NNPGs to meet the deadline. The issues standing on the way for resolution are the Naga flag and constitution. The GOI rejects Nagas' demand for the flag and the constitution. Meanwhile the working committee of the NNPGs accepted to forego the Naga national flag and Naga constitution, but the NSCN (IM) stood their ground. Alezo Venuh, who coordinates with the Centre on behalf of the NNPG, spells out the position of the group thus, "We (NNPGs) have resolved all issues, and the Government of India has decided to conclude the talks on October 31. We are prepared for it."[9] As usual, the GOI resorted to their old divide and rule policy by engineering division among the Naga national groups. The differences seriously jolted the peace process and threatened even to breaking down of the over 22 years old hard earned peace process. The GOI used all possible tactics to intimidate and coerce the Nagas by deploying its armed forces personnel to the fullest including "fighter aircraft were seen hovering over Dimapur a few days ago in a 'wartime preparedness drill' that covered six civilian airports in the northeast under the Eastern Air Command."[10] The NSCN (IM) accused India of creating fear psychosis by creating wartime situation in Nagalim and warned that Nagas will oppose any move for "forced union."[11] The peace talks was hanging on a life support. The NNPGs having already agreed to sign the deal without the flag and constitution, all attentions were turned to the break or make it talks between IM and the GOI interlocutor Ravi. On October 31, 2019, the two camps finally agreed to continue with the talks for final resolution on the basis of the Framework Agreement, having not been able to find agreeable solution on the contentious issues of Naga flag and constitution. To the relief of everyone, it gave a breather to the peace process. At

---

[9] "Govt may sign Naga pact even without NSCN(I-M) on Oct 31" https://timesofindia.indiatimes.com/india/govt-may-sign-naga-pact-even-without-nscni-m-on-oct-31/articleshow/71781225.cms (20/04/2020).

[10] "Govt's Security Overdrive in Nagaland Takes Locals by Surprise, Fuels Rumours," https://www.news18.com/news/india/govts-security-overdrive-in-nagaland-takes-locals-by-surprise-fuels-rumours-2361515.html (20/04/2020).

[11] Government of India is creating fear psychosis in Nagalim: Q Tuccu, President of NSCN-IM https://economictimes.indiatimes.com/news/politics-and-nation/government-of-india-is-creating-fear-psychosis-in-nagalim-q-tuccu-president-of-nscnim/articleshow/71666130.cms?utm_source=contentofinterest&utm_medium=text&utm_campaign=cppst (20/04/2020).

the same time, everyone is anxiously awaiting to know when the end will finally take place.

Meanwhile, there have been pressures from all quarters for all the Naga national groups to work together for lasting peaceful settlement with the GOI. However, till date that is not happening and this is one serious hurdle in bringing about resolution to the decades old Naga issue. Unfortunately, as the stalemate continues, there are already further divisive elements working against the long desired unified resolution among the Naga people. There are forces working and inciting divisions between Nagas of Nagaland state and the rest to the extent of advocating solutions only for the Nagas of Nagaland state. This is another serious problem confronting the Nagas in their search for honorable and lasting resolution to their decades old national issue.[12]

Manipur

Manipur was a princely state before the merger with India in 15th October 1947; it was however, opposed by some among the Meities. In mid 1960s, there were growing resentments among Meiteis with India. These resentments finally gave birth to the formations of a number of insurgency groups in Manipur to fight for the independence of the Meiteis from the forceful Indian occupation. In 1964 the United National Liberation Front (UNLF) was formed; however, only in 1991 that the group decided to take up arms for resistance. While the People's Liberation Army (PLA) was formed in 1972, Peoples Revolutionary Party of Kangleipak (PREPAK) was formed in 1981. Kangleipak Communist Party (KCP) is another Meitei insurgency group besides many more others. All of them profess to work for the liberation of Meitei people from the colonial rule of Indian government. There are also a number of hill based insurgency groups in Manipur. Some of the known groups include Kuki National Front (KNF), Kuki National Army (KNA), Zoumi Revolutionary Army (ZRA), Hmar Peoples' Liberation Front (HPLA), etc. Most of these groups have entered into ceasefire and in peace dialogue with the state government. The Naga insurgency groups, especially NSCN–IM and NSCN–K are equally active in Manipur as well.

Today Manipur is literally burning. Empowered by the Armed Forces Special Powers Act (AFSPA) 1948 amended in 1950, Indian army and state law enforcements have been literally running the show: abusing of human rights at will, making arbitrary arrests without warrants, killing of innocent people on mere suspicion, etc. Killing by fake encounters are happening on daily basis. The killing of one, Chongkham Sanjit on July 23, 2009 by the state police was the classic example of murder in plain sight. He was a victim of fake encounter. The

---

[12] This is unfortunate. This is the time for everyone to rise above narrow regional politicking and parochial tribal interests; time for everyone to exercise prudence and proactively work for the unified Indo-Naga peace resolution.

camera picture captured by Delhi based Tehelka News Magazine[13] showed the gruesome killing of Sanjit by the Police – Police dragged Sanjit into a pharmacy and killed in cold blood. On that fateful day, a young pregnant mother Rabina Devi was also killed in front of her young son.

Since that fateful day, life in Manipur has come to a stand still-protest rallies, bandhs and continued violence have become the norms. Schools and colleges in Manipur plains remained closed for several months until they were reopened in January 2010. As a result, many children and college going students have been greatly affected; there is a genuine fear that unless something is done soon, the collateral damage caused will become simply irreparable. For years the people of Manipur state have been living in fears and helplessness, under the mercies of these armed forces and insurgency groups. Extortion, murder, rape, bomb blasts, bandhs and protest rallies characterize the contemporary life realities of Manipur state. People are caught up in these vicious cycles of violence. The nearly 16 year old fast unto death by the former Iron Lady of Manipur Irom Chanu Sharmila Devi – who broke her fast on August 9, 2016 to the disappointment of many people[14] - is a stark reminder of the violent and volatile living realities of the people of Manipur.

Manipur, along with other Northeast states, continue to reel under AFSPA with no sign for withdrawal in the foreseeable future. According to the annual report of the Ministry of Home Affairs (MHA) 2018-19 Manipur remained the most violent state, accounting for about 50% of the total insurgency-related violence. The state which still has several insurgency groups witnessed 127 insurgency related violence. The report further states that Meitei insurgent groups were found involved in 57% incidents - which included killings of six security personnel and five civilians.[15] In the latest development, the Assam Rifles and the Manipur Police have created war-like situation in Kashung and Bungdung villages on April 21, 2020 under Kashom Khullen block in Kamjong district in the name of flushing out the NSCN-IM cadres who are camping in the border areas of the district.[16] The astonishing fact is that this has been happening when the whole

---

[13] Refer to *Tehelka,* 8 August 2009, vol. 6, Issue 31 & 15 August 2009, vol. 6, Issue 32; both the issues carry the pictures showing the murder of Sanjit and the body of Rabina Devi lying next to Sanjit's.

[14] "As announced Sharmila ends 16 years fast with a drop of honey... Says she will contest polls against Chief Minister," http://e-pao.net/GP.asp?src=1..100816.aug16; "Manipur's Iron Lady Irom Sharmila ends 16-year-long hunger strike," https://timesofindia.indiatimes.com/india/Manipurs-Iron-Lady-Irom-Sharmila-ends-16-year-long-fast/articleshow/53616970.cms?from=mdr (20/04/2020).

[15] "NE insurgency down, Nagaland and Manipur still a worry," in Deccan Herald. https://www.deccanherald.com/national/east-and-northeast/ne-insurgency-down-nagaland-and-manipur-still-a-worry-773082.html (25/04/2020).

[16] "Stand off between NSCN (IM) and Assam Rifles at Kamjong UNC seeks intervention of Union Home Minister," http://e-pao.net/GP.asp?src=3..250420.apr20 (27/04/2020).

world including Manipur is in lockdown situation combating the deadly corona virus, Covid -19 pandemic. The villagers, especially the courageous women folks in hordes blocked the advancing security forces at the Hongbei junction. This stand off is a repeat of the Shirui village stand off (2009) and Shihai Khullen stand off (2019) in Ukhrul district between the Assam Rifles and the NSCN-IM. For now, thanks to the timely intervention of the state government and the Naga civil society headed by United Naga Council, the impasse seems to have been resolved.[17] But, one wonders, what could happen in the next few days, once the lockdown is withdrawn.

Mizoram

Mizo people boycotted 15th August, 1947 in protest against the forceful occupation by India. In early 1960s gained momentum for independent Mizoram under Mizo National Front (MNF) led by Laldenga. MNF declared Mizoram independent from India in 1965 or 68? But things did not let up for a long time; instead it worsened the situation. In 1986, MNF under the leadership of Laldenga signed a Peace Accord with India; Rajiv Gandhi was then PM of India. India has signed a number of failed peace accords with many Northeast groups. In this case, the peace accord is successfully implemented. Most of the former insurgent leaders were absorbed into the political stream in the state. Mizoram is one the most peaceful states in India today. In recent times, there are cases of ethnic conflicts between the Mizos and Reangs/Brus. The militant outfits such as Bru National Liberation Front (BNLF) and Bru Liberation Front of Mizoram are active in Mizoram. The Brus who were forced out of the state to neighboring Tripura in 1997 on alleged atrocities on them by the dominant Mizos were housed in six relief camps in the Kanchanpur subdivision of North district in Tripura and they are awaiting their repatriation.[18]

Other outfits like the Hmar People's Convention-Democracy (HPC-D), mostly operate their activities from neighboring states of Assam and Manipur. Then there is a new outfit called Singlung Tiger Force later changed into Singlung People's Liberation Army (SPLA) was formed in 2007, to defend the rights of the indigenous Singlung people affected by the proposed construction of Tuirial and Tipaimukh multi-purpose hydel project in their area including the adjoining border areas of Manipur and Mizoram. In 2009, 64 SPLA cadres surrendered to the Mizoram Government.[19]

---

[17] "Posers over COVID-19 protocol: Stand off at Kamjong - The Sangai Express Editorial 27 April, 2020 –," http://e-pao.net/epSubPageExtractor.asp?src=news_section.editorial.editorial_2020.Stand_off_at_Kamjong_TSE_20200427 (27/04/2020).

[18] "Overview: Insurgency & Peace Efforts in Mizoram," *Centre for Development and Peace Studies* (available from http://cdpsindia.org/mizoram_insurgency.asp, 10/03/2010).

[19] *Ibid.*

Assam

Assamese fear of becoming minority in their land due to great influx of immigrants from other parts of India and Bangladesh gave birth to the "Assam for Assamese" movement led by Assam Sahitya Sabha and All Assam Students' Union (AASU) in the late 1970s. The United Liberation Front of Asom (ULFA) was formed in 1979 but formally constituted in 1981 in order to fight for independent Assamese nation. Then there are a number of tribal ethnic movements such as Bodos, Karbis, Dimasas, etc., each group demanding for greater autonomy, or statehood and active in their own respective regions. These tribal communities have been ignored and discriminated for so long by the state and Union Governments. Some of the dominant ethnic insurgency groups include Bodo Liberation Tiger Force (BLTF); National Democratic Front of Bodoland (NDFB-Dhiren Boro) and (NDFB-Ranjan Daimary); United Democratic People's Solidarity (UDPS); Karbi Longri National Liberation Front (KLNLF); Dima Halom Daoga (DHD-Nunisa) and (DHD-Jewel Garlosa, popularly known as the Black Widow); etc.

Assam in recent years has been experiencing escalations in violence and killings: bomb explosions taking place at regular intervals which have led to loss of many innocent lives. Then there are conflicts which are by and large ethnic by nature. The recent ethnic conflicts between Dimasas and Zemi Nagas, Kukis/Hmars and Dimasas, Bodos and Adivasis, etc. have claimed many lives and properties from all communities. Then there are the unending armed feuds between the various factions among the various insurgency groups among Bodos, Karbis, Dimasas, etc., besides the military offensive, and killings by fake encounters. According to a source estimate, between 1992 and 2009 (till July), 7, 277 insurgency related fatalities were reported in Assam. During this period, 3, 867 civilian and 778 security force personnel were killed in terrorist violence. On the other hand, the number of insurgency cadres killed in Assam during the same period is 2, 621.[20]

In recent times, there are signs of peace in the state with most of the insurgency groups opting for ceasefire and dialogue with the state and central governments for finding solutions to their long standing demands. The groups which are already on ceasefire and in dialogue with the governments include the UPDS, KLNLF, DHD (N) & DHD (J), and NDFB (Dhiren Boro group), Adivasi Cobra Militant force (ACMF), Birsa Commando Force (BCF) and ULFA. ULFA split between the pro-talk camp let by its Chairman Arabinda Rajkhowa and the hardliners under its Commander-in chief Paresh Baruah in the early part of 2011.[21] Under Paresh Baruah ULFA (Independent) was formed and the group refused to join the peace talks. ULFA (I) continues to carry on the movement and

---

[20] "Overview: Insurgency & Peace Efforts in Assam," *Centre for Development and Peace Studies* (available from http://cdpsindia.org/assam_insurgency.asp, 10/03/2010).

[21] "Ulfa splits, Paresh Baruah rejects talks," https://www.news18.com/news/india/ulfa-split-paresh-baruah-rejects-peace-talks-359885.html (20/04/2020).

its activities till date. In recent years, while talks have been progressing well with most of the groups in Assam including the Karbis and the ULFA,[22] the Bodos have signed a peace deal with the state and central government. The tripartite peace deal between the National Democratic Front of Boroland (NDFB), the government of Assam and Central government was sealed on January 27, 2020 in the presence of Shri Amit Shah home minister, Sarbananda Sonowal chief minister of Assam and hosts of dignitaries from all the parties.[23] The All Bodo Students' Union (ABSU), which has been spearheading a movement for a Bodoland state was also signatory to the accord. Efforts are on afoot to bring the Paresh Barua led ULFA (I) as well to the peace deal in the wake of the Bodo peace accord.[24]

Meanwhile, there are several groups seeking for Scheduled Tribe (ST) status in Assam. "The Union Cabinet has approved Scheduled Tribe (ST) status to six communities of Assam namely Tai Ahom, Koch Rajbongshi, Chutia, Tea Tribes, Moran and Matak."[25] However, so far the bill has not yet been introduced in the parliament. This move to grant ST status has been vehemently opposed by the tribal communities in the state.[26] Besides all this, one of the most potent issues which has been lingering and confronting the people of Assam has been the issue of illegal immigrants (often dubbed as foreigners issue) from the neighboring country, Bangladesh. The recent introduction and passing of Citizen's Amendment Bill/Act (CAA) 2019 coupled with the National Registration of Census (NRC) have further added fuels to the woes and angers of the people as demonstrated by violent protests and demonstrations.[27] The CAA which is passed in Parliament in December 11, 2019 came into effect on January 10, 2020.[28]

---

[22] "Assam: Centre to sign peace deal with Ulfa & 3 militants," https://timesofindia.indiatimes.com/city/guwahati/assam-centre-to-sign-peace-deal-with-ulfa-3-militant-groups-soon/articleshow/71885114.cms (20/04/2020).

[23] "Govt signs historic Bodo peace accord, Amit Shah says golden future awaits Assam," https://www.indiatoday.in/india/story/amit-shah-historic-bodo-peace-accord-sign-assam-1640584-2020-01-27; "Govt Signs 'Historic' Peace Accord with NDFB, ABSU to Resolve Assam's Decades-old Bodo Issue; PM Hails Move," https://www.news18.com/news/politics/assam-govt-signs-tripartite-peace-accord-to-resolve-bodoland-issue-2475347.html (20/04/2020).

[24] "Assam: Centre to sign peace deal with Ulfa & 3 militants."

[25] "Cabinet Approves ST status to 6 Assam communities," https://www.business-standard.com/article/news-ani/cabinet-approves-st-status-to-6-assam-communities-119010801462_1.html.

[26] "Tribals call shutdown in Assam after govt grants ST status to 6 ethnic groups," https://news.abplive.com/news/india/tribals-call-shutdown-in-assam-after-govt-grants-st-status-to-6-ethnic-groups-894223 (20/04/2020).

[27] "CAA protests in Assam: Why it is different from the rest of the country," https://economictimes.indiatimes.com/news/politics-and-nation/caa-protests-in-assam-why-it-is-different-from-the-rest-of-the-country/articleshow/72844673.cms (21/04/2020).

[28] "Citizenship Amendment Act comes into effect from January 10," https://www.indiatoday.in/india/story/citizenship-amendment-act-comes-into-effect-january-10-home-ministry-1635833-2020-01-10 (21/04/2020).

Tripura

Tripura presents a classic case where indigenous/tribal inhabitants have been literally reduced to minority by the immigrant outsiders. A princely state which merged with Indian union in 1949 used to be the home of the tribals before they were displaced by the successive influx of refugees from Bangladesh since the partition of the country in 1947. The following statistics will indicate how the demographic explosion ultimately reduced the tribals to minority status (36.85% in 1951, 31.53% in 1961, 28.95% in 1971, 28.45% in 1981, 30.95% in 1991, 31.1% in 2001 and 31.8% in 2011). From 80% to 30% tribals in Tripura have been decimated to minority status in their own homeland. The progressive alienation of their land and traditional forest rights has rendered the original inhabitants landless and without rights.[29]

In the face of such tribal alienation, in 1967 a regional tribal political organization called Tripura UpoJati Juba Samity (TUJS) was formed to fight for the cause of the tribals. Later in 1978 TUJS was changed to Tripura National Voluteers (TNV) under the leadership of B. K. Hrangkhawal. After a decade of violent insurgency activities TNV finally decided to come over-ground and signed a tripartite peace accord of 1988 with the Union Home Ministry and the state government. However, when the peace accord could not provide peace and security to the tribals, insurgency activities reemerged with the formations of two new outfits: the National Liberation Front of Tripura (NFLT) formed in 1989 and All Tripura Tiger Force (ATTF) formed in 1990 respectively. Both the groups espoused expulsion of all Bengali speaking immigrants from Tripura as their main objective, besides fighting for the rights and causes of the tribals.

Meghalaya

In Meghalaya the problems are mostly dominated by identity issues, the divide between tribals and non tribal settlers and the influx of immigrants from across the border. Here in Meghalaya too the insurgency movements are ethnic based. In the beginning, insurgency movement in the state targeted the outsiders (dkhars) – the domination of the outsiders. The Hynniewtrep Achik Liberation Council (HALC) before their split in 1992 represented the interests of the Khasis, Jaintias and the Garos.[30] The following insurgency groups are active in the state. The Garo/Achik movements include The Achik Liberation Magtnik (ALMA), and Achik National Volunteer Council (ANVC) formed in 1995. Their main agenda is the formation of Achik Land in Garo Hills. Where as, the Hynniewtrep National Liberation Council (HNLC) espoused to work for the protection of the Khasi-Jaintia communities from Garo domination. Additionally, the state is embroiled

[29] "Overview: Insurgency & Peace Efforts in Tripura," *Centre for Development and Peace Studies* (availble from http://cdpsindia.org/tripura_insurgency.asp, 11/03/2010).

[30] "Overview: Insurgency and Peace Efforts in Meghalaya," *Centre for Development and Peace Studies* (available from *http://cdpsindia.org/meghalaya_insurgency.asp*, 11/03/2010).

from time to time with violence triggered by communal tensions between the local and immigrant settlers mostly the Bengalis.

Arunachal Pradesh

Arunachal Pradesh, home to a number of tribal ethnicities, may be the only North East state which does not have ethnic insurgency movements unlike in other neighboring states. The only group Arunachal Dragon Force (ADF), which was rechristened as East India Liberation (EILF) in 2001, was neutralized by the state police forces.[31] However, that does not mean the state is free from problems related with insurgency activities; it is being said that in the two Naga districts of Tirap and Changlang, both the NSCN factions are actively engaged. Moreover, given the long international borders the state shares with China and Myanmar, the various insurgency groups from the region have used as a safe passage to and from Myanmar. And so the presence of a number of insurgency groups from the neighboring states bring their share of problems with it. Then of course, there are tensions due to Chinese claim over certain part of Arunachal Pradesh especially, Tawang which is the birth place of the Dalai Lama. The issues of border dispute have again cropped up with China in recent years; Arunachal Pradesh, being internationally an important strategic place for India, it has its share of problems related with it. The state remains as frontier as ever for India.

North East India and CAA 2019

The foreigners or the illegal immigrants issue has been a decades-long standing problem in the northeast India. The region has been overwhelmed for decades by the presence of foreigners and the unabated influx of illegal immigrants from across the borders, especially from Bangladesh and Myanmar. This has been a very sensitive and emotive issue for the people of northeast India. Time and again, the region has witnessed wide spread violent protests and demonstrations over this issue. Assam and Tripura have been the most affected states. Tripura stands as classic example in which the indigenous people of the state has been reduced to minority in their own home state. According to 2011 census, the indigenous (scheduled tribe) population stands at 31.8% of the total state population.[32] In Assam, the famous Assam Movement or Assam Agitation (1979-1985) spearheaded by the powerful All Assam Students' Union (AASU) and the All Assam Gana Sangram Parishad (AAGSP), which culminated in the signing of the famous Assam Accord in August 15, 1985 over the foreigners issue remains a stark reminder to all. Unfortunately, the Accord does not result in resolving the issue. Assam continues to be bogged down by this foreigners issue. In fact, the whole of northeastern states have been unduly enduring this problem till date with no clear

[31] "Overview: Insurgency and Peace Efforts in Arunachal Pradesh," *Centre for Development and Peace Studies* (available from http://cdpsindia.org/arunachal pradesh_insurgency.as*p*, 11/03/2010).

[32] https://tripura.gov.in/demographics.

solution insight. Under this trying circumstances, the Citizen's Amendment Act (CAA) 2019 (passed in the parliament in December 11, 2019 and came into effect from January 10, 2020) has come as the final blow to the people of the region. The whole of northeast, along with the rest of the country, have been protesting against the proposed Citizen's Amendment Bill (CAB) and subsequently on passing it in the parliament as CAA 2019. While, the protests in the rest of India is focused against the politics of religious nationalism and constitutionality of the Act, the resistance in northeast, especially Assam and Tripura has more to do with ethno-linguistic identity.[33] What is CAA 2019 all about?

> The Citizen's (Amendment) Act, 2019 ....amended the Citizenship Act of 1955 allowing Indian citizenship for Hindu, Sikh, Buddhist, Jain, Parsi, and Christian religious minorities who fled from the neighboring Muslim majority countries of Pakistan, Bangladesh and Afghanistan before December 2014 due to 'religious persecution or fear of religious persecution.' However, the Act excludes Muslims. Under 2019 amendment act, migrants who entered India by December 31, 2014...were made eligible for citizenship by the new law. These type of migrants will be granted fast track Indian citizenship in six years. The amendment also relaxed the residence requirement for naturalization of these migrants from eleven years to five.[34]

The northeast people, especially the Assamese and Tripura's indigenous people rightfully fear that the Act will lead to lakhs of Hindus from the neighboring countries, especially Bangladesh "swamping indigenous communities, burdening resources and threatening their language, culture and tradition."[35] This has resulted in mass scale violent protests and demonstrations against the Act by the people in northeast India. While, the indigenous people in most northeastern states including the indigenous people in Assam, have been protected by the Inner Line Permit (ILP) under the constitution, Assam and Tripura have been left at large with no such constitutional provisions to protect them.

---

33 "FOCUS: Assam's complicated tryst with CAA," https://www.livemint.com/mint-lounge/features/focus-assam-s-complicated-tryst-with-caa-11577418654545.html; "CAA protests in Assam: Why it is different from the rest of the country," https://economictimes.indiatimes.com/news/politics-and-nation/caa-protests-in-assam-why-it-is-different-from-the-rest-of-the-country/articleshow/72844673.cms?from=mdr (22/04/2020).

34 "What is CAA?," https://timesofindia.indiatimes.com/india/what-is-caa/articleshow/73153785.cms; "The Citizenship (Amendment) ACT, 2019," http://egazette.nic.in/WriteReadData/2019/214646.pdf (22/04/2020).

35 "Citizenship Amendment Bill: Why Assam is protesting?" https://economictimes.indiatimes.com/news/et-explains/citizenship-bill-why-is-assam-protesting/articleshow/72483294.cms (22/04/2020).

Religion's Ambiance for Peace: Religio-Theological Response

Religion and spiritual resources of the people are central to finding peace and reconciliation in conflict and oppressive situations. In this section, a brief religio-theological reflection is given vis-à-vis the struggles of the people for liberation and reconciliation, especially the indigenous-tribal people of the northeast India.

At the outset, liberation, reconciliation, and healing are the gifts and graces of the living Jesus just as they are the values and strengths of the best of the northeast people's traditions; they are interrelated and inseparably linked. There cannot be true liberation without reconciliation, just as there cannot be true reconciliation without freedom; they are like the two sides of the same coin. Liberation will encompass all that constitute a condition of *shalom*, where justice, peace, and harmony prevail. Jesus' declaration that he came into the world so that people might have life in fullness (John 10:10) speaks of a liberated life, a life also reconciled in Christ.

Having said this, it must be pointed out that there is no easy way to reconciliation and freedom. The notion of forgive and forget does not work unless the persons who are responsible for the wrongs committed are ready to own up their responsibility. There can be no genuine reconciliation and freedom without the recognition and acknowledgement by the perpetrators of the wrongs committed. There can be no reconciliation without first coming to terms with the realities of the past. Confronting the past is never easy, it is an agonizing and painful process but the healing that comes about through such process is real and worthwhile. The perpetrators must not only recognize the wrongs committed, they must also claim their culpability and express sincerely their intention to improve their ways. In the Northeast people's search for freedom and healing it is critical that India recognize and accept the wrongs she has inflicted during decades of aggression against and domination of the people. It is true that healing within and among the people in the region, must be sought and dealt with by the people themselves in ways consistent with their cultures and values. However, given the fact of the people's suffering and loss are linked directly to India's aggression and occupation, the people's healing must be accompanied by the healing of the Indians. Speaking in the context of American Indian people, George E. Tinker argues convincingly that:

> While the internal healing of American Indian communities may be Indian business at one level, any real healing or liberation in the world of American Indians must be paralleled by healing in the world of euro-americans in order for the healing of Indian peoples to be sustained.[36]

---

[36] George E. Tinker, *Spirit and Resistance: Political Theology and American Indian Liberation* (Minneapolis: Fortress Press, 2004), 5.

This is very true in the case of the Naga people vis-à-vis decades of Indian colonization. In order for the healing to take place, India must not only recognize the identity of the Nagas as a people with a unique history as a sovereign nation, but they must also take responsibility for the decades of Naga peoples' suffering. The 2001 recognition of the unique history of Naga people, important as that is, cannot ameliorate the genocidal crimes committed against the Naga people for over 60 years. It is critically important for the healings of both the Naga communities and Indians that India own up its aggression rather than resorting to the usual denials and subsequent intimidation.

A vital and affirming belief in Christ makes for not only a liberated life, it also provides for a life at its fullest. The goal of liberation is to make possible the wholeness of life but this wholeness is dependent on the Naga people being free from the reality of oppression they endure under India's occupation. Freedom must be experienced in the real physical world as well as in the spiritual life of the Naga people. The Northeast people, especially the indigenous people must be allowed to reclaim their past with a view to dreaming their own future. There is indeed power in naming and reclaiming; the healing process then must begin with naming and reclaiming. Winona LaDuke asks:

> How does a community heal itself from the ravages of the past? . . . I found an answer in the multifaceted process of recovering that which is "sacred." This complex and intergenerational process is essential to our vitality as Indigenous peoples and ultimately as individuals.[37]

In a similar manner, Taiaiake Alfred, reminds indigenous communities the importance of reclaiming their traditional values for their survival and future.

> The only way we can survive is to recover our strength, our wisdom, and our solidarity by honoring and revitalizing the core of our traditional teachings. Only by heeding the voices of our ancestors can we restore our nations and put peace, power, and righteousness back into the hearts and minds of our people.[38]

Alfred concludes saying, "The challenge for us is to commit ourselves to those teachings and to walk those indigenous paths."[39] Speaking in the context of Naga people's search for healing and recovery, Longchari also expresses the importance of reclaiming their stories.

---

[37] Winona LaDuke, *Recovering the Sacred: The Power of Naming and Claiming* (Cambridge: South End Press, 2005), 11. For LaDuke "Sacred" means the whole web of relationship with the land, Creation, and nature, it means the freedom to practice one's own spirituality in sacred lands.

[38] Taiaiake Alfred, *Peace, Power, and Righteousness: An Indigenous Manifesto* (Ontario: Oxford University Press, 1999), xii.

[39] Alfred, *Wasáse: Indigenous Pathways of Action and Freedom*, 236.

> I believe to move forward, we must first begin to understand where we came from and where we are today! In order to do so, we must reclaim our heritage, reclaim our stories, erase the myths that have distorted our identity and begin addressing our history in a way that embraces the richness of our cultures and one that will liberate us from the parochial systems that continue to suffocate us.[40]

The healing process for the northeast people must begin with the naming and reclaiming of neglected stories and traditions. Reclaiming their history and regaining the vision to dream their own future are essential to any efforts to bring wholeness back to the people.[41]

The people of northeast India deserve the freedom to determine the kind of future they want without any interference from outside forces. St. Paul says in Galatians, "For freedom Christ has set us free. Stand firm, therefore, and do not submit again to a yoke of slavery."[42] Freedom for which Christ has set us free includes the indigenous-tribal people's freedom to reclaim their histories and the ability to dream their own future. The liberation and healing of the people must take place on two fronts: reconciliation between and among the people themselves, and the reclamation of their stories and subsequent opportunity to dream their own future in a way that is consistent with their cultures and values. It is fundamental that the people of the region unite themselves for the just cause of their struggles and to keep alive in themselves the right to dream their own future.

Finally, the physical and psychological effects of the oppression, domination, and genocide inflicted on the people of the region, especially the indigenous-tribal people by the British and India require a power that can only be provided by a Christological belief and understanding which is infused with the reconciling and healing potential of the combined values of the people's tradition and the living Jesus.

---

[40] Longchari, "Challenges and Opportunity of Church for Nation Building."

[41] Essential to this effort will be the reinstitution of traditional democratic system of requiring a consensus in political decision making and implementation. Traditionally in Naga villages everyone has a voice in decisions that affect the community. This is still practiced today in most villages. This represents an Indigenous version of what has been referred to as "deep democracy" as it is articulated by Haider Khan in *Technology, Development and Democracy* (Cheltenham: Edward Elgar, 1998), 92-95, 101-102.

[42] Gal. 5:1.

Chapter 9

Rethinking Mission from Tribal-Adivasi Perspectives Shifting of Missional Footing

Introduction

I have been asked to write about mission from Tribal-Adivasi perspectives by the organizers of the Consultation. We are indeed meeting on this momentous occasion to mark the almost 52 years gone by Tribal Awakening movement of the Tribal-Adivasi people of the country. We stand at the threshold of making another historic contribution to the history and life of adivasi/tribal people in India. We gather here to once again look to the past with a grateful heart and learn from the past with the view to dream the future we want to build.

Keeping this in view, I have decided to revisit the history of colonization and missonization and the impacts it made among the tribals of northeast India. This will be followed by a discussion on understanding mission from Adivasi-Tribal people's perspectives.

1. An Overview of the Past: Colonization and Missionization

The British colonization of India in the 18th century which eventually led to the British control over the Northeast region in the 19th century – the region mostly inhabited by the indigenous populations – basically opened up the doors for the missionaries to the region. The pioneer missionaries who came to Northeast India in the 19th century belonged to the American Baptist Foreign Mission and Welsh

Presbyterian Mission.[1] Though the Roman Catholic missionaries did cross the path on their way to Tibet and China prior to the protestant missionaries as early as 1626, they did not start any mission work in the Northeast region.[2] They began their mission work in the region only in the early middle part of the 20th century.

Collusion among state, missionaries[3] and Western trained anthropologists, at least at the level of perception, in perpetuating the colonial naming of the native people was obvious in many instances. After all, most of those so-called ethnographers and anthropologists who had written so much about the tribals in Northeast India were in fact colonial administrators who compiled tribal people's ethnographies while serving the colonial state in their official capacity.[4] Secondly, there was an understated common goal of the colonial powers and Christian mission which was to embark on civilizing mission which is sometimes known as "white man's burden." The most potent weapon behind the civilizing mission was the philosophy that not only entertained but created the idea of superiority over the native race. It is regarded that the idea of civilizing mission first originated from the French *mission civilistrice* which was rooted in the "idea of mastery."[5] This was further based on the twin fundamental assumptions "of the superiority of French culture and the perfectibility of humankind." Of course, this became the imperial ideology of the British colonizers from the late eighteenth century onwards. The civilizing mission subsumes what the English called "improvement" or "betterment" and, later on, "moral and material progress." According to Michael Mann:

> Basically, the *mission civilistrice* rested upon the idea of mastery – or, in other words, "to be civilized was to be free from specific forms of tyranny: the tyranny of the elements over men, of disease over health, of

---

[1] Prior to the American Baptist Missionaries, the British Baptist and Serampore Missions were already in lower Assam but their mission did not last for long and the BMS rather decided to donate its Guwahati property to American Baptist missionaries. F. S. Downs, *The Mighty Works of God: A Brief History of the Council of Baptist Churches in North East India: The Mission Period 1836-1950* (Guwahati: Christian Literature Center, 1971), 10-13.

[2] Jesuit missionaries, Frs. Stephen Cacella and John Cabral were said to have traveled to Goalpara and Kamrup in Assam looking for a passage to Tibet and China. Milton S. Sangma (*History of American Baptist Mission in North-East India (1836-1950),* vol. 1 (Delhi: Mittal Publications, 1987), 14.

[3] For a detailed discussion on the relationship between colonial powers and Christian mission refer to my article, "Colonialism, Missionaries, and Indigenous: A Critical Appraisal," in *Journal of Tribal Studies*, vol. XII, no. 2, July-December 2007, 1- 22.

[4] For example, Hutton and Mills who have extensively written on Nagas were both senior officers in the British Administration.

[5] Michael Mann, "'Torch Bearers Upon the Path of Progress:' Britains Ideology of a 'Moral and Material Progress' in India: An Introductory Essay," in Harald Fischer-Tine and Michal Mann, eds., *Colonialism as Civilizing Mission: Cultural Ideology in British India* (London: Wimbledon Publishing Company, 2004), 4.

> instinct over reason, of ignorance over knowledge and despotism over liberty." However, in spite of this "enlightening agenda," the concept of the *mission civilistrice* was used above all for the self-legitimation of colonial rule.[6]

My purpose here is to bring to light the crucial question of who defines who is primitive, and who is civilized? Who determines what qualifies as "higher" or "lower" civilizations? Throughout modern Western history and to this very day the arbiter is always the West. It has always been the Western nations, who have had military and economic power to claim the patronizing responsibility of naming and categorizing all non-Western peoples and places. They follow a simple and yet a very exclusive exemplar, Euro-american culture as the "universal culture." Gramsci describes this claim "an audacious heretics of modern age." Other cultures are significant "only in so far as they have become constitutive elements in European culture."[7] Anything that is different and does not conform to that cultural norms and practices was considered of lower civilization or primitive or even to the extent of discrediting it as no culture. Further, and by extension, diversity and difference are attributes which are not tolerated easily, if at all. This imagined ideal that is Euro-american culture makes it extremely difficult to accept anything that is non-Euroamerican.

At the heart of the issue is the claim of European superiority. Following Gramsci's concept of *hegemony,* Edward Said stated that, "The component in European culture is...the idea of European identity as a superior one in comparison with all the non-European peoples and cultures,"[8] an idea that was aggressively advanced as an indispensable means for the world domination. He described this whole process of a Europe bent on hegemony over non-Europeans as a function of Orientalism.[9] This idea of superiority encompasses all aspects of life including political, cultural, social, intellectual and even moral.

According to George E. Tinker, the European hegemonic notion over the indigenous peoples went as far back as to 1492 when Columbus for the first time landed the western hemisphere across the atlantic. Tinker quotes from Columbus' own diary entry as evidence for this.

> [October 12, 1492] They ought to make good and skilled servants, for they repeat very quickly whatever we say to them. I think they can be made Christians, for they seem to have no religion. If it pleases Our Lord, I will take six of them to Your Highnesses when I depart.... [October 14] ... these people are very unskilled in arms. Your

---

[6] *Ibid.*

[7] Quoted in Suresh Sharma, *Tribal Identity and Modern World* (New Delhi: Sage Publications, 1994), 37.

[8] Edward Said, *Orientalism* (New York: Vintage Books, 1979), 7.

[9] *Ibid.*, 12.

> Highnesses will see this for yourselves when I bring to you the seven that I have taken. After they learn our language I shall return them, unless Your Highnesses order that the entire populations be taken to Castile, or held captive here. With 50 men you could subject everyone and make them do what you wished.[10]

Colonialism, Ethnography, and Indigenous

The attitude of Western colonizers and ethnographers regarding the tribal people was for the most part negative as illustrated by their need to name and define the tribals as primitive, uncivilized, and a people with no character. Indeed, much of what has been written, *The Naked Nagas* is emblematic, makes crystal clear the views held by Western anthropologists and writers.[11] In his description of the Sema Nagas, an ethnographer stated that "in treachery and lying they were and are quite unsurpassed, even among Nagas" and adds, "A Sema oath is worth less than the oath of any other Naga tribe."[12] Another colonial ethnographer described the Lotha Nagas as "a sullen race" who "are alike filthy in their persons and habits, and have a pompous mode of addressing one which might in some cases be interpreted as insolent."[13] Still another colonial writer denigrated them as "uninteresting people with dirty persons and villages."[14] On the other hand, a more realistic and unbiased view about the Lotha tribe is presented in the following comments:

> Though the tribe contains a few habitual criminals, on the whole, they are very honest. Petty theft is rare, and a man can leave his spear and cloth by the side of a village path knowing that he will find his property untouched when comes to pick it up on his way home.[15]

The element of tribal culture about which critics have been most vociferous is their practice of "head-hunting." Most writers, past and present, have depicted tribals as war-mongers and savages whose daily lives were consumed by waging war against each other and taking enemy heads. Here again, the most realistic assessment is expressed in the following observation: "War between Lhota villages was rare, and a powerful village surrounded by friends would regard defenses

---

[10] George E. Tinker, *Missionary Conquest: The Gospel and Native American Cultural Genocide* (Minneapolis: Fortress Press, 1993), 8.

[11] Christopher von Fürer-Haimendorf wrote extensively about/on the Nagas and two of them he named *The Naked Nagas* and *Return to the Naked Nagas* respectively. Cf. H. H. Presler, *Primitive Religions of India* (Madras: Christian Literature Society, 1971).

[12] Davis, *Census of Assam*, 1891, part II, 247.

[13] Quoted in J. P. Mills, *The Lhota Nagas: With an Introduction and Supplementary Notes by J. H. Hutton* (London: Macmillan and Co., Ltd., 1922), 2.

[14] Shakespear, *History of Upper Assam, Upper Burma and North-Eastern Frontier*, 202.

[15] Mills, *The Lhota Nagas*, 19.

as unnecessary."[16] After all, if waging war had been the daily order of their lives the Naga race would have been reduced to few survivors or even extinct by now. There is no denying the history of Naga war-making, but it cannot compare with the near constant state of war which characterized European society from the tenth through the eighteenth centuries. In addition European armies travelled hundreds, even thousands, of miles to wage war in what was called the "holy" crusades against Muslims, and their ships crossed seas and oceans to prosecute the conquest of the native peoples of the Americas, Africa, and Australia; yet these Europeans, the people who denounced the Nagas for their "head-hunting" practices, were/are unable or unwilling to acknowledge the hypocrisy so apparent in the fact that they would also travel miles and miles to wage a war of conquest against the Nagas. Furthermore, it was the Europeans who enlisted the Nagas for the Labor Corps twice in a span of twenty-five years in the twentieth century for wars waged by Europeans against Europeans. The pretence was further reified in that these European wars were dubbed "World War I" and "World War II."

What is bothersome is the way detractors have portrayed the Nagas, particularly the "holier than thou" attitude they assumed toward the Nagas and the double standard they applied as they passed judgment on them. The self-critical observation rendered by a British army officer who served in the Northeast region, specifically the so-called NEFA (North East Frontier Area) which is now Arunachal Pradesh state, echoes the concerns of many people. He said, "In our indignation at the Naga for taking a few heads in battle, we gloss over the shortcomings of modern culture as manifested in the barbarities of gas chamber and germ warfare."[17] In a similar vein a British administrator also called attention to European hypocrisy. "So-called civilized countries, which can destroy whole populations with a single atom bomb, can hardly afford to look down on a method of ritual warfare which, at the most, involved the loss of a few hundreds of lives every year."[18] Further, what is more damaging is the perpetuation of the stereotype of Nagas as "head hunters" while there is no such stereotyping of the Europeans and Americans as blood-thirsty holy crusaders, slave traders, or even perpetrators of genocide! In a response to the continued labelling of the Nagas as "former head-hunters" by powerful press agencies such as BBC, CNN, Reuters and others, the Naga International Support Center (NISC) issued a press release on November 15, 2004 offering these scathing remarks:

> First of all head hunting as a term has been used by the colonial powers. It was invented by colonialists to denounce tribal peoples.

---

[16] *Ibid.*, 22.

[17] Nari Rustomji, *Imperilled Frontiers: India's North-Eastern Borderlands* (Delhi: Oxford University Press, 1983), 4.

[18] Verrier Elwin, *Nagaland* (Shillong: Adviser's Secretariat, 1961), 11. Of course, even "a loss of few hundreds of lives" is quite exaggerated.

And, through its implicit appeal (connotation) on understanding these tribes, rather than peoples, as barbarians, they were thus described as lower kind. Similar to people living in caves that bash each other heads with clubs, head hunters are seen as people of a lower kind. Although, only partially true, may be you don't call your people Dutch former slave drivers or slave dealers. Is it okay to describe Americans as former slave drivers or, the Dutch as former slave traders, or the Germans as former Jew exterminators, etc. How would you feel if CNN becomes popularly nicknamed as former slave drivers, now trying to dictate the world in journalism? Also considering the term head-hunting to be factual, if only from the European perspectives, seems to be ridiculous because if people were really out to be hunting heads, they would be already extinct, for having exterminated both others and the last others themselves.[19]

Missionaries in Northeast India: Attitude, Intention and Impact

For the great majority of non-Christian tribals, the background is one of animism, of a belief in spirits and demons.... This background is nothing to be ashamed of, if people have not learned anything different. Indeed, if we go back far enough, we find that Europeans and Americans have the same background of belief in spirits and in nature-gods; this was the condition of our forefathers until Christian monks and missionaries came among them, with the good news of Jesus Christ.[20]

These were the words of Gordon Jones, a missionary who worked in Northeast India, in his address at the inaugural service of the Eastern Theological College, Jorhat, Assam on 18th July 1971. The missionary attitude towards the tribals since their arrival in the late 19th century seemed to have not changed much in the 1970s, even after decades have gone by. They have persistently continued to portray the religion of tribal people as animism, belief in spirits and demons. While Jones and others had begun to recognize the need for taking the context of the tribal people in the presentation of the good news of Jesus Christ, their over all premise and assumption about the tribals have not changed. Jones went on to ask, "What, then, can be good news to people of animistic beliefs?"

The Christian missionaries saw the Nagas and other tribals of the region as primitive, uncultured, uncivilized and savages. Their description of the people ranges from people with no culture to inferior culture, life styles and ways of life.

---

[19] Naga International Support Center (NISC), Amsterdam. Press Release November 15, 2004.

[20] Gordon Jones, "Good News for North-East India," in Renthy Keitzar, ed., *Good News for North East India: A Theological Reader* (Guwahati: Christian Literature Center, 1995), 4.

Their religion was derided as demonic, superstitious and evil. The opening page of M. M. Clark's *A Corner in India,* writing about the American Baptist mission in Naga areas, particularly among the Aos, begins with "…these strange, uncivilized men…."[21] And she goes on to describe their religion as animism or demon worship. The people's characters and virtues also came under severe criticism and they were held at the lowest esteem. This is the general attitude of the missionaries who worked among the indigenous people in the Northeast India.[22]

Such negative portrayal of the native people is part of the larger essentializing process or "the othering of the other" that is often employed by the colonial powers. This process of essentializing the natives were actively employed by the colonial powers with the Indians, Africans, the aborigines in Australia, the American Indians in North and South America.[23]

Unfortunately, in spite of the good intentions and work, the missionaries in many respects failed to understand and appreciate the religious and cultural ethos of the tribal people. The condemnation of tribal histories and ways of life has had far reaching psychological consequences for tribal people which manifests in feelings of inferiority and self debasement. People are often led to develop the sense of insecurity and inadequacy because of the repeated negation of their ways of life. In addition, an attitude of distrust and distain develops regarding everything that was or is of their own cultural.[24]

Identity: The Interpretive Principle

F. S. Downs was right when he stated that the role of Christianity in Northeast India cannot be studied in isolation. One needs to take into account the political, social, economic, cultural and religious change as well. In Downs' own words, "The history of the Christian movement in the North East can only be understood as an integral part of a larger process of change - political, social, economic, cultural and religious change."[25]

Following Downs' lead, O. L. Snaithang examines the role of Christian mission among the Khasi-Jaintia of Meghalaya state and concludes that Christianity played the role of "preserving a distinctive identity" of the people.[26]

[21] M. M. Clark, *A Corner in India* (Guwahati: Christian Literature Center, 1978), 1.

[22] *Pettigrew's Mission Reports and Letters*, 35-36.

[23] Refer to Ashis Nandy, *The Intimate Enemy Loss and Recovery of Self under Colonialism* (Delhi: Oxford University Press, 1983); Franz Fanon, *The Wretched of the Earth* (New York: Grove Press, 1963); Albert Memmi, *The Colonizer and the Colonized*, Expanded Edition, Introduction by Jean-Paul Sartre (Boston: Beacon Press Books, 1967).

[24] For a detailed discussion on the impact of missionaries on the tribal people refer to my article, "Emerging Vision of Indigenous/Tribal Theology," in James Massey and Shimreingam Shimray, eds., *Dalit-Tribal Theological Interface: Current Trends in Subaltern Theologies* (Jorhat: TSC/WSC; Delhi: CDS, 2007), 16-55.

[25] F. S. Downs, *Christianity in North East India: Historical Perspectives* (Delhi: ISPCK, 1983), 3.

[26] Snaithang, *Christianity and Social Change*, 62.

With the coming of the British colonial power and under its administration the people saw the gradual break down of their traditional social and economic life, administrative, judicial and political structures. On the other hand, Hinduism was perceived to be a threat to the identity of the people. Although people, especially people of the War areas and Jaintias had been exposed to Hinduism for decades, and with the exception of Jaintia kings who became Hindu, the people held on to their primal religion. It was during such time and context that Christian missionaries arrived and began their mission among the people. As people began to embrace Christian faith they also began to see Christianity as an alternative order as opposed to changes that were taking place under British administration. They perceived Christianity served as a means of preserving their own identity in the midst of the occurring changes unlike Hinduism which tend to assimilate tribals into that religion.[27] While this is true to a certain extent, it must be pointed out that Christianity also contributed in the demise of tribal cultures. The missionaries "felt every ceremony should be abolished ....The tendency was to abolish the old things and substitute individualism for the strong community feeling....The result was a conflict not necessarily of arms but of culture...."[28]

According to Downs, the single most contribution of Christianity to the tribals in Northeast India is the development of tribal identity. In his article "Identity: The Interpretive Principle,"[29] Downs argues that Christianity is responsible for bringing together the tribals into a unified group of people who were otherwise known for their fiercely guarded village autonomy with hardly any unified tribal consciousness. In a number of his writings,[30] Downs repeatedly reiterates that Christianity helped dismantle the traditional antagonisms and barriers that existed within and among the tribals and inculcated in them the sense of tribal solidarity and oneness. He used the terms like tribal ecumenism, tribal solidarity and tribal integration interchangeably in referencing to Tribal identity.[31] Downs identified four ways by which Christianity played central role in the development of tribal ecumenism and solidarity: (a) through the creation of standard languages, (b) through its educational work, (c) through its ideology,

[27] The Meiteis of Manipur and the tribals of Assam were case in point who were assimilated into Hinduism.

[28] M. Alemchiba, "Problems of Readjustment to New Situation with Special Reference to Naga Tribes," in *Highlander*, vol. 4, 1 & 2 (March-April), 3.

[29] F. S. Downs. *"Identity: The Integrative Principle,"* In *Asia Journal of Theology* 6 (1980), 238-249.

[30] ________., "Tribal Ecumenism in Northeast India: The Christian Role in Tribal Solidarity," in ed., Renthy Keitzar *Good News for North East India: A Theological Reader* (Guwahati: Christian Literature Center, 1995), 8-21; "Christianity as a Tribal Response to Change in Northeast India," in *Missiology: An International Review* 8 (October 1980), 407-416; "The Christian Role in Tribal Solidarity Movements in Northeast India," in *Bangalore Theological Forum*, vol. 20, 1-2, 1988.

[31] By Tribal ecumenism Downs means "the development of positive relationships" emerging between and among the various tribes and with those outside tribal community.

and (d) through its ecclesiastical structures.[32] Christianity brought a whole new outlook and life orientation through the proclamation of the good news of Jesus Christ.

Downs also points out that the native converts played a vital role in this whole process of change; he attributes this positive change to Christian ideology of universalism taking root in and among the tribal people.[33] They themselves became the messengers of the Gospel to their own people and others. They went evangelizing the neighboring villages including those regarded to be hostile due to traditional enmity between the two villages and where in ordinary circumstances people would dare not take a chance.

The visiting of villages by the native itinerant evangelists help begin the healing process of the warring villages and consequently the bonding relationship among them. The initiatives for evangelizing were not limited within the same tribe. There were also inter-tribal evangelistic activities taking place - where an evangelist belonging to a tribe would take the gospel to people of different tribe(s). Many Tangkhul Nagas went to neighboring tribes including Maring, Maram and other tribes to evangelize them. Likewise, many tribes in Nagaland including Konyak, Chang, Sangtam and others were missionized by the Ao Christians.

On the other hand, Christianity was guilty of sowing division between and among the Naga villages when the missionaries founded Christian villages separating the newly converts from the rest of the villagers.[34] Such divisions inevitably resulted in the feuding among the villagers. The new converts were forbidden from maintaining any contact with their fellow villagers; they were forbidden to attend or participate in any of the village ceremonies or festivals which was deemed by some as a direct challenge to the old faith. In fact, the various festivals where the dancing, singing, and general hilarity occurred were considered to have had a cathartic effect on the people. Clark, himself the pioneer missionary to the Nagas acknowledged the mistake of founding Christian villages. In his letter to Home Board in March 1877, he wrote, "Their village government is a government higher than even from the civilized nations. To build another village separate from the others for the sake of the Gospel creates division."[35] In another letter he wrote, "To build a new village with the believers separate from non believers will not be fair to the Gospel. What I have done may have been a mistake…."[36]

---

32 Downs, "Tribal Ecumenism in Northeast India," 15-19. Cf. Merithung Tüngoe, *Administrators Missionaries and a World turned Upside Down* (Delhi: ISPCK; Jorhat: ETC, 2000), 86-87.

33 *Ibid.*, 17-18.

34 E. W. Clark, *Assam Baptist Conference Report, 1913*, 54.

35 Quoted in Imchen, *Ancient Ao Naga Religion and Culture*, 157.

36 *Ibid.*

Whereas, according to J. H. Thumra, the break from the cultural heritages and way of life for the new converts to Christianity was helpful. He argues that from psychological point of view:

> It was necessary and expedient that at least the first generation converts have to undergo a radical break from their old way of life and religious rituals. If this is not done, due to the human nature of 'psychology of association' they may be drawn back to their old religion.[37]

While there is some kernel of truth in it, such argument simply goes on to indicate that tribal way of life before the advent of Christianity was nothing but evil and damned. It reinforces the negative images of the indigenous people. Of course, Thumra acknowledges that since the Naga people have embraced Christian faith, it does not mean that they are free from the vices of drinking, corruption and other permissive life styles, rather they "have assumed a dangerous proportion" in contemporary Naga Christian society.[38]

Missionary Theologies and Indigenous

It is simply not possible for me to discuss the specific theologies of those missionaries who worked among the Naga people in particular and Northeast India in general for a number of obvious reasons. The primary reason concerns with the non availability of the materials necessary for our examination. The other factor is the diversity of their theologies. Supposing even if there are materials within our reach, the very fact that the missionaries came from diverse theological backgrounds and periods of time makes it even more difficult to discuss their particular theologies. My intention here is then to provide a general overview of missionary theology to which the missionaries were in general associated with and influenced by.

Missionaries who came to Northeast India in the 19th and 20th centuries were generally the products of Pietistic movements in Europe and the concomitant movement in North America known as the Great Awakening. Connected to this was the Puritan movement in Europe and later in North America.

Pietism in general was associated with the Lutheran reform movement in Germany under the leadership of Philip Jacob Spencer.[39] Spencer and his followers considered the Protestant church as preoccupied with ecclesiastical demands and not with the important spiritual well being of the followers. The church was seen to be spiritually bankrupt and in need of spiritual reform within. Similarly, Puritanism which had its origin in Great Britain and later went on to

---

[37] Thumra, *Impact of Christianity*, 48.

[38] *Ibid.*

[39] Pietism in wider context includes the Dutch Pietism, Puritanism, the Wesleyan Revivals and Methodists and the Great Awakening. Trond Enger, "Pietism," in *The Oxford Companion to Christian Thought* (Oxford University Press, 2000), 540.

flourish in North America as a religious reform movement called for purification of the visible church through the "teaching of Reformed doctrine, and a revival of discipline and evangelical piety in clergy and laity alike."[40] Puritan theology was a great deal influenced by Reformed theology, especially of Calvinistic theology and covenant; the idea that the believers both at the church and individual levels have covenantal relationship with God. The heart of covenant theology was the:

> Insistence that God's predestination decrees were not part of a vast impersonal and mechanical scheme, but that, under the Gospel dispensation, God had established a covenant of grace....This was to be appropriated in faith, and hence was irreducibly personal.[41]

Both Pietist and Puritan theologies emphasized on the experience of spiritual rebirth and individual holiness. Following Calvinistic theology they insisted on the inner transformation and subsequently leading a sanctified life.[42] They strongly believed in the experience of salvation through grace.

> In the concept of rebirth we find the Pietists' main concerns: it expresses humanity's absolute passivity in salvation, just as in natural birth; it expresses the total change, the new status as God's child; it focuses on the necessity of development and growth.[43]

Bible was central to Pietist and Puritan's faith and understanding. In a way, they were a Bible movement. They believed that intensive Bible study was essential if change had to occur in humanity, the church and the world. They strongly believed in transforming the world through changing humanity. Mission was thus defined in terms of affecting change in the world through humanity's transforming experience. Of course, the underlying motive for missions was rescuing as many perishing souls as possible.[44] To a certain extent, the origin of modern Protestant missionary movement can be traced to the pietistic-puritan movements. As D. W. Brown rightly states the newly formed University of Halle "became an international center for the dissemination of pietist literature, missionaries and beliefs to Russia, Scandinavia, Britain and the new World."[45]

---

[40] Sydney E. Ahlstrom, *A Religious History of the American People* (New Haven: Yale University Press, 1972), 125.

[41] *Ibid.,* 131.

[42] For Calvin placed a special emphasis on pneumatology: "The work of the Spirit in the human soul, renewing the inner life, and the Spirit's activity of renewing the face of the earth." Bosch, *Transforming Missions*, 256.

[43] Enger, "Pietism," 540; Cf. W. R. Ward, *The Protestant Evangelical Awakening* (Cambridge: Cambridge University Press, 1992), 57.

[44] Dunn, *Missionary Theology*, 52.

[45] D. W. Brown, "Pietism" in *New Dictionary of Theology* (Leicester: InterVarsity Press, 1988), 516; Cf. Ward, *The Protestant Evangelical Awakening*, 62-63.

The love for neighbor and charitable service was another important tenet of pietist faith. Equally prominent in their theology was their emphasis on the otherworld and ascetic practices.

Puritanism on the other hand, gave a great deal of emphasis on law and discipline both at the church and personal levels. Applying and observing the disciplines as taught in the scripture became a way of Christian life for the puritans. Coupled with this was the emphasis on the reformation of character and obedient godliness.[46]

The pietist-puritan theology was carried over and further picked up during the Great Awakening in the eighteenth century in New England, America. Jonathan Edwards became the most prominent leader of the revival movement. It was the preaching of the "plain gospel truths" centering on "God's absolute sovereignty, man's total depravity, and Christ atoning love" which sparked the spiritual fire in the hearts of the listeners.[47] The first and second Great Awakenings inspired many believers and spurred them to the formation of mission societies - Home and Foreign missions. American Board of Commissioners for Foreign Missions sent Adoniram Judson and Luther Rice as their missionaries to India but ended up landing in Burma and they both converted to Baptist views. Initially, the Baptists were a weak and dispirited denomination but they turned out to be the greatest beneficiaries of the Great Awakening. The "awakened" Christians began to question the validity of infant baptism given the significance of the decisive Christian experience. This and other factors led many believers to join the Baptist denomination and Baptists grew in numbers.[48]

The theologies of those missionaries who worked among the Northeast Indian peoples generally fall within the wide spectrum of pietist-puritan evangelical theologies. The theology that is rooted in the belief of the seriousness of individual sin and salvation of the individual soul were deeply entrenched in the theological thinking of the missionaries. The message of repentance from sin and putting a break to one's past life served as the core theologies of the missionaries. Forsaking one's habits and life styles as a sign of a changed person – "a new creation in Christ" – was given a great deal of emphasis. The abandoning of the past was not limited to one's habits and lifestyles but regrettably it also meant dissociating from the family and loved ones, cultural festivities and religious ceremonies. In order to ensure that the new converts were free from influences from their non-Christian folks the converts were severed from their loved ones and settled them in a newly founded settlement often called Christian compound or village. The villages were thus divided up into the old village and new Christian village respectively. To this day, the villages

[46] Ahlstrom, *A Religious History of the American People*, 129.

[47] *Ibid.*, 417.

[48] *Ibid.*, 292-293.

have continued to maintain the division in spite of the fact that everyone has embraced Christianity.

The experience of personal conversion and the awakening of the people's spiritual consciousness was further enthused by the waves of revival movements that swept through the tribal hills of Northeast region in the early and mid 20th century.

Second, missionaries' emphasis on strict observance of church disciplines including strict observance of Sunday worships reflect the pietist-puritan evangelical insistence on law and discipline. Not too long ago, in fact, even to this day, most Christians in most Northeast regions observe Sundays as a holy Sabbath and other than attending church worships normal activities including travels are suspended.

Third, true to the pietist-puritan evangelical tradition the missionaries held on to the primacy of the Bible for all faith edification and instructions. They believed the Bible is the word of God and hence it's free from human agency and error. They believed in the literal interpretation of the Bible. In short, Bible was central to the missionaries' theology and faith. They believed in the transforming power of the Bible for humanity, church and society. The tribal Christians have held on to this extreme conservative view of the Bible. In the tradition of the missionaries, they believe that the Bible is inspired by God and hence it is the word of God.[49]

Finally, missionary theology was highly individualistic and anthropocentric. The aspect of creation-centered theology was sorely absent in their theology. The anthropocentric theology has influenced the theological thinking and understanding of the tribal Christians. Such privileging of humanity over creation and nature goes contrary to the traditional tribal understanding and belief.[50]

2. Mission from Tribal-Adivasi Perspectives

We have learned how colonization and missionization had and have impacted the indigenous people in India. The western missionaries, in spite of their good intentions, contributed to the destruction of tribal cultures and traditions. Tribal people till this day continue to suffer psychologically and socially. Psychologically, they continue to have that feeling of inferiority complex and low self esteem. Socially, they are looked down upon by the main land Indians.

Religiously, people continue to accuse Christianity to be a foreign religion. Influenced by missionary theologies, tribal Christians have a narrow understanding of mission and Christian faith. Mission is largely viewed in terms of sending out missionaries and to preach the good news of salvation to the "unreached" people.

---

[49] They believe that the Bible is dictated by God word for word and therefore free from human agency and error.

[50] For a detailed discussion on the impact of missionary theology refer to my article, "Emerging Vision of Indigenous/Tribal Theology," 16-55.

Salvation and spirituality are understood in terms of spiritual salvation and privatization of faith respectively. The dualist worldview of the west continues to have sway over the people's understanding of faith and spirituality. This is very true even in people's understanding of mission. And much of the churches' articulation of mission and its activities are to a great deal influenced by such worldviews and ideals.

There is a serious need for tribal Christians in Northeast India to examine their overall understanding of faith, mission and spirituality again. Today Christian society is, unlike other times, beset with innumerable problems like corruption, bribery, violence and all forms of social evils one can imagine. Ecological crisis is another serious concern. On the top of all this, the church is facing a stiff challenge from other religious groups, especially the Hindu fundamentalist groups like Rashtriya Swayamsevak Sangh (RSS) on the one hand, and the Muslim jihadists on the other. The RSS and its associates are working relentlessly to promote and penetrate hindutva ideology in northeast Christian states. This is also the case with Muslim fundamentalist groups. The alarming truth is that they are making headway already. The question is whether the church is caught unaware or the church has been complacent about the whole thing? One thing seems to be clear: it seriously questions the quality of Christian faith and the spiritual life of the people. It seriously questions the church's understanding of mission. All this is nothing but a manifestation of spiritual decay.

Re-casting Mission Today: Shifting of Missional Footing

Mission Mandate

Traditionally, Christians have regarded the **Great Commission** found in Matthew 28 as the "only" mission mandate. "Then Jesus came to them and said, 'All authority in heaven and on earth has been given to me. Therefore, go and make disciples of all nations, baptizing them in the name of the Father and of the Son and of the Holy Spirit, and teaching them to obey everything I have commanded you. And surely I am with you always, to the very end of the age'" (Matthew 28: 18-20). Following the Great Commission, Christian mission has for long, focussed on sending out missionaries to proclaim the good news to the unreached people. And often, the emphasis is given to saving the lost soul – spiritual salvation of the person.

While we acknowledge the necessity of spiritual salvation, the gospel of Jesus Christ is for the whole person, inclusive of both spiritual as well as physical. The **Nazareth Manifesto** which is recorded in Luke 4 is very often overlooked and neglected. "'The Spirit of the Lord is on me, because he has anointed me to preach good news to the poor. He has sent me to proclaim freedom for the prisoners and recovery of sight for the blind, to release the oppressed, to proclaim the year of the Lord's favour'" (Luke 4: 18-19). God sent His Son Jesus Christ to the world so that we might be saved from both physical and spiritual bondages of sin.

Christian mission is a continuation of God's mission. Holistic mission calls for proclaiming the gospel of Jesus Christ for the salvation of the total person. Christian mission therefore must be grounded on the **Great Commission** and the **Nazareth Manifesto**. Together they constitute the **Mission Mandate**! Emphasizing one over the other would result in one-sided understanding of God's mission and we must therefore guard against such misconceived view of mission.

Life in Abundance

The West's dualist worldview which makes sharp distinction between sacred and mundane, spiritual and physical, heavenly and worldly/earthly, etc., need to be jettisoned. The indigenous people's holistic worldview which affirms unity of all things and views life in totality must be reclaimed and affirmed. Holistic mission is possible only when we embrace holistic vision of life. In the words of our Lord Jesus: "I came that you may have life, life in abundance" (John 10:10). Jesus came to the world so that the world and everything in it might have fullness of life. Traditional understanding of mission, regrettably, failed to understand this very promise of Jesus Christ as part of the mission mandate of our Lord Jesus Christ. Life in abundance was conceived and proclaimed narrowly limiting it to spiritual salvation. The quality of life which Jesus promised includes both spiritual and physical. It is about shalomic life in Christ. Mission then is about building shalomic life here on this earth as much as it is about life eternal with Christ in heaven. Holistic mission calls for embracing both the physical as well as the spiritual, the mundane and the sacred, the earthly and the heavenly. Jesus came to proclaim the good news of the Kingdom of God here on this earth. And the disciples and the believers are entrusted to carry out that mission of proclaiming the good news of God's Kingdom on earth. The church is called to carry out this mission of our Lord Jesus Christ on His behalf.

Cosmic Christ Cosmic Mission

The traditional human centred theology must give way to creation centred theology. For too long, Christian theology has proclaimed the primacy of humans over the rest of God's creation. And accordingly, salvation and mission have been understood in terms of saving human beings only. Nature and creation have been simply treated as mere objects to be exploited for human use. The idea is that nature and creation are not part of the redemptive plan of God.

St. Paul in his epistle to the Colossians clearly spells out that Christ is the agent of creation and that in Him every being and thing in the universe will be reconciled (Col. 1: 15ff). Mission is God's mission and not our mission. We must for God's sake, do away with our human pretence and arrogance and be honest to God and to ourselves. Cosmic Christ calls for cosmic mission.

Human's Together with the Whole of Creation

The Bible is replete with the universal understanding of salvation – salvation of the whole cosmos in which humans and creation are together. Starting from God proclaiming the goodness of His creation (humans and creation) in Genesis to proclamation of the New Heaven and New Earth in Revelation, humans and creation are always inseparably connected together. Few of the biblical passages and stories are cited here to substantiate the biblical affirmation of the universal understanding of salvation.

God's Covenant with Creation (Gen. 8:20-22): God made covenant with Noah after the great flood. The covenant was made not only with humans but the whole of God's creation. Perhaps, going further back we find that God not only saved Noah's family but also the rest of creation pair by pair, male and female together (Gen. 6:18-22; 8:18-19). God is surely the God of all beings and creations. God enters into covenant wilfully and freely with the whole of God's creation. Humans are part of the covenant along with the rest of creation.

The Year of Jubilee (Lev. 25): Jubilee is for all creation including humans and the rest of creation. Rest is for all including humans and creation. Rights are meant for all including humans and creation. This abundantly demonstrates that God is concerned not only for the well-being of humans but for the whole His creation.

Isaiah's Ultimate Vision (Isaiah 11:6-7; 65:25): Envisions every creation, foes and friends, eating and living together in peace and harmony. 'The wolf will live with the lamb, the leopard will lie down with the goat, the calf and the lion and the yearling together; and a little child will lead them" (Isaiah 11 6). "The wolf and the lamb will graze together, and the lion will eat straw like the ox; and dust will be the serpent's food. They will do no evil or harm in all My holy mountain," says the Lord," (Isaiah 65:25).

God's Love is for the Cosmos (John 3:16): "For God so loved the world (cosmos) that He gave His only begotten son...." God's love is for the universe including all creation and humanity; God's love is not limited to human beings alone.

The Whole Creation Longs for the Coming Redemption (Rom. 8:19-22): The suffering of the whole creation is compared with that of the mother's experience of pain in giving birth. And that the whole creation is subjected to futility not of their own making. And then St. Paul goes on to affirm that the whole creation waits expectantly for the revealing of the sons of God and that they will be redeemed from the corrupt bondage of corruption and into the glorious liberty of the children of God.

In Christ all Things Hold Together (Col. 1:15ff): The text is very clear: every being-human and creation – have the same destiny in Christ. In Christ all beings and things in the universe will be reconciled. "For God was pleased to have all His fullness dwell in Him and through Him to reconcile to himself all things, whether things on earth or things in heaven by making peace through his blood, shed on the cross," (Col. 1:19-20). Salvation is all about sharing life together in Christ and with one another and the whole of creation.

New Heaven and New Earth (Rev. 21:1-6): God is going to establish new heaven and new earth. New heaven and new earth do not simply replace the old one. The world, God's good creation, is not replaced but rather redeemed and renewed. God makes all things new. "He who was seated on the throne said, 'I am making everything new!'" (Rev. 21:5).

Communitarian Narrative

Adivasi-Tribals have for long been affirming the oneness of humans with the rest of God's creation. The idea that we humans have symbiotic relationship with the whole of creation is not a new thing for the indigenous people. The indigenous people around the world believe that life is interconnected. Every being is connected and there is no being which is not connected. The saying of the indigenous people, "We are all relatives" sums up the whole life philosophy as well as the vision of the indigenous people – Tribals-Adivasis. They lived in harmony with nature and environment.

Most Tribals did not believe in heaven or hell as Christians do. They believed when they die they would go to the land of dead which was the extension of present earthly life. They believed they would continue to live in the land of the dead together with the rest of God's creation. The basic belief is this: even in life, dead and after humans and creation are destined to be together. In Christ all will be reconciled!

Conclusion

Mission is God's mission. It is the triune God - God the Father, God the Son and God the Holy Spirit – calling the church to celebrate life and to witness the love of God not only to humans but the whole of God's creation. I would like to conclude with the following faith affirmation:

> We believe in the Triune God who is the creator, redeemer, and sustainer of all life. God created the whole *oikoumene* in God's image and constantly works in the world to affirm and safeguard life. We believe in Jesus Christ, the Life of the world, the incarnation of God's love for the world (John 3:16). Affirming life in all its fullness is Jesus Christ's ultimate concern and mission (John 10:10). We believe in God, the Holy Spirit, the Life-giver, who sustains and empowers life and renews the whole creation (Gen. 2:7; John 3:8). A denial of life is a rejection of the God of life. God invites us into the life-giving

mission of the Triune God and empowers us to bear witness to the vision of abundant life for all in the new heaven and earth. How and where do we discern God's life-giving work that enables us to participate in God's mission today?[51]

---

[51] "Together Towards Life" – The New WCC Affirmation on Mission and Evangelism Commission on World Mission and Evangelism (CWME), 2013.

Chapter 10

Climate Change and Climate Justice in the Context of Tribal Worldview

Introduction

The question of climate change and climate justice inevitably leads us to the question of why all this. What is the underlying cause of all this? What is the role of humanity in all this? And why do humans behave and act the way they are? Or do we have to blame the natural law? Things happen as they are because they are beyond human control? These are some of the basic questions that come to mind as we deliberate on this important question of climate change and climate justice.

On the whole, from the point of view of indigenous-tribal people, climate change and climate justice are about disruptions of relationships between and among the whole of creation including humanity. It concerns with the diminishing quality of life of all creation due to irresponsible human actions and ways of life. And most of all, such human actions are driven by the underlying worldviews and values of life people hold on to and profess. This chapter looks at the important question of tribal worldview(s) and its implications for addressing the issue of climate change and climate justice in our society today. For this, I have decided to focus on the indigenous astronomical knowledge, which is a natural extension of tribal worldviews, to illustrate how humans according to indigenous-tribal people relate with the sky world in order to maintain balance and harmony in the world.

Indigenous Worldview: Basis of Indigenous Knowledge and Ways of Life

Understanding Indigenous worldview is key to understanding Indigenous knowledge, ways of knowing and ways of life. Worldviews both inform and are informed by the thinking and understanding of a people about the world and how it operates. This is of particular importance for indigenous peoples because theirs is fundamentally different from that of Western culture. What follows is a brief but essential discussion of indigenous worldviews. According to Gregory Cajete, an American Indian scholar:

> A worldview is a set of assumptions and beliefs that form the basis of a people's comprehension of the world. The stories, symbols, analogies, and metaphors that express a worldview in coded form are called mythology. Worldviews are conveyed via mythology in informal, art, media, economic, spiritual, governmental, and educational institutions.[1]

A worldview is thus an underlying foundational principle that holds together peoples visions, orientations and thinking in life as a community. It is a foundational principle that informs and directs all aspects of a peoples' existence: how people relate to one another as well as how they interact with nature, and creation, and God(s). The worldview thus shapes and is shaped by attitude and orientation toward life and the world. Ninian Smart thinks worldviews can be maps of how to live and explains, "From one perspective different worldviews are maps of how to live. From another they themselves depict those powers in human experience and the cosmos that stir people to action."[2] Smart explains further that worldviews are comprised of belief systems and ideologies to the extent that the study of religions and ideologies can be regarded as "worldview analysis."

Indigenous worldviews can be described as the recognition of the undifferentiated unity of all things, meaning, there is no distinction drawn between the spiritual and physical, material and immaterial, sacred and profane, and spiritual and earthly. Nor does an indigenous worldview recognize any structure of hierarchy in creation. They see the world and all its surroundings in holistic perspective. While a Western worldview is essentially anthropocentric, an indigenous worldview is creation-centered and is characterized by understanding the interdependence and the inter-relatedness of *all* creation, including human beings. Therefore, indigenous peoples all across the world believe that the whole of creation are our relatives. The Lakota nation of American Indians has an

---

[1] Gregory Cajete, *Native Science: Natural Laws of Interdependence* (Santa Fe: Clear Light Publishers, 2000), 62.

[2] Ninian Smart, *Worldviews: Crosscultural Exploration of Human Beliefs*. Third Edition (Upper Saddle: Prentice Hall Inc., 2000), 54.

expression which describes beautifully all that concerns the indigenous worldview, "We are all related." According to Standing Rock Sioux scholar Vine Deloria, Jr, the similar phrase, "All my relatives" is not merely a religious sentiment which many people have supposed, but it also "describes the epistemology of the Indian worldview, providing the methodological basis for the gathering of the information about the world."[3] Deloria goes on to explain the implication of this worldview when he states:

> "We are all relatives" when taken as a methodological tool for obtaining knowledge means that we observe the natural world by looking for relationships between various things in it. That is to say, everything in the natural world has relationship with every other thing and the total set of relationships makes up the natural world as we experience it. This concept is simply the relativity concept as applied to a universe that people experience as alive and not as dead or inert.[4]

Here then is another key characteristic which distinguishes an indigenous worldview and its knowledge from a Western worldview and its scientific methods. In a similar vein, Leroy Little Bear observes that the indigenous "paradigm is comprised of and includes ideas of constant motion and flux, existence consisting of energy waves, interrelationships, all things being animate, space/place, renewal, and all things being imbued with spirits."[5]

As noted above, indigenous "peoples do not differentiate their world of experience into two realms that oppose or complement each other. They seem to maintain a consistent understanding of the unity of all experience."[6] Referring to Naga religious view, J. H. Thumra asserts that "unlike many modern Christian belief in the dichotomy of the 'sacred' and the 'secular' or the 'spiritual' and the 'material', the traditional Naga religion does not have such a dichotomy. For them the 'sacred' and the 'secular' are one."[7] In "An Emerging Asian Theology: Tribal Theology," Wati Longchar makes a useful comparison between dominant Christian worldview and traditional tribal worldview in which he underscores their differences.[8] Indigenous peoples around the world view reality in its wholeness and perceive life as one single web and many smaller webs of relationships which

---

[3] Vine Deloria, Jr, *Spirit & Reason: The Vine Deloria, Jr., Reader*, Eds. Barbara Deloria, et al (Golden: Fulcrum Publishing, 1999), 52.

[4] *Ibid.*, 34.

[5] Leroy Little Bear, "Foreward," in Gregory Cajete, *Native Science*. x.

[6] Deloria, *Spirit and Reason.* 354.

[7] Jonathan H. Thumra, "The Naga Primal (Traditional) Religion and Christianity: A Theological Reflection," in V. K. Nuh, ed. *In Search of Praxis Theology for the Nagas* (New Delhi: Regency Publications, 2003), 54.

[8] For a detailed comparison see A. Wati Longchar, *An Emerging Asian Theology: Tribal Theology: Issue, Method and Perspective* (Jorhat: Tribal Study Center, 2000), 64.

is the antithesis of the dominant Christian dualistic and individualistic views. Further, their cultural and religious values are governed by respect for one another and reciprocity is the norm for their day-today interactions.

The well-being of all creation including that of human beings depends upon preserving and restoring the harmonious inter-relationships of all creation. All living creatures including humans are meant to work toward maintaining balance and harmony and these are to be seen as the ultimate concern of all beings. Indigenous peoples do not believe in the superiority of humans over against the rest of creation. In fact, most indigenous people believe, as their stories and mythologies attest, humans are thought to be at the lowest strata of creation order.[9] Arguing against the Euro-western theories of evolutionary ascendancy, Tinker asserts that:

> Rather than elevate human beings to the apex of an evolutionary ascendancy (i.e., common descent), the lack of human privileging over against these other life forms means that Indians understand that all life shares equal status and that value, personhood, intelligence, and the like must be recognized in all life. If there is a hierarchy of beings in the Indian experience of the world, humans are found at the bottom rather than at the top, the youngest and least wise of all living things.[10]

Indeed, indigenous peoples consider animals, other living creatures, and all created as "'people' in the same manner as the various tribes of human beings are people."[11] Indigenous peoples claim they have reciprocal relationships with all living things, which includes the so-called "inanimate" objects such as rocks, plants, and other natural forms.[12] Everything is imbued with spirit so all is sacred for indigenous peoples. Because all creation is sacred the very land we walk and till must be treated with respect and reverence. Therefore, they treat life and creation with respect and reverence. One reason land is sacred for indigenous peoples is that it is the dwelling place of the spirits; the ancestors have lived and worked the same land and they take their final rest and their bones become the land.[13]

Indigenous worldview is further characterized by being spatially oriented

---

[9] *Ibid.,* 131.

[10] George E. Tinker, "The Stones Shall Cry Out: Consciousness, Rocks and Indians," *Wicazo Sa Review* 19(2) (January 2004), 107.

[11] Vine Deloria, Jr, *God is Red: A Native View of Religion.* 2nd ed. (Golden: North American Press, 1992), 89.

[12] Walking Buffalo articulates this truth: "Did you know that trees talk? Well they do. They talk to each other, and they'll talk to you if you listen. Trouble is, White people don't listen. They never learned to listen to the Indians, so I don't I suppose they'll listen to other voices in nature. But I have learned a lot from trees: some times about the weather, some times about animals, sometimes about the Great Spirit." Quoted in Deloria. *Ibid.,* 90.

[13] M. Horam, *Nagas Old Ways New Trends* (Delhi: Cosmos Publications, 1988), 15f.

rather than temporally focused as is of the Euro-american worldview. This worldview of spatiality essentially accentuates and locates the all important life qualities of relationships among and between human beings and the whole of creation. This understanding extends and embraces the way indigenous peoples view the world and relate themselves to the spirits and God(s). In "Full Circle of Liberation: An American Theology of Place," Tinker argues that the traditional Christian Euro-centric notion of God's action in time, which incidentally, is also embraced by Black theologians and Latin American theologians, is not how American Indians could understand a relation to God. God acts in space and in place. Tinker explains, "God reveals God's self in creation, in space or place, not in time."[14] For Tinker and other indigenous thinkers, the traditional linear thinking of temporality that is fundamental to the Western intellectual tradition is quite alien to indigenous peoples and is in fact destructive to their livelihood.

Indigenous Astronomy: A Brief Overview[15]

Native astronomies are predicated upon a participation-resonance-creative imagination-relational orientation that characterized the participatory nature of native interaction with other aspects of the natural world. In other words, Native cultures applied a participatory consciousness to their conception of the heavens, whose goal was to establish a kind of resonance with what they perceived in the night sky and their activities on Earth. They approached the stars with their creative imaginations as well as their skills of observation and astronomical technology.[16]

Indigenous people are avid observers of nature and their surroundings. They are sensitive to the happenings around them and their world. They are acutely aware of the fact that they are part and parcel of the totality of the universe and human life is understood in this wider context of relationships. Knowledge about space and astronomy is thus a natural extension of their worldviews that define their relatedness to the world of space and time.

Indigenous astronomy refers to the traditional astronomical observations and practices of the indigenous peoples around the world. Different scholars have used different names but some of the common names include archaeoastronomy, traditional astronomy, ethnoastronomy, naked eye astronomy[17] and so on.

---

[14] George E. Tinker, "The Full Circle of Liberation: An American Theology of Place," in David G. Hallman, ed., *Ecotheology: Voices from South and North* (Geneva: WCC Publications, 1994), 221; *Spirit and Resistance*, 91-92.

[15] For my work I have heavily relied on sources from the indigenous peoples (American Indians/Native Americans) of South, Central and North America besides the indigenous peoples of the Northeast India.

[16] Gregory Cajete, *Native Science: Natural Laws of Interdependence*, Forward by Leroy Little Bear (Santa Fe: Clear Light Publishers, 2000), 216.

[17] While Anthony F. Aveni and others generally refer to as "archaeoastronomy" Ray A. Williamson and Claire R. Farrer refer to it as "naked-eye astronomy," Ray A Williamson and Claire

Indigenous peoples are known to have accurate and highly intelligent knowledge about nature and space including astronomy. This is abundantly obvious from the recent studies of indigenous understandings of nature and astronomy as Stephen C. McCluskey points out in his penetrating article, "Science, Society, Objectivity, and the Astronomies of the Southwest."[18] McCluskey underscores the dilemma that rather defines western scientific community's attitude toward indigenous ways of knowing and their reluctance to accept indigenous knowledge about astronomy to be scientific. McCluskey comments:

> We have increasingly come to realize the richness, complexity, and even accuracy of the understandings of nature developed by "primitive" peoples. Recent studies of early astronomies have been exceptionally illustrative in this regard. Yet there is a strange reluctance to apply the words science or scientific to these intellectual activities.[19]

Underlying this observation is the idea that all indigenous knowledge about nature and astronomy cannot be regarded authentic or acceptable unless it is subjected to the rigorous scrutiny of modern science. What is being assumed and led to believe is that since indigenous knowledge about nature or astronomy is not based on mathematical or theory based as modern science is, indigenous knowledge is nothing more than a mere superstitions and therefore it cannot be regarded as science or scientific. Anthony Aveni questions such assumptions and he rightly maintains that it is wrong to subject indigenous knowledge to the modern western European standards since both operate and function from different assumptions. The application of modern western scientific methods effectively undercuts the whole dynamics of traditional astronomies including other elements of culture of which they form an integral part.[20] Leroy Little Bear also argues that it is wrong to assume that western science is free from western

---

R. Farrer, eds., *Earth and Sky: Visions of the Cosmos in Native American Folklore* (Albuquerque: University of New Mexico Press, 1992), 3. In the preface to *Lakota Star Knowledge: Studies in Lakota Stellar Theology*, Ray Williamson writes the importance of naked eye astronomy to the indigenous people as follows, "Naked eye observation allows one to construct a highly accurate calendar using the ordered patterns and motions of the celestial bodies. Native American groups also watched the motions of the planets, and other appearances, including comets, meteor showers, and lunar and solar eclipses, in order to guide their lives." Ronald Goodman, *Lakota and Star Knowledge: Studies in Lakota Stellar Theology* (Rosebud: Sinta Gleska University, 1992), 1.

[18] Stephen C. McCluskey, "Science, Society, Objectivity and the Astronomies of the Southwest" in *Astronomy and Ceremony in Prehistoric Southwest* , no. 2. eds., John B. Carlson and W. James Judge (Albuquerque: Maxwell Museum of Anthropology), 1987, 205-217.

[19] *Ibid.*, 205.

[20] Anthony F. Aveni, "Archaeoastronomy in the Maya Region: A Review of the Past Decade." *Archaeoastronomy* 3 (JHT 12), 51-S16.

culture or worldview. The fact of the matter is that all sciences whether western/ modern or other sciences are all culturally relative.[21]

And to those who try to discredit indigenous traditions by describing it as "figments of primitive imaginations" and "an intellectual creation designed to account for natural processes or human reactions to human problems," Deloria has this to offer:

> We can transcend their complicated interpretations to recognize that our species has generally been fairly practical in approach to the natural world. We have not cringed before winds and rain storms; and we recognized in the unusual events of nature a reality that transcended mere mechanical explanations. In recognizing that primitive myths and the oral traditions of tribal peoples contain memories of past events, we give them a respectable status. These people preserved a knowledge of the history of our planet, and our recognition of this accomplishment enhances their sense of pride in traditions and cultural values.[22]

McClusky makes a useful distinction between traditional astronomies and modern western astronomies.[23] While modern astronomy functions within a theoretical framework and often considered as an abstract enterprise, traditional astronomies have close linkage with larger society. And the close relations of traditional astronomies with the society can be seen in several fronts. First, traditional astronomies take religious overtones and manifest in religious worldview of the people. They are practiced as part of "ritual, and their astronomical concepts are expressed in sacred terms."[24] Secondly, unlike the scientific astronomy which tend to maintain that it is free from religion and society "traditional astronomies and cosmologies often serve as models for social structures."[25] Finally, the relations of traditional astronomies with the society is obvious from the fact that they have practical utility for the people. This is most clearly seen in determining religious and agricultural calendar. As Vincent Malstrom notes for pre-columbine Mesoamerica,

> ...bound up with the calendar are many if not all of the more sophisticated aspects of the region's early intellectual life: the awareness of a cyclicity in the movement of celestial bodies, the evolution of mathematical skills by which they could manipulate the numbers

---

[21] Leroy Little Bear, "Foreward," in Cajete, *Native Science.* ix.

[22] Vine Deloria, Jr, *The Metaphysics of Modern Existence* (San Francisco: Harper & Row Publishers, 1979), 173.

[23] McCluskey, "Science, Society, Objectivity." 206.

[24] *Ibid.*

[25] *Ibid.*

> derived from those cycles, and the development of a system of hieroglyphics for the results.[26]

Most indigenous peoples' religious and agricultural calendars are thus organized based on their readings of the movements of the celestial bodies. Moreover, the movements of the heavenly bodies served as the organizing principles of social groups.[27] For example, the Hopi Soyal ceremony occurs during the winter solstice while the Inca and Maya people relied on the calendar system for their political leadership transitions in their communities. It is also true that the Pawnees organized their villages according to the patterns of stars in the sky. In this way, the cycles of nature played a very vital role in the life of the indigenous people since it functions as the organizing principle of intellectual inquiry and social organization.

The study and observations of celestial bodies is not merely an intellectual activity but an important aspect in the life of the indigenous people for maintaining the necessary balance and harmony in the universe. Studying the movements of the celestial bodies, the stars and the moon, enables them to align themselves and model their earthly activities accordingly. Ben Sherman underscores the importance of this dynamic relations when he comments on the traditional Lakota belief system.

> Through their observations of celestial phenomena, the Lakota people designed their movements, ceremonies and actions on earth to be in alignment with the movements of the sun and stars. This sacred unity of earth and sky is an essential element of the traditional Lakota belief system.[28]

Sherman goes on to argue that native peoples' knowledge about stars and heavenly bodies in general is quite ancient and that there are "valid methods of measuring the antiquity of this ancient star knowledge through the concept of stellar 'precession,' which dates parts of Lakota star traditions at 2,000 to 3,000 years old."[29] In fact, it may not be wrong to assert that the traditional astronomies are as old as their existence here on earth.

Indigenous peoples' knowledge of heavenly bodies and their relationship with the sky world is largely contained and found in folklore and mythology. The examinations of folklore and mythology often provide new insights about the indigenous peoples' cultures and belief systems. And this aspect of reflection

---

[26] Vincent Malstrom, *Cycles of the Sun, Mysteries of the Moon* (Austin: University of Taxes Press, 1997), 14.

[27] Clara Sue Kidwell, "Archaeoastronomy as the Key to Human Intellectual Development and Social Organization." TMs, 3.

[28] Ben Sherman, "Watchers of the Ancient Skies," in *Winds of Change,* Summer 1998, 21.

[29] *Ibid.*

and examination is a significant means toward constructing "alternatives to the prevailing scientific definition of reality."[30]

Most indigenous peoples' cosmological myths relate that there was agreement between their ancestors and the Earth and Sky/Sun in the very beginning of time. The agreement was concerned with the roles of the Earth and Sky/Sun in the lives of the people and how the earth people could mutually reciprocate their goodness. The Navajo creation story as explained by Rik Pinxten and Ingred van Dooren contains the content and nature of the agreement.

> As the result of an agreement between the ancestors and the Earth and Sky at the dawn of this world, both Earth and Sun (Sky) keep giving force to living beings on a continuous and daily basis. However, they have to get something in return in order to be able to continue this transfer; each and every day Earth and Sun takes lives: that is, the vital force of dying beings return to them. Because of this cosmological gift-recuperation system, the Earth and the Sun will continue the transfer of life forces to new generation of living beings.[31]

Place and Astronomical Orientation

In the indigenous peoples' worldview space and place take precedence over time.[32] The sense of space and place pervades the whole thinking patterns and life orientation including their relationship to the environment around them. They are acutely aware of the fact that the universe including earth and sky and everything is interconnected and consequently affect each other. The sky world has a great deal of influence on those living on the earth including humans and creation. In fact, indigenous people has the mirroring image of the relationship between earth and sky as it is aptly described in the Lakota stellar story, "What is in the stars is on the Earth and what is on the Earth is in the stars."[33] This understanding goes right to the heart of indigenous peoples' dualistic worldview that regards dualism as a necessary reciprocal pair, spiritual and material, sky and earth/above and below for the purpose of maintaining, restoring and recreating balance and harmony.[34]

---

[30] Ray A. Williamson and Clare R. Farrer, *Earth and Sky*, 1.

[31] Rik Pinxten and Ingred van Dooren, "Navajo Earth and Sky and the Celestial Life-Force." In *Earth and Sky: Visions of the Cosmos in Native American Folklore.* ed. Ray A. Williamson and Claire R. Farrer (Albuquerque: University on New Mexico Press, 1992), 103.

[32] For a detailed discussion on indigenous peoples' worldviews refer to my essay, "Emerging Vision of Indigenous/Tribal Theology," in James Massey and Shimreingam Shimray, eds. *Dalit-Tribal Theological Interface: Current Trends in Subaltern Theologies* (Jorhat: TSC/TWC, 2007), 16-55.

[33] Sherman, "Watchers of the Ancient Skies," 21.

[34] This dualistic worldview is widely known among many American Indian nations. The Tewa and Osage Indian nations are typical representations of this dualistic structure of the society.

Describing about Osage society Tinker thus writes, "Like many cognate tribes, the Osage world was (is) one of thorough-going dualism of reciprocity."[35] The Osage people organize their socio-religious structures based on the dualistic understanding of their worldview. In a similar vein Francis La Flesche says, "Like the Omahas, Poncas, Quapaws, and other related peoples, an Osage village was divided into two parts: the *tsi zhu,* or Sky People division, and the *hon-ga* or Earth People division with mandated cross-divisional marriage."[36] Further, the community architecture (both permanent towns and hunting camps) was divided by an east-west roadways, the *tsi zhu* constructing their lodges to the north and the *hon-ga* to the south. This spatial arrangement is repeated in the seating of the *hon-zhin-ga,* the council of elders inside a lodge prepared for ceremonial observance.[37]

The traditional Osage social, political and religious institutions were said to be highly integrated so much so that they constitute a single unified system. Patterned according to the image of cosmos, typical Osage village have two chiefs, one representing the Earth people division and the other representing the Sky people division. The houses of the two chiefs were built in the middle of the village. While the house of the chief of the Earth people division stood on the south, the Sky people division chief's house stood on the north. The houses of the chiefs were sacred because they symbolically represented the:

> Two life giving powers – the Earth and the Sun (Sky). The house stands for the earth and must have two doors, one opening toward the rising sun and the other toward the setting sun. The fire that is placed midway between the two doors represents the sun, whose pathway symbolizes endless life, and thus passes through the middle of the house that stands for the earth. The fire place was also consecrated and the fire taken there from by the people to start their home fire was thought of as holy and as having the power to give life and health to those who use it.[38]

Similarly, the Khasis of Meghalaya believed that their ancestors descended from heaven/sky world. According to the Khasi origin story, God created sixteen families in heaven and allowed them to live with Him in heaven.[39] God also gave

---

While the Tewa society is broadly divided into summer and winter moieties based on their myth of origin, the Osage society is divided into Sky people and Earth people reflecting their cosmological image.

[35] George E. "Tink" Tinker, "God, Gods, Goddesses, and Indians." TMs, 7.

[36] Garrick A. Bailey ed., *The Osage and the Invisible World: From the Works of Francis La Flesche* (Norman: University of Oklahoma Press, 1995), 29.

[37] Quoted in Bailey, *The Osage*, 43.

[38] Tinker, "God, Gods, Goddesses, and Indians." 7.

[39] R. Tokin Roy Rymbai, "Evolution of Modern Khasi Society (Babu Jeebon Roy)," in J. N. Chowdhury, ed. *The Khasi Canvas: A Cultural and Political History* (Shillong: Srimati Jaya

them the freedom to move between heaven and earth through a golden ladder. On one such occasion, seven families decided to settle down on earth leaving behind the nine families in heaven. "These seven families came to be known as *Ki Hynniew Ha Tbin* (The Seven Below) and those who remained in heaven as *Ki Khyndai Ha jrong* (The Nine Above)."[40] The Khasis claim they are the descendents of these seven families.[41]

The Stars are Our Relatives: Implications for Climate Change and Climate Justice

The Stars are Our Relatives

Indigenous peoples around the world have rich and diverse stories about the sky world that have been passed down to them from generation to generation.[42] The stories in one way or the other underscore indigenous peoples' deep connections with the various heavenly bodies. They do not regard the heavenly bodies as mere objects that appear night after night rather they identify them with their own relations who had passed away from the earth. In some cases, they relate and identify them with their spiritual worldviews. The Sumi Nagas of Nagaland believe that the stars (*ayeh*) are "men who have been translated to the heavens after their deaths."[43] They regard a comet as the souls of some great warrior. The Rengma Nagas regard Milky Way as meeting place of souls, they call it spirits *morung*, while Pleiades is identified with souls carrying a large rice pounding-table. The Sumis call the Pleiades *Ayeniklimini*, "The Star Princesses."[44] According to Sumi legend, these star princesses were a group of pretty girls who were killed in a sudden raid of a village by the enemies while they were spinning and making local wine in a rich man's house. It is believed that these pretty girls continue to dance in heavens as they did while on the earth.[45] The Thadou Kukis of Manipur instead identify the Pleiades with the seven brothers trying to cover themselves

---

Chowdhury, 1978), 415.

[40] *Ibid.*

[41] For more detailed discussion on astronomical space and location refer to my article, "The Stars are Our Relatives: Some Musing of Indigenous People's Stellar Theology," in *JTCA: The Journal of Theologies and Cultures in Asia* (vol. 6, 2007), 111-130.

[42] Jean Guard Monroe and Ray A. Williamson in their, *They Dance in the Sky: Native American Star Myths* (Boston: Houghton Mifflin Company, 1987) said that stories about stars are found in abundance from ancient Greek to Aborigines of Australia. I may even add from American Indians of North and South America to Indigenous peoples of Northeast India including Nagas, Khasis, Mizos, Kukis and others.

[43] J. H. Hutton, *The Sema Nagas*, Foreword by Henry Balfour (London: MacMillan and Co., Ltd., 1921), 250.

[44] Hutton, *The Sema Nagas*, 251.

[45] J. P. Mills, *The Rengma Nagas* (London: Macmillan, 1937); Reprint (New York: AMS, 1979), 244.

with only a piece of cloth they had. More over, they regard the shooting stars as stars going to the *daka chang*, the bachelors' dorm; and they have a song which speaks of inviting other stars to join them in the bachelors' dorm.[46]

Another constellation that prominently figures among the Naga tribes of Northeast India is the Belt of the Orion. They call it *Phoghwosülespifemi*, the "Rooftree-carriers." Here again according to legend the three men carrying the roof beam were suddenly attacked and killed by their enemies. And they identify the small stars that form the sword or scabbard with the enemies that killed the three men.

Eclipses of sun and moon are believed to have been caused when animals, especially frog and tiger are trying to devour the sun or the moon. This belief is held by most Naga tribes including the Sumis, the Konyaks and the Tangkhuls. For the Konyak Nagas, eclipses of sun and moon represent a symbolic re-enactment of significant social tensions between the commoners identified as frog clan (*Lukyim*) and the aristocratic/ruling clan identified as Tiger clan (*Angh*).[47] While the frog clan supports the animal by shouting "eat it all," the tiger clan shouts against being eaten by saying "don't eat it, this is our sun."

While we recognize the richness of native myths about the sky world and human relations with the various heavenly bodies, by far star myths constitute the largest of them all.[48] Myths about stars range from inter-marriage between human beings and stars, Peublo myth about Long Sash leading the journey, Lakota story of the Fallen Star to stories that identify stars with ancestors, and Naga people's identification of stars with young girls dancing in the sky. There are myths that talk about how stars came to be where they are and how their movements have great influence on the life activities of the earth people. I think the list of stories about stars and their relationships with humans goes on and on; the stories are quite extensive. And they all convey profoundly the relational nature of indigenous peoples' worldview and life; how profoundly indigenous world and peoples are connected with the heavens above. There is a strong sense of connectedness between the two worlds.[49] In the essay, "The Celestial Skiff: An Alabama Myth of the Stars," Ray A. Williamson describes how sky people and earth people were connected through the marriage of a sky woman and earth man

---

[46] Hutton, *The Sema Nagas*, 251.

[47] Julia Jacobs, *The Nagas: Hill Peoples of Northeast India: Society, Culture and the Colonial Encounter* (New York: Thames and Hudson, 1990), 86 f.

[48] According to Cajete, "After myths about animals and human relationships with animals, the second largest group of myths are those of the stars." *Native Science*, 227.

[49] According to the Pawnee Indian belief the stars are the carriers of the wisdom of Tirawahat, the Pawnee's Supreme Being. And so they watched carefully the movements of the stars, especially of Morning Star and Evening Star to find the clues for their living pattern. The earth lodge of the Pawnees is patterned after the sky. Monroe and Williamson, *They Dance in the Sky*, 44-47.

and subsequently through their children.[50] From this story Williamson goes on to connect the sky woman with the Corn Woman who provides corns/foods to the earth people. "She is the Sky being who represents corn and the coming of agriculture."[51] Such stories of marriage between star world and earth people are also prominently found among the indigenous peoples of Northeast India.

According to the Navajo belief, Black God created and arranged the stars including North Star out of crystals and everything he had created have names.[52] The numerous stars whose names are not known are said to have been the handiwork of Coyote who snatched the pouch away from Black God and scattered the remaining crystals randomly. By observing the positions of the stars including their appearance and disappearance the Navajos like many other indigenous peoples have developed a highly practical stellar calendar. They are also able to determine "when to plant and when to harvest."[53]

The story of the Pueblo culture hero Long Sash who is believed to have brought his people to the place where they inhabit today after a long strenuous and difficult journey and his instructions about hunting skills and skills concerning other activities is being told again and again in the Pueblo community. "The evidence of the journey of Long Sash and his people is written in the stars, for Long Sash is Orion, the never-ending trail is the Milky Way, and places that the people stopped are Castro and Pollux and the constellations of Cancer and Leo."[54]

Another fascinating story comes from the Lakota Indians who primarily reside in South Dakota and Nebraska in the United States– the story of the Fallen Star.[55] According to the story, the Fallen Star was born to one of the two Lakota women who were married to the stars. Fallen star was born when his mother was killed attempting to escape from the star world to the earth. He was thus raised by a meadowlark who happened to speak Lakota. Fallen Star grew to an extraordinary size and matured in a matter of days. "Fallen Star, the protector, the bringer of light and higher consciousness, travels from one Lakota band to another, and everywhere he is recognized, expected, and reverenced."[56] According to the story, Fallen Star killed the eagle that was killing a girl-child everyday near Harney Peak in the Black Hills. Altogether the eagle had already killed seven little girls. Fallen Star placed the spirits of the little girls in the sky as

---

[50] Ray A. Williamson, "The Celestial Skiff: An Alabama Myth of the Stars," in Williamson and Farrer, ed., *Earth and Sky*, 54 ff.

[51] *Ibid.*, 63.

[52] Monroe and Williamson, *They Dance in the Sky*, 33.

[53] *Ibid.*, 44.

[54] Gregory Cajete, *Native Science*, 227.

[55] Ronald Goodman, *Lakota Star Knowledge*, 3,4. There are many versions of the Fallen Star stories and what is described here is based on just one of them.

[56] *Ibid.*, 3.

a constellation. And Pleiades is identified with the "seven little girls," *wicincala sakowin*. He also rescued a young brother and sister from a ferocious bear by raising the ground higher and that raised tower is identified with the Devil's Towers in Black Hills.

Black Hills which is located in the western South Dakota is widely recognized as a place of spiritual significance for the Lakota Indians. It is one of the sacred places of the American Indians. According to Ronald Goodman, Lakota people regard the Black Hills to be a consecrated enclosure that encloses land forms including Winter Camps, Harney Peak, Tayamni, Pe Sla and Devil's Tower besides others.[57] And according to the sacred stories the Lakota constellations on the ecliptic correlated to distinct land forms in the Black Hills.[58] Goodman describes the significance of the Black Hills and the constellations to the Lakota people as follows:

> The constellations were the visible "scriptures" of the People at night; and the related land forms mirrored those stellar scriptures during the day. The stars were understood to be, "The holy breath of the Great Spirit," the woniya of Wakan Tanka. The constellations expressed the basic symbols of the people, which in turn evoked their sacred stories and beliefs. Both night and day the Lakota lived between stories and symbols written in the sky and mirrored on the earth, which through the mediation of Fallen Star taught them how to establish an authentic relation to the spirit world.[59]

The Lakota stellar stories not only reveal how indigenous peoples are profoundly connected with the star world but also they reveal how the people can establish an authentic relation with the spirit world. The stories affirm the unity of human beings and the star world in a fashion that is characterized by reciprocity.

The Stars are Our Moral Guardians

In his, "The Hooghan and the Stars," Trudy Griffin-Pierce examines star patterns and moral teachings of the Navajo Indians in order to find connections between the two.[60] The Navajos believe that the constellations, sun and moon are supernatural beings or Holy People who share human "emotions and are tied genealogically through the clan organization to the Earth Surface People."[61] The constellations depicted in sand paintings by a Navajo chanter correspondingly

---

[57] *Ibid.*, 9.

[58] *Ibid.*, 29.

[59] *Ibid.*, 9.

[60] Trudy Griffin-Pierce, "The Hooghan and the Stars," in Williamson and Farrer, eds., *Earth and Sky*, 110-130.

[61] *Ibid.*, 112.

convey moral examples for the Navajo people. These constellations – Big Dipper and Cassiopeia – revolve around Polaris, which represents central fire in the *hooghan*. These constellations represent "old people" or "women folks" and they are telling the people to "stay at home, to stay around your fire." Here "the implication is that these constellations set a moral example for the Earth Surface People to be at home with their families to carry out their familial responsibilities."[62] Secondly, they are also reminding the leaders of their responsibilities towards their people. On the whole, "the visual depiction of constellations in sand paintings transmits and reiterates the Navajo emphasis on order, balance and, circularity and reciprocity."[63]

In the case of the Cahuilla, a California Indian tribe, it is moon which plays the role of moral or ethical teacher.[64] Cahuilla people believe that moon is one of the earliest of beings who resided with them in the beginning itself. "Moon is the mother of all Cahuilla people. She was the first woman and remains a great culture heroine, a reference point for Cahuillaness."[65] It is believed that while moon was on Earth as a *nukatem* she was actively involved in the moral and ethical life of the people as their guide. She was also known as the organizer of Cahuilla people's social and ritual life; she was attributed as responsible for the assigning of Cahuilla people to their respective moieties.[66] Until this day, the Cahuilla people regard moon as a significant symbolic representation of their history and identity.

Balance and Harmony

The sky world including stars and moon remind the earth people to maintain good relations with every creation, animate and inanimate for the sake of maintaining balance and harmony. In the context of today's environmental crisis, global warming, desertification due to deforestation, the depletion of ozone layers, air and water pollutions and the more frequent natural calamities like the recent Tsunami disaster and Hurricane Katrina in the United States, the frequent flash floods, climate change, etc., in and around the world including our northeast region, indigenous people's wisdom such as this become ever more relevant and significant. According to Mescalero Apaches' creation myth, which is also true with other indigenous creation myths, human beings are considered to be the weakest link in the chain of creation and so they need

---

62 *Ibid.*, 116.

63 *Ibid.*, 126.

64 Lowell John Bean, "Symbolic Representation of Cahuilla Women," in Williamson and Farrer, eds., *Earth and Sky*, 167.

65 *Ibid.*, 166.

66 *Ibid.*, 167 f.

the cooperation of other creatures for their existence.[67] It is therefore very important for human beings to carefully chart out their relationships with others in creation. The Milky Way which is also known as the Scattered Stars[68] serves as nightly reminder of the importance of maintaining good relationships with one's fellow human beings and the rest of creation. The consequences of the failure to live properly:

> Are messy, unordered, scattered, and imperfect....The messages are very clear to Mescalero Apaches: either live according to the Creator's plan or disrupt the balance and harmony of the universe; either cooperate with one another or lose your status as a separate Tribe. It is right up there in the sky to see; one cannot forget.[69]

This cautionary advice to the Mescalero Apaches applies to all the indigenous peoples around the world: either live according to the Creator's plan or disrupt the balance of the universe. Maintaining good relationships goes along way for maintaining balance and harmony in the universe.

Conclusion

Indigenous peoples' astronomy in many ways, is the embodiment of indigenous knowledge or science. It incorporates the whole spectrum of indigenous people's ways of knowing and its application to life. It is the extension of indigenous worldview that embraces wholeness, relationship and reciprocity. Indigenous astronomy encompasses and reflects all that concerns indigenous peoples' ways of knowing including their cosmology, stories of creation and the evolutions of human beings.

Unlike Western science that prides in objectivity, indigenous knowledge affirms the unity and integrity of all ways of knowing. There is no pretension in indigenous peoples' claim for respect for all forms of life and knowledge contrary to Western science's claim for universality and truth. Indigenous stellar theology, as it is aptly demonstrated, deals with the concrete and larger society rather than focusing on the abstracts as Western science does. Indigenous stellar theology is concerned with the practical utility it has for the larger society: by observing the movements of stars, sun and moon they are able to develop their yearly calendar. Further, indigenous stellar theology enables indigenous peoples to maintain close relations with the spirit world. Indigenous stellar theology most of all, affirms the

---

[67] Claire R. Farrer, "...by you they will know the directions to guide them:" Stars and Mascalero Apaches," in Williamson and Farrer, ed., *Earth and Sky*, 71.

[68] According to Mascalero Apache's myth, Milky Way resulted out of the fight between the Twin Warrior Gods. While they were fighting they by mistake hit the seeds which resulted in the scattering of seeds all across the sky. Now the Creator did not fix the rupture caused by their fighting, instead left as it is as a reminder for the people to remain in good relationships. *Ibid.,* 71-72.

[69] *Ibid.*, 72.

importance of maintaining good relations with fellow humans and the whole of creation which is critical for the purpose of maintaining balance and harmony in the universe. In sum:

> Native astronomies are expressions of the universal process of human inquiry into the nature of nature in order to make human life possible and more meaningful. By attempting to see the cosmos through the eyes of Native skywatchers, we can allow ourselves a perspective that may better equip us as we search for a more sustainable life.[70]

Theology is all about relations, how humans are related with God, the world, creation and fellow human beings. The study of indigenous astronomy serves as a valuable source for our theological articulation and reflection, after all indigenous people's astronomy in a way, is the embodiment of indigenous people's knowledge.

[70] Cajete, *Native Science*, 257.

Chapter 11

Exploring the Theme of Liberation in the Works of Some Selected Theologians

The chapter intends to explore the theme of liberation as a theological enterprise in the writings of some selected theologians. I would particularly examine the works of St. Augustine, Martin Luther, Reinhold Niebuhr, Gustavo Gutierrez and James Cone. These theologians come from a wide spectrum of theological traditions representing differing theological view points and time. While selecting the works of these theologians, I certainly recognize the magnitude of the diversified understandings of the usage and meaning of liberation. While some have employed the term liberation as their main theological theme (Gutierrez and Cone), many others did not even refer to the term liberation. However, I intend to use liberation in relation to the theme of salvation, sin and human freedom. So, in what follows we will find the themes like salvation, Christian freedom and sin being discussed as those inevitable themes related to liberation. The question of the relationship between salvation and human liberation will receive a critical attention in our discussion. For the sake of maintaining this perspective, the paper begins with a brief introduction about the emergence of liberation as a theological theme in liberation theology.

Liberation as a Theological Theme

Liberation as a theological theme came to its prominence only in the late 60s and early 70s with the emergence of liberation theology in Latin America. Gustavo Gutierrez is widely regarded as the father of liberation theology. His first ever book on liberation theology, A *Theology of Liberation,* appeared in 1971. Meanwhile, black theology of liberation also emerged almost at the same time in the United States of America under the leadership of James H. Cone. In fact, Cone's first book on black theology, *Black Theology and Black Power,* was for the first time published in 1969. Liberation theology emerged out of the context of the socio-economic and political exploitations of the poor. The poor peoples' experience of economic exploitations and political oppressions is the basis of liberation theology. In the case of black theology, it is the blacks' experience of slavery for decades and their continued experience of discriminations in the hands of the white oppressors which served as the context of their theological reflection. Liberation theology follows praxis, the method of action-reflection, as its methodology. Theology is accordingly defined as the critical reflection on praxis "based on the gospel and the experiences of men and women committed to the process of liberation in the oppressed and exploited land....It is a theological reflection born of the experience of shared efforts to abolish the current unjust situation and to build a different society, freer and more human."[1] In the same manner, James Cone defines, "Christian theology is a theology of liberation. It is a rational study of the being of God in the world in light of the existential situation of an oppressed community, relating the forces of liberation to the essence of the gospel, which is Jesus Christ."[2]

Liberation theology begins with the claim that all theology is contextual. No theology is universally valid for all people and for all time. James Cone states categorically thus:

> Theology is not a universal language about God. Rather, it is human speech informed by historical and theological traditions, and written for particular times and places. Theology is contextual language - that is, defined by the human situation that gives birth to it. No one can write theology for all times, places, and persons.[3]

Accordingly Cone and Gutierrez regard peoples' experience along with the scripture as sources for doing theology. Reading scripture in the light of peoples' experience of suffering and their struggle for liberation is the point of departure for liberation theology. According to Cone, the Bible is "one witness to God's empowering presence in human affairs, along with others important testimonies."[4] And the other testimonies include sacred documents of African-American experience such as peoples' speeches and writings, music and arts, and

---

[1] Gustavo Gutierrez. *A Theology of Liberation.* 15th Anniversary Edition with a new introduction. (Maryknoll, New York: Orbis Books, 2000). xiii.

[2] James H. Cone. *A Black Theology of Liberation* (Twentieth Anniversary Edition). (Maryknoll, New York: Orbis Books, 1990), 1.

[3] *Ibid.*, xi.

[4] James H. Cone. *God of the Oppressed.* Revised Edition. (Maryknoll, New York: Orbis Books, 1997), xi.

liberating stories, myths, and legends.[5] Both Cone and Gutierrez take seriously the importance of history and peoples' traditions for theological articulations. It is in history that God encounters humanity and the world. In the light of this understanding, Gutierrez talks about the task of theological reflection. "Theological reflection would then necessarily be a criticism of society and the Church insofar as they are called and addressed by the Word of God; it would be a critical theory, worked out in the light of the Word accepted in faith and inspired by a practical purpose - and therefore indissolubly linked to historical praxis."[6]

Identifying people's experience from socio-economic exploitations and political unfreedoms, liberation theologians appropriately employ liberation as a theme for their theological reflection. Liberation thus becomes the heart and soul of their theological thinking and aspirations. What is liberation and what do they mean by it in the light of Christian understanding of salvation is being discussed in the following.

Salvation and Liberation

What is liberation? Is liberation part of the comprehensive Christian understanding of salvation? How is liberation related to salvation? These are some of the important questions I intend to address while discussing the views of the following theologians.

Gustavo Gutierrez

According to Gutierrez, there is no distinction between liberation and salvation. He equates liberation with salvation. For Gutierrez, to liberate is to give life, life in its fullness. "The historical process in which Latin America has been involved, and the experience of many Christians in this process, led liberation theology to speak of salvation in Christ in terms of liberation."[7] Of course, Gutierrez understands liberation in a comprehensive manner as "an integral reality from which nothing is excluded." Accordingly, Gutierrez distinguishes three levels or dimensions of liberation in Christ.[8] The first dimension consists of liberation from socio-economic and political situations of oppressions and marginalization which contradicts God s will for the life of the poor people. The second dimension concerns with transformation of the personal life and the third dimension consists of liberation from sin. Sin is the "deepest roots of all servitude;" it is the "breaking of friendship with God and with other human beings, and therefore cannot be eradicated except by the unmerited redemptive love of the Lord whom we receive

[5] *Black Theology of Liberation.* Twentieth Anniversary Edition. (Maryknoll, New York: Orbis Books, 1990), 23-30.

[6] Gustavo Gutierrez. *A Theology of Liberation.* 9.

[7] *Ibid.,* xxxvii.

[8] *Ibid.*

by faith and in communion with one another."[9] So, for Gutierrez liberation encompasses all these three dimensions: liberation from social situations, personal transformation and liberation from sin. By liberation then Gutierrez means salvation in its totality, spiritual as well as physical.

Further, Gutierrez talks about the quantitative view of salvation and the qualitative view of salvation in Christian theology. He is critical of the quantitative view of salvation which is generally held by traditional Christian theology according to which salvation is understood in terms of saving from sin for the life hereafter. Salvation is thus considered essentially as otherworldly. "The notion of salvation implied in this point of view has two very well-defined characteristics: it is a cure for sin in this life; and this cure is in virtue of a salvation to be attained beyond this life."[10] According to Gutierrez, this understanding of salvation is "moralistic, and the spirituality is one of flight from this world." This is a narrow view of salvation and it reduces salvation to spiritual salvation alone ignoring the physical and earthly dimension of salvation. Gutierrez thus argues for a qualitative view of salvation which includes and embraces the totality of the person including the present reality. Gutierrez affirms:

> Salvation is not something otherworldly, in regard to which the present life is merely a test. Salvation - the communion of human beings with God and among themselves - is something which embraces all human reality, transforms it, and leads it to its fullness in Christ: Thus, the center of God's salvific design is Jesus Christ, who by his death and resurrection transforms the universe and makes it possible for the person to reach fulfillment as a human being. This fulfillment embraces every aspect of humanity: body and spirit, Individual and society, person and cosmos, time and eternity. Christ, the image of the Father and the perfect God-Man, takes on all the dimensions of human existence."[11]

Accordingly for Gutierrez, sin is not merely a private or interior thing rather it is both a personal and intra-historical reality. Sin is a historical reality. It is the breaking of relationship with God and with other fellow human being. "Sin is regarded as a social, historical fact, the absence of fellowship and love in relationships among persons, the breach of friendship with God and other persons, and therefore, an interior, personal fracture."[12] Gutierrez argues that such an understanding of sin enables us to see the collective dimensions of sin which is essential for understanding the complexities of the reality of human existence. It enables us to see sin in the social situations wherever there are oppressive structures,

---

[9] *Ibid.*

[10] *Ibid.*, 84.

[11] *Ibid.*, 85.

[12] *Ibid.*, 103.

exploitations of humans by humans, dominations and slavery of peoples, races and social classes. It enables us to recognize that all forms of social injustices and exploitations are concrete manifestations of sin. Sin is not merely a spiritual affair that concerns only the individual, rather sin includes the whole gamut of human reality - spiritual and physical. Salvation in this sense is wholeness of the totality of the person and community. All forms of brokenness that we experience in our human society is sin for Gutierrez. Likewise mending the broken relationship is liberation.

Since sin is a historical reality and deeply rooted in the social-political structures of the society, in the same token sin demands radical liberation. This then necessarily implies a political liberation. For Gutierrez the liberation of Israel from Egypt is a political action. "It is the breaking away from a situation of despoliation and misery and the beginning of the construction of a just and comradely society. It is the suppression of disorder and the creation of new order."[13]

Gutierrez affirms, that for Christians the basis of liberation is Jesus Christ. Jesus Christ is the embodiment of and the ground of human liberation.

James H. Cone

The ground of human liberation for Cone is Jesus Christ.[14] And this Jesus Christ is the God who was, is and will be actively engaged in the liberation of the oppressed. Without Jesus there is no human freedom and consequently the struggle for freedom will have no meaning. People, especially the oppressed are willing to suffer in their struggle for liberation precisely because of their faith in Jesus Christ. Cone affirms the humanity and divinity of Jesus Christ and on this basis he affirms that "the pain of the cross was God suffering for and with us so that our humanity can be liberated for freedom in the divine struggle against 'evil.'"[15] He goes on to say that God is free to love and to be for us. Therefore, "the biblical God is the God whose salvation is liberation.

Agreeing with Jürgen Moltmann who states that "Christian theology speaks history eschatologically," Cone asserts that the struggle for liberation is based on the hope of the future.[16] Cone believes that God's promise of liberation is the strength and enduring power that keeps people to fight on for their liberation. This hope for the future coming of Jesus Christ, enables the blacks to keep struggling "against inexplicable evil in their existence.[17] Liberation is certainly a gift of God. Freedom thus belongs to God and it is not human made.

---

[13] *Ibid.*, 88.

[14] James H. Cone. *God of the Oppressed.* Revised Edition. (Maryknoll, New York, Orbis Books, 2000), 127.

[15] *Ibid.,* 128.

[16] *Ibid.*

[17] *Ibid.,* 129.

Cone understands liberation as freedom and he means four things by liberation as freedom.

First, liberation as freedom is to be in relation to God. To be in right relationship with God is the primary content of human liberation and this freedom must precede the freedom to be in relation to self and community. And to do so one must experience personal conversion. This is the vertical dimension of liberation. "The conversion experience in black religion is a radical, transforming encounter with the One the people believe to be the foundation of their existence."[18] Apart from community worship, prayer is an integral part of their faith-life to keep them in constant fellowship with God. Prayer for Cone is "not an escape that leads to passivity. Rather, it is the beginning of Christian practice of liberation."[19] Community worship is a liberating event and therefore, it is a celebration of the freedom the oppressed people enjoy in God.

Secondly, liberation is freedom in relation to self and community of the oppressed. For Cone, the experience of liberation includes freedom of the self and the community and the two are inseparably related. There can be no authentic freedom of the self unless it is related to the freedom of the community. It means that one is not fully liberated until the whole community of the oppressed is liberated.[20] According to Cone, black theology of liberation derives from the dialectic of freedom and oppression as they are related to political praxis. He affirms the paradox that says "freedom is the opposite of oppression, but only the oppressed are truly free."[21] This paradox is significant because Jesus (in the dialectic of death and resurrection) has connected his liberation with the struggles of the wretched of the earth."[22] Christianity is then inevitably a community that chooses to be oppressed. A true Christian community belongs to the oppressed community. Cone is quite clear: the oppressors claim that they are also part of the oppressed community is nothing but "hypocrisy and blasphemy." According to Cone, by claiming themselves to be part of the oppressed community the oppressors are trying to justify their own particular status in the society. Cone does not deny the fact that the oppressors are oppressed too. But, the truth of the matter is that to understand that they too are oppressed, their consciousness need to be defined in the light of the social existence of the poor. In other words, "for the oppressors to understand liberation, they must be liberated from being political oppressors."[23] There is no other way to understand the phrase "all are oppressed" except from the perspective of the poor. The poor are in a better

---

[18] *Ibid.*, 130.

[19] *Ibid.*

[20] *Ibid.*, 135.

[21] *Ibid.*

[22] *Ibid.*

[23] *Ibid.*, 137.

position to understand the universal dimension of the gospel of liberation. And this means working for the liberation of all including the oppressed community.

Thirdly, Cone understands liberation as the project of freedom in history. Liberation is not an object, it is the project of freedom in history. It is in human history that the project of freedom has to be sought. In this sense, liberation cannot be separated from the historical struggle of freedom in this world. It is biblical, Cone asserts. The Exodus event is a historical event in which the Israelites were freed from social-political bondage. The mission and ministry of Jesus is historical. Jesus proclaimed freedom to the captives, good news to the poor, ministered to the least of these, and invited the sinners to Kingdom banquet. In this sense "salvation is granting of physical wholeness in the concreteness of pain and suffering."[24] This is the reason why black preachers like Martin Luther King Jr. preached freedom from political bondage and fought for civil liberties. This is the reason that "the identification of divine justice with civil justice became the central theme of the civil rights movement in the 1950s and 60s."[25] Cone strongly believes that liberation is not a theoretical proposition, it is a historical reality for the oppressed. It is a project of freedom that resists any oppressive force that prevents a person from becoming fully human. Liberation is also a project of freedom that recognizes that God is struggling with the oppressed community in the fight for liberation.

Finally for Cone, liberation is the project of freedom in hope. Liberation is not limited to historical freedom but it goes beyond here and now. It is also a future event which is yet to come. The fullness of liberation belongs to the other world - beyond this world. This does not in any way mean escaping from the present realities rather it is an affirmation of the vision of a new heaven and a new earth" which is "not made with human hands but grounded in the liberating promises of God."[26] It also means that the divine future breaks into their social existence, bestowing wholeness in the present situation of pain and suffering and enabling black people to know that the existing state of oppression contradicts humanity as defined by God's future.[27]

Cone recognizes the fear of freedom and the risks involved in the struggle are real and they are "ever-present realities" but "the transcendence of freedom, granted in Jesus' resurrection, introduces a factor that makes a significant difference."[28] In fact, the belief in the resurrection of Jesus Christ enables the oppressed people to transcend death and interpret freedom from death as a heavenly, eschatological reality. Cone believes that "liberation is not simply what oppressed people can do

[24] *Ibid.*, 140.

[25] *Ibid.*, 142.

[26] *Ibid.*, 145.

[27] *Ibid.*, 146.

[28] *Ibid.*, 148.

alone; it is basically what God has done and will do to accomplish liberation both in and beyond history."[29]

Reinhold Niebuhr

Niebuhr is often regarded as a neo-orthodox theologian although he does not like himself to be described that way. For Niebuhr sin is primarily pride, "man's pride and will to power disturb the harmony of creation."[30] According to him, the biblical view of sin contains both the religious and moral dimensions. In religious terms sin is rebellion against God, an effort to become like God. Where as the moral and social dimension of sin is injustice.[31]

Niebuhr sees the necessity of making a distinction between group pride and individual egotism basically on two accounts! a) the group enjoys certain authority over the individual, and it results in unconditioned demands upon the individual, b) the pretensions and claims of a collective or social self exceed those of the individual ego."[32] The collective or social egotism is most prominently expressed by the national state. The national state perceives itself as representing the collective will of the people and when it develops an "organ of will as part of the state apparatus there is always the unconditioned demands upon the people. The national state is not "merely an expression of the natural impulse for survival" but has its "spiritual life" which is often characterized by the lust for power, pride, contempt toward the other, and finally the moral autonomy by which the self-deification of the social group is made explicit by its presentation as the source and end of existence."[33] Most of all, the pride of the state includes its pretension to be divine. And perhaps the state resorts to such claims when the people are confronted by the fact that they are limited and finite. In short, for Niebuhr, the collective egotism has to do with the glorification and deification of the state and the exacting of total loyalty from the individuals. Niebuhr argues that the only ethical tradition that can challenge such collective egotism is the ethics of the "prophetic religion" (prophetic Christianity and qualifiedly, Judaism).

In Niebuhr's view of human nature, the aspect of anxiety as a concomitance of freedom is vital. Human beings are both limited and limitless, bound and free and this dialectical nature makes human to be anxious.

> Anxiety is the inevitable concomitant of the paradox of freedom and finiteness in which man is involved. Anxiety is the internal

[29] *Ibid.*, 147.

[30] Reinhold Niebuhr. *The Destiny and Nature of Man.* Vol. 1. (Upper Saddle River: Prentice Hall, 1964), 179.

[31] *Ibid.*

[32] *Ibid.*, 208.

[33] *Ibid., 211.*

> precondition of sin. It is the inevitable spiritual state of man, standing in the paradoxical situation of freedom and finiteness.[34]

According to Niebuhr, anxiety cannot be identified with sin, anxiety is not sin. "Partly because it is its precondition and not actuality, and partly because it is the basis of all human creativity as well as the precondition of sin."[35]

Anxiety is not sin and yet freedom from anxiety is critical to the understanding of human salvation from sin. Whereas freedom from anxiety can happen only by faith in God, this understanding becomes clear when Niebuhr begins to discuss on the important doctrine of the original righteousness.

Niebuhr argues that there is over-exaggeration on the total depravity of human nature in Christian theology due to the literal understanding of the fall story in Genesis as an historical event. Niebuhr makes a distinction between the essential nature of human being and the virtue and perfection that correspond to that nature. In order to show that "sin neither destroys the structure by virtue of which man is man nor yet eliminates the sense of obligation toward the essential nature of man, which is the remnant of his perfection."[36] Niebuhr maintains that the image of God is not lost despite the fall. Rather the original righteousness or perfection is present in sinful human as law. However, Niebuhr places the consciousness of the original righteousness outside of history (in the sense that human being transcends history) but "yet it is in the man who is in the history."[37]

Niebuhr further identities the content of original righteousness with the law of, love." By this he refers to a) the perfect relation of the soul to God in which obedience is transcended by love, trust and confidence, b) the perfect harmony of the soul with itself in all of its desires and impulses and, c) The perfect harmony of life with life.[38] The first concerns with the love of God, the second with the love of self and the last with the love of the neighbour. In Niebuhr's scheme of thought the love of God is foremost and the love of self and the love of other are derivative of their faith and trust in God. Faith in God is integral to the freedom of a person. Further, "faith in the wisdom of God is thus a prerequisite of love because it is the condition without which man is anxious and is driven by his anxiety into vicious circles of self-sufficiency and pride."[39]

The law of love is thus the requirement of human freedom. However, since the law of love is beyond history, Niebuhr asserts that no historic structure of justice can fulfill the law of love. Niebuhr thus holds a pessimistic view about utopia, the idea of ushering in the Kingdom of God here on earth by fulfilling

[34] *Ibid.*, 182.

[35] *Ibid.*, 183.

[36] *Ibid.*, 272.

[37] *Ibid.*, 280.

[38] *Ibid.*, 288.

[39] *Ibid.*, 289.

the law of love. To those utopian proponents Niebuhr has to say "they do not realize that the law of love stands on the edge of history and not in history, that it represents an ultimate and not an immediate possibility."[40] Whereas, in contrast to the view of the total depravity of human nature, the law of love as original righteousness is always present in the human as a possession but now in "the sense of something lacking."[41]

St. Augustine and Martin Luther

Augustine basically understands salvation as God's gift. He believes in the original sin and the universality of sin. He believes in the total depravity of human nature as a result of the fall. According to Augustine, sin is biologically transmitted from parents to the children so that everybody including the new born child is a sinner. No one is innocent in the sight of God. Because of his belief in the original sin, Augustine holds that human being is not able not to sin. This is in contrast to Pelagius who believes that human being has the ability not to commit sin. Pelagius identifies God's grace with human freewill. Grace is the God-given human capacity and the will is "the power of choice, unbiased and neutral. Whereas, Augustine believes in the total depravity of human nature because of the fall of Adam. According to Augustine, Our wills at each moment are not neutral, but better or worse as a result of what has come before."[42] Accordingly he believes that sinners have no ability to obtain salvation on the basis of merits.

Salvation is purely God's gift to the sinner. Salvation for Augustine is possible through faith and this faith is identified as grace, given *gratis,* not because of past good works or foreseen future ones. For Augustine, grace is a God-given thing something that freewill cannot do itself.[43] Augustine is clear, that without this grace, we do not have the ability to do the good that we recognize we ought to do. "Unless the mercy of God in calling precedes, no one can even believe, and so begin to be justified and to receive power to do good works. So grace comes before all merits."[44] At the same time Augustine believes in the doctrine of predestination. Augustine argues that although everyone deserves punishment for sin and yet God in his mercy chooses to save some, to make them "vessels of honour" (Romans 9:21). God calls them knowing fully well that those called will not refuse His call. "He calls the man on whom he has mercy in the way he knows will suit him, so that he will not refuse the call." This is the idea of the "congruous call", the *vocatio congrua.* In fact, Augustine sees in his own calling the nature of the congruous call.

---

[40] *Ibid.*, 298.

[41] *Ibid.*, 296.

[42] Joan O'Grady, *Early Christian Heresies* (New York: Barnes and Noble Books, 1985), 122.

[43] *Ibid.*, 123.

[44] Saint Augustine, *Four Anti-Pelagius Writngs: On Nature and Grace.* Trans. John Mourant and William J. Collinge (Washington D.C.: The Catholic University of America Press, 1992), 60.

Martin Luther like Augustine believes in the total depravity of human nature. In fact, Luther is greatly influenced by St. Augustine and his theology. They both hold the primacy of the individuality of human nature and sin. Likewise salvation is understood in terms of individual salvation. Luther affirms the famous Pauline assertion in Romans, which says "justification by faith alone." Luther's theology and faith is founded and shaped on this cornerstone of God's grace alone. And the only source of theology and faith is scripture. While Erasmus based his theological view on combination of Scripture, church authority, church tradition and human reason, Luther believes only in the authority of the Scripture - *Sola Scriptura.* According to Luther, human reason is totally inadequate and church authority and tradition in opposition to the plain reading of the scriptures is a perversion of the faith.

The debate with Erasmus on the role of freewill amply indicates that Luther does not believe in the role of human freewill on matter pertaining to God and eternal life. Erasmus defines freewill "as a power of the human will by which a man may apply himself to those things that lead to eternal salvation, or turn away from the same."[45] On Erasmus' affirmation on freewill, Luther counters by arguing that freewill makes unnecessary the sacrifice of Christ. "But, what is here left to grace and the Holy Ghost? This is plainly to ascribe divinity to 'free will'! For to will the law and the gospel, not to will sin, and to will death, is possible to divine power alone...."[46]

Luther appeals to Paul in Romans and John in the Gospel in refuting the role of freewill on one hand and on the other in affirming justification by grace through faith alone. It is by God's grace alone that a sinner receives salvation. Human being has no power whatsoever when it comes to matter of salvation. "There is no such thing as merit at all, but all that are justified are justified freely, and this is ascribed to nothing but the grace of God. And when righteousness is given, then the kingdom and eternal life are given with it."[47] So, it is all God's doing none of ours.

Conclusion: Evaluation and Comparison

In so far as the discussion goes it is quite obvious that we have broadly two theological strands of thought whose theological convictions and views do not even come close to each other and whose priorities are as polarized as any other. While liberation theologians in this case, Gutierrez and Cone employ liberation as their main theological theme, Niebuhr, Augustine and Luther did not ever use the term liberation in their theological expressions. This being the case, one might argue that there is no justification for having chosen to examine their works

---

[45] *Ibid.*

[46] Martin Luther, *The Bondage of the Will.* Trans. J. I. Packer & O. R. Johnston (Grand Rapids: Fleming H. Revell), 136.

[47] *Ibid.*, 140.

under the theme of liberation. However, I argue that despite the fact that some of them did not employ liberation in their works, it is still useful for the sake of examining the related themes such as salvation, sin and human freedom or free will, as all of them have dealt with them in their works. I argue that looking at them from this perspective allows us to bring in the theme of liberation as a point of departure on the part of the liberation theologians to view salvation differently - to broaden the Christian concept of salvation, although liberationism is alive in the Old Testament - than it is being understood in traditional Christian theology. Likewise, the theme of liberation allows us to view sin or human freedom for that matter in a much more comprehensive manner than they are being viewed in traditional Christian theology. In other words, what I am trying to argue here is that the examination of the works of these theologians enables us to get into the premise and theological convictions of each of these theologians. And for that purpose, taking the theme of liberation is enormously helpful.

While liberation theologians like Gutierrez and Cone begin their theology with the peoples experience of socio-economic and political exploitations, traditional Christian theology focuses on the experience of individuals. Augustine, Luther and others begin their theology with the assertion of the primacy of the individual. Accordingly, as already discussed in the preceding sections, their understanding of sin and salvation are very individualistic. And they understand them as matters of spiritual concerns that has nothing to do with social situations of the people. They view sin in terms of individual immorality and individual disobedience to God. It is the matter of individual person breaking his/her relationship with God. Further they believe in the total depravity of human nature according to which the human has nothing good except by the grace of God alone. That is the reason why Augustine and Luther do not believe in the human freewill, at least with regard to salvation. Salvation is purely God's free gift.

I would think Reinhold Niebuhr stands in between liberation theologians and Augustine and Luther. By this I mean Niebuhr is closer to Augustine and Luther in so far as Niebuhr understands sometimes sin and salvation in individualistic terms. But Niebuhr is on the other hand closer to Gutierrez and Cone in so far as he recognizes the collective pride or egotism. In this sense, Niebuhr's perception of sin which he identifies as the pride of the state can be identified with liberation theologians' understanding of the collective dimension of sin - the structural and systemic evil of the society that continues to keep the people from enjoying life in its fullness. Of course, unlike Gutierrez and Cone, Niebuhr does not talk about the preferential option of the poor. Further, his understanding of freedom is limited to the freedom of the individual person. Niebuhr should be credited for his views about the original righteousness which he identifies with the law of love as being present in a person as a law and requirement. Christian freedom is thus understood in the light of the loving God, self and neighbour.

Niebuhr is definitely a more complicated theologian than any other. Niebuhr appears on the one hand to be quite pessimistic about human condition and on the other, he speaks so profoundly affirming the positive side of humanity. Niebuhr asserts, "There are no limits to be set in history for the achievement of more universal brotherhood, for the development of more perfect and more inclusive mutual relations....The freedom of man makes it to set any limits of race, sex, or social condition upon the brotherhood which may be achieved in history."[48] It may not be wrong to describe Niebuhr as a "pessimistic optimist"[49] as Robert McAfee Brown calls him. Brown believes that the mixture of grace and sin in Niebuhr's thought, in both individuals and cultures, works as a potentially redemptive rather than an inevitably destructive element in our political life. That is why Brown concludes, "Niebuhr is not an optimist pessimist but a pessimist optimist."[50]

Liberation theologians in this case, Gutierrez and Cone, no doubt question the very theological methods of the existing theologies especially that of the western Christian theologies. For Gutierrez and Cone, the datum for doing theology is the totality of the realities of life. They both situate their theological reflections in the social, economic and political realities of the world especially that of the oppressed and the poor. While Gutierrez works from the perspectives of the poor in Latin America, Cone does so from the context of the black peoples' experience of suffering from centuries of slavery and political discriminations. From the perspectives of the poor and the oppressed, Gutierrez and Cone are rereading the Scriptures to find relevance and meaning for those poor and the oppressed. For them sin is not individualistic, sin has social dimensions. Sin is not merely spiritual, rather sin is very much historical. Sin is thus social and historical. All forms of injustice and exploitation that people experience in their life-situations is a manifestation of sin. Wherever there is oppression, exploitation and unjust structure, systemic sin is actively at work. Liberation from all these oppressive, and unjust structures of the society is then an integral part of the salvific work of God in the world.

Gutierrez equates liberation with salvation. For him liberation is salvation. Whereas, Cone regards liberation as an integral part of salvation. In that sense, for Cone, liberation comes within the larger understanding of salvation. However, both Gutierrez and Cone recognize the seriousness of sin and its far-reaching consequences in human society. As a result they both recognize the necessity for radical liberation from the wretchedness of sin. Resistance and struggle against oppressive forces and forces of domination, Gutierrez and Cone, believe is an integral part of the mission of Jesus Christ. In the words of Gutierrez, in our

---

[48] *Ibid.*, 292.

[49] Reinhold Niebuhr, *The Destiny and Nature of Man.* Vol. 2 (New York: Charles Scribner's Sons, 1943), 85.

[50] *Ibid.*, xiii.

insertion into the process of liberation in which the peoples of Latin America are now engaged, we live out the gift of faith, hope, and charity that makes us disciples of the lord. This experience is ours as well.[51] Jesus Christ is the ground of liberation and so in our struggle for justice and liberation we are participating in extending God's Kingdom here on earth. Of course, God is the author of liberation. And so liberation is a gift of God.

Liberation theology in general has been criticized for adopting Marxist economic analysis and accused of Marxism in religious garb. In the same vein liberation theology is criticized for employing the term liberation on the ground that it advocates and condones violence. In my readings of Gutierrez and Cone it is not apparent to me that any of them is advocating violence or for that matter trying to politically advocate Marxism, despite the fact that they might have employed Marxist analytical tools for understanding the socio-economic reality of the world. It appears to me that both are sincerely engaged in the demands of the gospel: to proclaim the good news to the poor, liberty to the captives and to proclaim life to those who have been deprived. In other words, both are attempting to make the gospel of Jesus Christ meaningful and relevant to the people in the context of the social realities of the people. My criticism against liberation theology concerns with its failure to take into serious consideration the cultural dimension of the people and the ecological issues in its theological reflection. This seems to be the case in the initial stage of liberation theology. Political and socio-economic liberation of the people became the central focus of liberation theology.

In the final analysis, liberation as a theological theme will continue to have its impact on the overall concerns of Christian theology, while many might not choose to employ the term liberation and yet the import of liberation as a theme will continue to be evident in their works, and many more will continue to benefit out of the theme of liberation.

---

[51] Gustavo Gutierrez, *We Drink from the Our Own Wells: the Spiritual Journey of a People* (Maryknoll: Orbis Books, 1984), 5.

12

Prosperity Theology
A Theological Critique

Synopsis

Prosperity theology refers to the understanding of faith that centres on wealth and riches, health and happiness as the blessings from God. It emphasizes on the individual ability, gifts, talents and success. Prosperity theology and prosperity gospel are used interchangeably for the same understanding of Christian faith. Generally, the prosperity gospel is a collective term for a group of teachings that liken Christian faith with material, and particularly financial success. They are mostly popular among charismatic preachers and Christians in the so called evangelical tradition. It is posing a serious challenge to the overall understanding of Christian faith and praxis. This calls for a serious reflection and consideration. The purpose of this chapter is to offer a theological critique on the overall prosperity theology movement. The chapter also briefly looks at the historical origin and development of prosperity theology, its meaning, and the kind of impact it makes to the overall Christian faith and practice.

Introduction

Prosperity theology is posing a serious challenge to the overall understanding of Christian faith and praxis. This calls for a serious reflection and consideration. The main purpose of this chapter is to offer a theological critique on the overall prosperity theology movement. The chapter will also briefly look at the historical origin and development of prosperity theology, its meaning and message, and the kind of impact it makes to the overall Christian faith and practice.

Defining Prosperity Theology

Prosperity theology refers to the understanding of faith that centres on wealth and riches, health and happiness as the blessings from God. It emphasizes on the individual ability, gifts, talents and success. Prosperity theology is sometimes known as prosperity gospel; they are interchangeably used for the same understanding of Christian faith. Generally, the prosperity gospel is a collective term for a certain group of beliefs that liken Christian faith with material, and particularly financial success. They are mostly popular among charismatic preachers and Christians in the so called evangelical tradition.

Prosperity theology is a certain kind of a Christian teaching and is concerned with Christian faith and practice. However, examining the history of its origin, we find that American metaphysical religions known as the New Thought contributed towards the development of prosperity theology, besides others as well.

A Brief History of Prosperity Theology: An Overview

According to David L. Smith, prosperity theology as an advanced and new development "arose as a religious philosophy concomitant to the charismatic renewal of the 1960s."[1] It is possible that the basic philosophy of prosperity theology emerged out of a North American socio-economic (dream) culture. In terms of its forms, they were packaged and marketed worldwide mostly by healing evangelists. And what is considered to be its apparent success in physical healings was extended to the material realm quite naturally and automatically.[2]

Broadly, there are three factors or thoughts which are behind the overall developments of prosperity theology as we know it today.

New Thought

To begin with, prosperity theology had its origin in the tradition of New Thought, a nineteenth-century spiritual movement popular with unorthodox thinkers like Ralph Waldo Emerson and William James.[3] New Thought gives priority on spiritual and mind over physical and matter. It is learned that not all practitioners of New Thought, are Christians. They generally held the divinity of the individual human being and the priority of mind over matter. In other words, if you could correctly channel your mental energy, you could harness its material

---

[1] David L. Smith, *Theologies of Success: Handbook of Contemporary Theology* (Illinois: Victor Books, 1992), 188.

[2] *Ibid.*

[3] Tara Isabella Burton, "The prosperity gospel, explained: Why Joel Osteen believes that prayer can make you rich: The long, strange history of a quintessentially American theology," 3. https://www.vox.com/.../prosperity-gospel-explained-why-joel-osteen-believes-prayer (7/1/2018).

results. New Thought, also known as the "mind cure," took many forms: from interest in the occult to splinter-Christian denominations like Christian Science to the development of the "talking cure" at the root of psychotherapy.[4]

New Thought represents a cluster of thinkers and metaphysical religions that emerged in the 1880s and early 1900s. The influential proponents of New Thought include those individuals and churches associated with the International New Thought Alliance (INTA), founded in 1899, and American metaphysical religions affiliated with Phineas Quimby, Mary Baker Eddy, and Emma Curtis Hopkins.[5] "New Thought adherents shared the idea that God is Mind, humans are spiritual beings, and thoughts can manifest change in the physical world."[6]

Generally, the movement claims that there is some "unity of God and human mind" which has the potential to manifest change in the world. All New Thought writers affirm that thought has substance. In the words of Ralph Waldo Trine, "Thoughts are forces, the most vital and powerful in the universe, that they have form and substance and power."[7] According to this idea, thinking about success could lead to materialization of success in the real form and substance.

According to Catherine Bowler, three aspects of New Thought became foundational to the formation of prosperity mental magic.[8] First, it taught that there is essential unity between God and humanity. Essentially, there is no difference between the two; humanity's separation from the divine was only a matter of degree. In Christian terms, this meant that "'salvation' would not be an act imposed from above by God, but rather an act of drawing out humanity's potential."[9] Second, New Thought taught that the world should be re-imagined as thought rather than substance. The basic assumption is the understanding that the spiritual world formed absolute reality, while the material world was the mind's projection. It must be noted that unlike Christian Science, New Thought never denied the reality of the material world, but saw it as contingent upon the mind. According to this understanding, right standing with the divine required sacred alignment, a mystical connection. This relationship is popularly

---

[4] *Ibid.*

[5] Dawn Hutchinson, "New Thoughts Prosperity Theology and Its Influence on American Ideas of Success," in *Nova, Religio: The Journal of Alternative and Emergent Religions*, Vol. 18, Issue 2, 2014, 29.

[6] *Ibid.*

[7] Quoted in Hutchinson, "New Thoughts Prosperity Theology and Its Influence on American Ideas of Success," 32.

[8] Catherine Bowler, "Blessed: A History of the American Prosperity Gospel," (PhD. Dissertation, Graduate School of Duke University, 2010), 43. https://dukespace.lib.duke.edu/dspace/bitstream/handle/10161/2297/D_Bowler_Catherine_a_201005.pdf (7/1/2018).

[9] *Ibid.* Cf. Hutchinson, "New Thoughts Prosperity Theology and Its Influence on American Ideas of Success," 29.

described by noted historian Sydney Ahlstrom as "harmonial religion."[10] Third, New Thought argued that human beings shared in God's creative power to create by means of thought. It is by their thinking that people shaped their own worlds, just as God had created the world using thought. New Thought affirmed that positive thoughts produced positive circumstances, and likewise, negative thoughts produced negative situations.[11] In the words of Bowler, "These three features—a high anthropology, the priority of spiritual reality, and the creationist power of positive thought—formed the main presuppositions of the developing mental magic."[12]

The consequential effect of New Thought, though, "was the quintessentially American idea that the individual was responsible for his or her own happiness, health, and situation in life, and that applying mental energy in the appropriate direction was sufficient to cure any ills."[13]

In the light of this, one of the New Thought thinkers Ralph Waldo Trine, paints an optimistic outlook for his readers when he exhorted them to "See yourself in a prosperous condition. Affirm that you will before long be in a prosperous condition."[14]

In addition to influencing Christian movements like the prosperity gospel, New Thought has made a far reaching impact on the "secular" aspects of American life. The tradition of positive-thinking self-help in America as well, is influenced by the New Thought.

Pro-Capitalist Protestant Work Ethic

A second factor behind the development of the American prosperity gospel was the teaching of the "Protestant work ethic." The leading proponent of this Protestant work ethic was none other than Max Weber. Weber's *The Protestant Ethic and the Spirit of Capitalism,* which was written in 1905, traced what he saw as the specifically Protestant approach to labor as integral to the development of capitalism and industrialization. In his introduction to *The Protestant Ethic*, Weber points out that "greed and the desire for personal gain, as well as trading and other economic enterprises designed to make a profit, exist everywhere and have been true of people in all walks of life and in all cultures of the earth. This human impulse to acquire wealth does not necessarily have anything to do with

[10] Sydney Ahlstrom, *A Religious History of the American People* (London: Yale University Press, 2004), 1019.

[11] Beryl Satter, *Each Mind a Kingdom: American Women, Sexual Purity and the New Thought Movement, 1875–1920* (Berkeley: University of California Press, 1999), 2.

[12] Bowler, "Blessed: A History of the American Prosperity Gospel," 43.

[13] Burton, "The Prosperity Gospel, Explained," 4.

[14] Quoted in Burton, "The Prosperity Gospel, Explained," 4.

capitalism."[15] Weber then went on to define capitalism. Virgil Hardgerink puts across succinctly Weber's definition of capitalism in the following words:

> As an economic action that expects to make a profit based on peaceful and mutually beneficial exchanges. He suggests that religious piety and capitalistic acquisition are compatible, and that both traits are characteristic of many of the most important Churches and sects in the history of Protestantism. He notes that in French Huguenot Churches monks and business men were particularly numerous. And the Spaniards knew that the Calvinism of the Dutch promoted trade which coincided with the capitalistic development of the Netherlands.[16]

Burton describes how Weber makes a historical analysis that finds the correlation between Protestant Calvinist's idea of predestination and the material success through hard work.

> In Weber's historical analysis, Protestant Calvinists — who generally believe in the idea of "predestination," or that God has chosen some people to be saved and others damned — felt the need to justify their own sense of themselves as the saved. They looked both for outward signs of God's favor (i.e., through material success) and for ways to express inward virtue (i.e., through hard work). While the *accuracy* of Weber's analysis is still debated by scholars, it nevertheless tells us a lot about cultural attitudes at the time Weber wrote it.[17]

What seemed to be generally obvious was the correlation between hard work and the material reward, "the idea that working hard and receiving material, financial reward for that work was integral to a certain strand of Protestant Christianity had entered the public consciousness."[18] This is still the general understanding of many even today. It is pretty obvious that Protestants and citizens of predominately Protestant countries tend to link labor with personal satisfaction more than those of other religious traditions.

Joer Rieger asserts that there is a strong connection between Christianity and capitalism.[19] Economics is not simply about money. It is more than that. In fact, our life is shaped and influenced by economics much more pervasively than we think. Our life and the way we think are greatly influenced by economic matters. Therefore, faith and religion are not exclusive to each other. Rather

---

[15] Virgil Hardgerink, "The Protestant Ethic of Prosperity," 1. http://www.christianitytoday.com/history/issues/issue-14/protestant-ethic-of-prosperity.html (21/1/2018).

[16] Hardgerink, "The Protestant Ethic of Prosperity," 1.

[17] Burton, "The Prosperity Gospel, Explained," 4.

[18] *Ibid.*

[19] Joerg Rieger, "Christianity, Capitalism, and Desire: Can Religion Make a Difference," in *Union Seminary Quarterly Review,* 64, no. 1, 2013, 1.

they are closely connected to each other. Substantiating his point, Rieger argues that prosperity theology represents the working relationship between faith and religion. Prosperity theology promises unprecedented wealth and happiness to the people. "The Gospel of prosperity resembles neo-capitalism in that it preaches limitless success endorsed by God, beginning with the elites moving from the top down. While this approach works for the few, there is little evidence that it has worked for the many."[20]

Charismatic Pentecostal Churches in America

The third and final factor behind the development of the prosperity gospel was the development of charismatic Pentecostal churches in America. Charismatic Pentecostal is an umbrella term for a decentralized group of churches — comprising over 700 churches.[21] These churches are characterized by an emphasis on what is known as "spiritual gifts" (or *charisms,* from which the term "charismatic" is drawn). Burton explains the characteristics as well as the implications of Pentecostal faiths to the prosperity gospel as follows:

> A worshipful Christian might experience, for example, the gift of healing, or might suddenly start speaking "in tongues." This tradition of worship meant that, for a believer, the idea that God would manifest Himself to the faithful in concrete, miraculous ways *in the here and now* was more prevalent than it would be in, say, a mainline Episcopalian church. In addition, the decentralized nature of these churches also meant that individual leaders, many of whom practiced faith healing or similar practices, had a particularly strong effect on their congregations and could build up individual personal followings.[22]

Traditionally, early Pentecostals were world affirming - the material world. Though better known for their "heavenly minded experiences of ecstatic worship, speaking in tongues, and focus on the Lord's imminent return, Pentecostals also distinguished themselves with radical claims about God's terrestrial blessings."[23] Following their radical evangelical predecessors, they preached a "four-fold" gospel of divine healing, personal salvation, baptism of the Holy Spirit, and Christ's soon return. Moreover they believed the human material body as a site of divine healing, blessing, and empowerment. Accordingly, John G. Lake, the noted Zion City evangelist observed that salvation was "an all-inclusive word, including all that God does for the spirit, soul, and body of man."[24]

---

[20] *Ibid.*

[21] Burton, "The Prosperity Gospel, Explained," 4.

[22] Burton, "The Prosperity Gospel, Explained," 3.

[23] Bowler, "Blessed: A History of the American Prosperity Gospel," 41.

[24] Quoted in Bowler, "Blessed: A History of the American Prosperity Gospel," 41.

In the context of Africa, in order to define the Pentecostal movement, the following six 'avenues' are listed by Gifford and Nogueira-Godsey.

> The first avenue is called 'motivation' and focuses on the 'drive and determination' that a positive message can create in terms of attitude. The second is 'entrepreneurship' which is overtly encouraged in most of the churches adhering to 'winning ways.' The third avenue draws attention to 'practical life skills' and includes focus on hard work, saving, investing, organising time etc. The fourth path towards success goes through the practice of 'sowing' or 'planting a seed' which points to donating funds to the church expecting that God in miraculous ways will reward you many times what you invest. The fifth avenue explains that in order to be prosperous the believer has to associate themselves with 'the man of God,' the leader chosen as a medium for God's blessing, both spiritually and materially. Finally, the pastor has the power to 'deliver followers from evil spirits', spirits who seek to distort the progress and success of the believer.[25]

The six avenues listed comprising attitude for positive change, entrepreneurship, skills, giving as investment, associating with a charismatic leader, and faith in the minister's power generally characterize the Pentecostal movement that are associated with prosperity theology everywhere.

In summary, these three strands, New Thought, Protestant Capitalist work ethics, and Pentecostal churches, collided throughout the twentieth century, as the prosperity gospel came into being. It started — like the "work ethic" Max Weber described — as a way to justify why, during the gilded Age, some people were rich and others poor. One of the early prosperity gospel proponents, Baptist preacher Russell H. Conwell, told his mostly-destitute congregation in 1915: "I say you ought to be rich; you have no right to be poor."[26] Prosperity gospel preachers like Conwell, viewed that individuals were responsible for their unfortunate state of life, whether rich or poor. Instead of blaming structural inequality, they would blame the perceived failures of the individual.

While all these factors are behind the development of prosperity theology, it is worth noting that, it was in Pentecostal churches, with their focus on immediate spiritual gifts and the power of God to confer favor (and wellness) immediately, that the prosperity gospel as we know it today took hold.[27] Behind this brand of Pentecostal movement is the "Word of Faith" movement. This movement represents the Pentecostal form of New Thought that teaches positive faith which

---

[25] Quoted in Tomas Sundnes Drenen, "Weber, Prosperity and the Protestant Ethic: Some Reflections on Pentecostalism and Economic Development," *Swedish Missiological Themes,* 100, 3 (2012), 325.

[26] Quoted in Burton, "The Prosperity Gospel, Explained," 5.

[27] Burton, "The Prosperity Gospel, Explained," 3.

is central to financial and material success. The Word of Faith movement emerged in the late 20th century with E. W. Kenyon as its founder, who came under the influence of metaphysical New Thought teachings of Phineas Quimby. But, it was Kenneth Hagin, a student of Kenyon, who became the most influential proponent of prosperity theology and through him the Word of Faith movement grew dramatically.[28] Hagin founded a Bible institute, the Rhema Bible Training Center in 1974 in Tulsa, Oklahoma and trained many ministers in the new form of faith. It's estimated that by 2008, the Rhema Center has trained nearly 30,000 ministers.[29]

Today, through the works of a number of influential figures like Kenneth Hagin, Kenneth and Gloria Copeland, Oral Roberts, Joel Osteen, T. D. Jakes, Creflo Dollar, I. V. Hilliard, Benny Hinn, Joyce Myers, Frederick Price, Eddie Long, Pat Robertson, and many others, prosperity theology is being promoted aggressively in America and beyond.[30] They are known for their high profile and celebrity lifestyles; they are business-savvy and unabashed about their "million-dollar personal portfolios and lavish lifestyles." As Bowler aptly describes, "Charming though not effusive, polished but not slick, these favored few could as easily have appeared on *Larry King Live* as behind their megachurch Sunday pulpits. Podcasts, Internet streaming, and daily television programming carried their sermons to millions."[31]

In the words of Shayne Lee, "The timely spread of the prosperity gospel in the 1980s resonated with millions of Americans already hypnotized by the burgeoning consumer culture of the Reagan era and the explosion of wealth inflamed by the rise of Wall Street, producing unprecedented financial prosperity."[32]

God as a banker

Proponents of prosperity theology have no problem envisaging God as a kind of banker. Throughout the twentieth century, God was portrayed "as a kind of banker, dispensing money to the deserving, with Jesus as a model business executive."[33] Both of these characterizations were, at times, literal. Take for example, in 1936,

---

[28] Kenneth Hagin also wrote books on prosperity theology, started Word and Faith magazine and introduced Radio ministries too. Bowler, "Blessed: A History of the American Prosperity Gospel," 24; cf. Shayen Lee, "Prosperity Theology: T. D. Jakes and the Gospel of the Almighty Dollar," in *Cross Currents*, 57 no. 2, Summer 2007; 227-229.

[29] Bowler, "Blessed: A History of the American Prosperity Gospel," 24.

[30] Apart from North America, prosperity gospel movement is making a strong impact in Africa, Latin America, and Asia. Bowler, "Blessed: A History of the American Prosperity Gospel," 232ff; Cf. Imas, J. B. Mboya, "Gift Challenges and Transforms Prosperity Gospel," *in African Ecclesial Review,* Vol. 58, Nos. 1 & *2*, 2016,

[31] Bowler, "Blessed: A History of the American Prosperity Gospel," 4.

[32] Shayen Lee, "Prosperity Theology: T. D. Jakes and the Gospel of the Almighty Dollar," 228.

[33] *Ibid.* 3.

New Thought mystic and founder of the Unity Church Charles Fillmore rewrote Psalm 23 to read, "The Lord is my banker/my credit is good."[34] Similarly in 1925, advertising executive Bruce Bowler wrote *The Man Nobody Knows* to argue that Jesus was the first great capitalist. The literal money quote reads, "Some day ... someone will write a book about Jesus. Every businessman will read it and send it to his partners and his salesmen. For it will tell the story of the founder of modern business."[35]

The Message of Prosperity Theology

According to Catherine Bowler, there are primarily four markers of prosperity theology.[36] First, faith is at the center of the movement. The faith of the individual believer becomes the focal point and it is the faith that is regarded to be the mover of things, including receiving material blessings, health, happiness and success in return. "It conceived of faith as an 'activator,' a power given to believers that bound and loosed spiritual forces and turned the spoken word into reality."[37] In other words, what counts is the quality and depth of a believer's faith. The rest of the markers including material wealth, personal health and success are the by-products of faith. Wealth and health constitute the second and third markers respectively of the prosperity gospel. According to their teaching, a believer's faith is demonstrated in wealth and health. "It could be measured in both in the wallet—one's personal wealth—and in the body—one's personal health—making material reality the measure of the success of immaterial faith."[38] Finally, the movement conceived that the faith of a believer ultimately leads to victory. The power of faith is experienced even here and now on this earth and nothing can prevent believers from living a victorious life. "Believers trusted that culture held no political, social, or economic impediment to faith, and no circumstance could stop believers from living in total victory here on earth."[39]

Though its origins lay in the late nineteenth century, the prosperity gospel took root mainly in the Pentecostal revivals of the post-World War II years. It reached maturity by the late 1970s as a robust pan-denominational movement, garnering a national platform and a robust network of churches, ministries, publications, and media outlets. As noted, generally speaking, faith, wealth, health, and victory or success served as the hallmarks of this American phenomenon.

---

[34] Quoted in Burton, "The Prosperity Gospel, Explained," 3.

[35] Quoted in Burton, "The Prosperity Gospel, Explained," 3.

[36] Bowler, "Blessed: A History of the American Prosperity Gospel," 3.

[37] *Ibid.*

[38] *Ibid.*

[39] *Ibid.*

Tithing as an Investment

One of the central teachings of prosperity gospel was the idea of tithing, or giving money to the church, ideally one's "first fruits" — or initial earnings. This money, many prosperity gospel preachers promised, was an investment. In other words, tithing is understood as investment in business sense rather than understanding giving as a faith commitment to God. The focus is on receiving more in return out of tithing. The understanding is that by showing faith, congregation members could have a "hundredfold" return on their investment, a reference to a verse in the Gospel of Mark about those who suffer for Christ receiving a hundredfold what they have lost (Mark 10:30). In the light of this, Ken Copeland could write in his *Laws of Prosperity*, "Do you want a hundredfold return on your money? Give and let God multiply it back to you. No bank in the world offers this kind of return! Praise the Lord!"[40] According to this view, tithing is a financially responsible thing to do. It's a demonstration of faith as well as a shrewd investment. It is also a wager on the understanding that God acts in the here and now to reward those with both faith and a sufficiently developed work ethic.[41]

A Theological Critique

Individual Success and Structural Inequality

Prosperity theology affirms physical health, wealth and riches. It affirms positive thinking as well as developing a positive outlook, developing personal potentials, etc.

Critics of prosperity theology are highly critical of the movement for promoting capitalistic ideology, consumerist culture and lavish lifestyles. Most of all, for compromising social justice concerns. Structures and systems of the society are hardly taken into consideration. When structural injustices and oppressions are the main causes of poverty and sufferings of many, prosperity gospel movement remains silent on this important issue. Rather, it proclaims gospel of individual ability and success. Success is lauded as the outcome of individual person's performance.

James Cone, who is regarded as the father of black liberation theology, explained how Jakes's conservative message avoids challenging those in power and this criticism could very well represent the general critique against prosperity theology.

> T. D. Jakes represents a black man who has strong crossover appeal but he also represents blacks who preach a gospel that... would make it very difficult for him to have an understanding of the gospel that would be conflictive and engaging politically in a sharp sense that

[40] Quoted in Burton, "The Prosperity Gospel, Explained," 5.

[41] *Ibid.*

would cause people to be challenged in a way that makes them feel uncomfortable.[42]

Jakes and many other prosperity gospel preachers like him are the metaphor of a new church that energizes audiences with ecstatic worship experiences, lively music, and prosperity preaching. They are business savvy and culture affirming. They and their brand of church unabashedly embrace modern high tech and utilize state-of-the-art technology. They and their ministries are adorned with the most colourful costumes and glitterati of the day. This brand of churches, by and large, prefer to remain officially non-denominational, though generally, most identify with Pentecostal denominations.[43] What distinguishes them is their ability to offer a vibrant otherworldly worship experience and a this-worldly message and ministry.[44]

One of the main problems with such Christianity is that, it does not work with the common masses. The majority people are left behind as the workers are often left behind in neo-liberal capitalism. It is also true with the middle class; more and more middle class are left out by neoliberal capitalism as it benefits only the rich few. "The other problem is that Christianity, which shaped by capitalism promotes the image of God that have fairly little in common with what we know of the God of Israel and the God of Jesus Christ."[45]

There is what is known as the claim for the common good. The pro-capitalist camp often makes a tall claim that creating wealth at the top is meant for the benefit of all. It is said that "'since the rising tide is going to lift all boats,' increasing prosperity of the super-rich is seen as the good sign for the country, even if it happens to fall in times of trouble for everyone else."[46] On the contrary, we are rather witnessing the ill impacts the neoliberal economy has upon the majority people at the bottom. Rather than benefiting everyone, the production of wealth at the top has resulted in the exclusion of more and more people from the benefit of the economy. When we examine the Scripture in regards to the common good, the Bible seems to suggest otherwise. St Paul advises the struggling community to suffer together and to help one another. "If one member suffers, all suffer together with it," (1Cor. 12:26). St Paul elaborates his intentions as follows: "On the contrary, those parts of the body that seem to be weaker are indispensable, and the parts that we think are less honourable we treat with special honor. And the parts that are unpresentable are treated with special modesty," (1 Cor. 12:22-23).

What is obvious is that one cannot expect to build the common good following the pro-capitalist's systems, from top down; the reverse should be the

---

[42] Quoted in Shayne Lee, "Prosperity Theology," 231.

[43] Bowler, "Blessed: A History of the American Prosperity Gospel," 19.

[44] Shayne Lee, "Prosperity Theology," 235.

[45] Rieger, Joerg, "Christianity, Capitalism, and Desire," 2.

[46] *Ibid.*, 4.

case, from bottom up. This is indeed, the overall expectations and teachings of the Bible throughout. The concerns for the poor, the needy, the stranger, the weak, the orphan, the downtrodden, etc., are categorically stipulated and charged in the Bible. The classic text is the Nazareth manifesto: "'The Spirit of the Lord is on me, because he has anointed me to preach good news to the poor. He has sent me to proclaim freedom for the prisoners and recovery of sight for the blind, to release the oppressed, to proclaim the year of the Lord's favour'" (Luke 4:18-19). With much certainty, one can proclaim that God is interested with the uplifting and liberating of these so called the least in the society. "Just as you did it to one of the least of these who are members of my family, you did it to me," (Matthew 25: 40).

Imas J. B. Mboya in his incisive article "Gift Challenges and Transforms Prosperity Gospel," offers a six point criticism against prosperity theology and I would like to reiterate them further here. "The Gospel of prosperity, especially when it emphasizes that material prosperity flows from the depth and quality of one's faith in God, undermines the following elements: The true worship of God; call and ministry; the gift of communion; the dignity and identity of the human person and the mission of the Church."[47]

God the Proper Object of Worship

The Bible clearly states that the proper object of worship is God alone and nothing else (cf. Matt 4:10). God, from the very beginning, is opposed to any worship of objects that have been created by human beings (cf. Acts 17:29). It is obvious the excessive love for money or wealth that is usually associated with the prosperity gospel is certainly a form of idolatry (cf. Col 3:5). The Gospel of prosperity has the subtle tendency to mask idolatry and false faith (cf. Luke 4:5-7). True Christian giving arises in thankful response to God who loved us first (cf. John 3:16), to Christ (cf. Gal 2:20) and to the neighbour (cf. 2 Cor 8:5, Gal 5:14 and Rom 12:1-2). The intent of giving is very significant. It is wrong to give or tithe in order that one might receive more in return rather than as a thankful response to God's blessings. "The human desire for physical things such as food, property, money, among others, is in fact a desire for the fulfilling beauty of the maker of those physical works of creation. These objects of human craving reflect the glory of God who truly deserves our worship."[48]

The Gospel of the Cross

Central to Christian faith is the cross - the suffering and death of Jesus on the cross. Prosperity theology, emphasizing so much on success and victory, to a large extent ignores the Gospel of the cross. It is true that physical well-being and

---

[47] Imas, J. B. Mboya, "Gift Challenges and Transforms Prosperity Gospel," *in African Ecclesial Review,* Vol. 58, Nos. 1 & 2, 2016, 35.

[48] *Ibid.*

happiness is integral to the Gospel of Jesus Christ. Jesus said, "I came that you may have life, fullness of life," (John 10:10). At the same time, He also asked his followers to live a life of self- denial (cf. Luke 14:33). There is a clear warning sounded to the believers of the dangers of the desire for riches and how it plunges people into ruin and destruction (cf. 1 Tim 6:9). Jesus urges us to live according to the Spirit not for flesh (cf. Rom 8:13). In as much as Christian life is about joy, happiness and victory, it is also about pain, suffering, sickness, and difficulties. We are united with Christ through these experiences. God is often encountered in moments of suffering and grief. The story of Job is a vivid reminder of this reality. It is a powerful message of the gift of faith in moments of suffering. "Embracing suffering or persecution as Job did enables us to suffer and die with Christ so that we may be raised to His glory by God the Father."[49] Of course, one should be careful to distinguish such suffering from the experiences of suffering due to structural inequality and oppression – suffering due to injustices. The prosperity gospel seems to ignore this truth about suffering. True freedom is found neither in health nor wealth but in surrender to and trust in God.

The Spirit of Community in the Church

One of the significant aspects of Christian faith that the gospel of prosperity undermines is the spirit of community in the church. Generally, "Those who allegedly obtain material wealth as a sign of blessing from God tend to classify themselves in a higher social status than those who have not received wealth."[50] There is a strong tendency to regard the poor and the majority who are at the bottom to be without God's blessings. To classify members of the church, based on their material endowments does not represent the true character of the church of God.[51] It rather perpetuates disunity in the church. This disunity leads to tensions and marginalization in the larger community. Additionally, it must be noted that prosperity theology teaches a materialistic view of the church. The church is thus only regarded as useful insofar as, it meets the material needs and expectations of the believers. One of the importance of having a church as a community is to nurture God-given potentialities towards the service of God and others. Without this community, a believer becomes a spiritual wanderer. Fellowship in the community is vital to encourage and strengthen one another's faith and the capacity to demonstrate faith in good works.

---

[49] *Ibid.*

[50] *Ibid.*, 36.

[51] According to the studies conducted in the US, megachurches of the prosperity gospel movement cater more to the middle class and upper class church goers and not the majority working class communities. "In 1985, an analysis of 23 top-rated religious programs found that prosperity televangelists catered to the upwardly mobile and middle class, rather than the working class (with the exception of blue-collar favorite Rex Humbard)." Bowler, "Blessed: A History of the American Prosperity Gospel," 230.

A One-person Centred Movement

Prosperity theology which gives importance to a one-person leadership undermines the gift of ministry. By and large, prosperity theology is a one-person centred movement in the sense that the church exits and revolves around the charismatic leader or minister. Practically, it becomes a one-person show. It undermines "the collective contribution of God's people working together, sharing their gifts for the common good."[52] On the contrary, the leader is treated with absolute reverence and authority. As a result, most of such movements assume to appear cultic. Mboya puts across this truth powerfully in the following words:

> Ideally, every gift and every member is needed for the Church to achieve its God-given purpose. However, prosperity Gospel ministers assume a "celebrity culture," where the leader is regarded as an indispensable authority of the Gospel message and manager of all of Church resources. In the process, the human agency becomes an end in itself. The Gospel is given by God as a gift. Ministry is the agency through which the Gospel is enabled to reach out to those who need it. The minister is, therefore, simply an agent. However, when the agent is regarded more than the message, then human pride soon sets in and disrupts the message and authority of the Church. This pride is what makes some ministers to exercise leadership without accountability (cf. Heb 13:17; 3:13). Humility goes hand in hand with Christian ministry (cf. Jn 3:30). In genuine ministry, Jesus Christ increases as the servants decrease.[53]

The source of joy in human life is Jesus Christ

One of the core aspects of Christian faith is God's invitation to us to be faithful to and find joy in Him. It is absolutely critical to note that our faithfulness to God does not always bring about material prosperity. Additionally, we need to recognize the difference between happiness and joy. While it is true that material blessings could offer happiness in this world, true joy can be experienced in and through Christ alone. "Happiness is fleeting, but joy is always present even in the middle of life's turmoils. We attain joy when we centre our lives around Jesus Christ, who is the source of life (cf. Jn 14:6)."[54] A serious problem with prosperity theology is to regard and measure joy and happiness in materialistic terms. In like manner, faithfulness is often directly linked with material rewards from God. Similarly, the success of a church is measured in terms of the number of congregants who

---

[52] Mboya, "Gift Challenges and Transforms Prosperity Gospel," 36; Cf. Bowler, "Blessed: A History of the American Prosperity Gospel," 5.

[53] Mboya, "Gift Challenges and Transforms Prosperity Gospel," 37.

[54] *Ibid.*

attend its services and by the amount of money they contribute. The ministers in such churches "parade their wealth and regard themselves as successful by the exorbitant lifestyles they lead. The measure of success of their ministry work is seen in the expensive cars, houses, clothes and many travels and endorsements abroad."[55] This is certainly not how Jesus exemplified and taught his disciples to be. Jesus said, "Foxes have holes and birds of the air have nests, but the Son of Man has no place to lay his head," (Matt. 8:20). Contrary to the teaching of Jesus Christ, the ministers and evangelists have embraced material wealth as their security, rather than the Lord God (cf. Matt 6:19ff). They teach the members how to get rich and become popular, rather than preaching the gospel. They centre their sermons on carefully selected favourite Scriptural passages that speak positively of wealth and riches.

God's Grace and Mercy

In Christian life and experience, we believe that we are sustained by God's grace and mercy alone. Unfortunately, prosperity theology severely undermines this truth. "It propagates a *quid-pro-quo* relationship with God."[56] It tends to assume that God's faithfulness to us is dependent on our faithfulness to Him and vice versa. As such, God becomes an instrument in the hands of people and an object of human manipulation. God the giver and sustainer is regarded less than the gifts of God themselves. In other words, prosperity theology elevates God's gifts above God, the giver. On the contrary, the sole purpose of human existence is to glorify God and it is in glorifying God that the value of a human being's life rests. This is possible only when we live by following God's will as revealed in Scripture. In this way, the soul and life of an individual is ordered by God and not the passing fancies of material property.[57]

Prosperity theology as we know it today therefore needs a serious reconsideration. The Gospel of Jesus Christ cannot be compromised nor reduced to material success and personal ability, gifts and talents. There are more questions than answers still lingering in the minds of many believers. Jonathan Baer aptly remarks:

> In an environment of relentless claims of miracles and changed lives, outsized expectations of endless and appropriable divine abundance create palpable excitement, but one suspects there is a deep well of sadness, fear, and personal anxieties. Unseen and unheard, forcibly silenced by a theology that insists the only plausible reason for their inability to grasp money, power, and health is their own failure to hold onto true faith, these folks carry on in the hope of better results or

---

[55] *Ibid.*

[56] *Ibid.*, 38.

[57] *Ibid.*

> slink away disillusioned.... If the power is in your hands and the results don't materialize, what then? Who do you have to blame but yourself? What does that do to one's faith in God?[58]

Conclusion

It is simply not possible to ignore the pervasive influence of prosperity theology today. The marks of prosperity theology such as happiness, wealth, healing and success are no doubt manifestations of God's blessings. Throughout Scripture we know God promises the people of Israel and every believer material blessings, physical wellbeing as well as success. We see God blessing people, and promising to bless people. At times, all these blessings are conditioned by their obedience to God. In all this, faith matters. Faith is at the centre of prosperity gospel. By faith, one can claim all the riches in the world. The depth and quality of a believer's faith is indispensable in prosperity gospel. However, to measure one's quality of faith in terms of material wealth and success is problematic. Such understanding reduces faith to as well as equates it with material success.

Though prosperity could be a sign of God's blessings to the people, what ultimately matters is how one receives them. As noted above, centring on individual's faith, ability and gifts masked the stark reality of our society characterized by poverty, disparities between the rich and the poor and suffering largely due to structural or systemic inequalities that exist in the world. Prosperity theology unfortunately refuses to address this vital issue and conveniently blame the faithlessness of the people as the cause of all their sufferings. Such understanding of faith, counts every material success as God's blessings, when that is not true. Many have amassed wealth and riches by unjust means and corrupt practices thereby perpetuating unjust systems in the society. Many have become rich and wealthy only because of the unjust structures and system which favour them. Jonathan Baer sums up the problem associated with it when he says that prosperity theology "has ridden several major cultural currents: incorrigible optimism, individualism, the consumer culture of advanced capitalism, our coddled self-esteem, and an undying conviction in the world-changing power of one's personal will."[59]

It is not right to equate abundant life with material wealth and to measure in terms of material success. Such understanding of theology poses a serious challenge to the overall understanding of Christian faith and life. Abundant life promised to us in the Bible is much more than that. Joy and happiness promised in the Bible is much more than what material success could provide us. Abundant life is not

---

[58] Jonathan Baer, "Book Review: Blessed: A History of the American Prosperity Gospel, by Kate Bowler" https://www.9marks.org/review/blessed-history-american-prosperity-gospel/ (15/02/2018).

[59] *Ibid.*

about what we have, what we get and what we claim. Ultimately, abundant life is about what we receive as a gift from the Lord and to live knowing we are stewards of the blessings of God.

What is critical is to know that we will not automatically receive material blessings and to acknowledge that we can be remarkably blessed, and live an abundant life, in the midst of difficult circumstances. Poverty and experiences of suffering in life can never overcome the prosperity that God provides for us in Christ. Abundant life in the Bible is about shalomic wellbeing – a life where peace, wholeness, completeness, justice, harmony, love, tranquillity and equality prevail.

13

A Theological Response to Corruption

Introduction

Corruption is likened with cancer. Like cancer spreads in a human body, corruption is wide spread in our society. Corruption is everywhere and in every level of life. From top to bottom, every layer is affected by corruption. Corruption is certainly a global phenomenon and no country is totally free from this problem. Secondly, corruption has existed from the very beginning of human existence in the world in different forms. Historically, however, corruption is said to be related to the "beginning of the creation of law and the state and was already in the antiquity considered an evil, which negatively affects the public administration and the functioning of the political system. The earliest records of corruption date back to the thirteenth century BC, to the time of the Assyrian civilization. From the found plates, written in cuneiform, the archaeologists managed to discern how and who accepted bribes."[1] What is alarming though is that today, the breadth, wide and depth of corruption have enormously increased. This has resulted in destroying the social fabric of the countries. We know that corruption has "permeated our national ethos, politics, civil society, public and private sectors of business and commerce, our educational system, moral preferences and the entire

[1] Štefan Šumah (February 21st 2018). "Corruption, Causes and Consequences," Trade and Global Market, Vito Bobek, Intech Open, DOI: 10.5772/intechopen. 72953. Available from: https://www.intechopen.com/books/trade-and-global-market/corruption-causes-and-consequences (25/04/2020).

economic machinery of our society."[2] Almost every sphere of our society and every walk of our life is infected with the cancer of corruption. From local leaders to central ministers, from peons to top bureaucrats, police officials, lawyers, judges, everyone is guilty of corruption. Without bribery, it is almost impossible to get things done. The service sectors like healthcare and education, NGOs, sports and entertainment business, etc. are all affected by corruption. We are painfully aware that church and religious institutions are not free from corruption, either. In fact, corruption is so pervasive in our society that it has become almost like part of our life; it has become a way of life. This is the tragedy of our faith as well as our life today.

Defining Corruption

What is corruption? It is not easy defining corruption. The term corruption, according to *Vocabulary.com Dictionary,* derives from the Latin root, *corrumpere,* which means "to break."[3] It refers to the breaking of integrity, morality, dishonesty of every kind, debasement and depravity. *Merriam-Webster*, likewise, lists the following as definition of corruption:[4]

a) dishonest or illegal behavior especially by powerful people (such as government officials or police officers); b) inducement to wrong by improper or unlawful means (such as bribery); c) a departure from the original or from what is pure or correct (such as corruption of a text or computer files); d) decay, decomposition (such as a corruption of carcass).

In the history, under Roman law the criminal offence of corruption was defined as "giving, receiving and claiming benefits in order to influence the official in connection with his work."[5] At the narrower sense corruption refers to the "misuse of public office for private gain."[6] According to this understanding corruption takes place whenever, public officials misuse their authority either for monetary or non-monetary gain for themselves, for their relatives, friends or acquaintances, etc. The broader view of corruption includes "the abuse of power

---

[2] Shaji George Kochuthara, "Indian Ethos and the Culture of Corruption: Moral/Psychological Perspective," in Francis Gonsalves and Shalini Mulackal, eds, *Corruption in Public Life: A Theological Response* (Bangalore: Indian Theological Association and Asian Trading Corporation, 2013), 68.

[3] "Corruption," in *Vocabulary.com Dictionary*, https://www.vocabulary.com/dictionary/corruption (25/04/2020).

[4] "Corruption," in *Merriam-Webster*, https://www.merriam-webster.com/dictionary/corruption (25/04/2020).

[5] Šumah, "Corruption, Causes and Consequences."

[6] According to Transparency International, "Corruption is the abuse of entrusted power for private gain," in "What is corruption?" https://www.transparency.org/what-is-corruption (25/04/2020).

for private gain at the expense of others or the society as a whole."[7] In addition, "In the ordinary parlance corruption simply means asking, giving or taking a fee, gift or favours as a condition for performance of one's legal or assigned responsibility."[8] This definition gives a broader picture and helps us to see human costs and relational aspects of corruption.

Manifestations of Corruption

Corruption takes many forms, namely, political, economic, corporate, legal, intellectual, police, and more. Corruption often refers to monetary corruption that may appear in various forms. However, it cannot be limited to monetary corruption alone. It is not only about taking bribes in government offices, but also about various forms of manipulation and blackmailing, political arm-twisting, physical elimination of political opponents or commercial competitors, silencing the voices of the weaker sections, using thugs for vacating land of the poor for mega projects, fixing matches, selling drugs and the like. Corruption also has reference to hidden deals, *hawala* transaction, unpaid salaries, underpaid employees, and unfair pressure. Monetary corruption in the limited sense of bribes, kickbacks and skimming or siphoning of funds is perhaps less a form of corruption than the inevitable consequence of policies that are deliberately skewed.[9]

Corrupt practices can be categorized as follows:[10] a) "petty corruption," which involves small amounts paid for frequent transactions; b) administrative corruption, when bribes are paid to escape taxes or to win relatively minor procurement contracts; c) "systemic", when corruption is prevalent through all levels of society, and d) "grand corruption," when it involves senior officials, ministers or heads of state. Grand corruption is also known as political corruption by some. When corruption occurs within corporation, it is sometimes termed as "Corporate corruption," where corporation officials use the corporation's resources for private gain, at the expense of the shareholders.

Causes and Consequences of Corruption

Factors causing corruption could be many and varied. Human greed for money and wealth, and in some cases for survival sake (economic poverty), moral laxity, and many more. However, one single factor which contributes most to corruption

---

[7] Shalini Mulackal, "Christian Witness in a Corrupt World," in Francis Gonsalves and Shalini Mulackal, eds, *Corruption in Public Life: A Theological Response* (Bangalore: Indian Theological Association and Asian Trading Corporation, 2013), 112.

[8] Kochuthara, "Indian Ethos and the Culture of Corruption," 70.

[9] Gautam Patel, "What We Talk About When We Talk About Corruption," in *Economics and Political Weekly* 46/17 (April 23, 2011), 13-16.

[10] Mulackal, "Christian Witness in a Corrupt World," 113; Cf. José G. Vargas-Hernández, "The Multiple Faces of Corruption: Typology, Forms and Levels," in *Studies of Changing Societies: Corruption Study*, Vol. 1' (6) 2012, 1-27.

is the structure or system of a society, state or institution. System or structure invariably refers to social system of a people and or a state or country, political and economic system and environment which includes professional ethics and legislation and their lack of, governance, issues of power and positions, systems of distribution of wealth and resources, justice system, etc. Besides, people's habits, customs, traditions, and demography,[11] play contributory roles to corruption and in perpetuating corruption in the world. At the personal level and from the faith perspective, corruption has to do with lack of integrity and moral strength.

While corruption affects every society and people, obviously it is the poor and the weak who have been disproportionately affected.[12] They are the most vulnerable ones in the society. On the other hand, it's the people in power and positions either in the government or private sectors, who are most likely beneficiaries of such corrupt dealings. As noted above, the forms of corruption includes bribes, exchange of goods and services, theft, etc. In one sense, the existence of so much of gaps between the rich and the poor in the world has a lot to do with corruption in the society. The poor and the vulnerable are disproportionately affected in all spheres of their lives – economic, education, health, etc. The Transparency International in its latest report reinforces the impact of corruption on the world population, especially on the poor and the powerless in the midst of Covid-19 pandemic. Raising alarm over serious corruption risks in Latin America's emergency response to corona virus or Covid-19 pandemic, Transparency International warns that "corruption could cost additional lives" and urges to follow recommendations of best practices from Latin America, as, "The measures aim to reduce the risk of hidden contracts, bribery, embezzlement, overpricing, lack of competition, collusion and other forms of corruption that would make national responses to the pandemic less effective."[13] On the whole, corruption leads to stagnation, rotting, underdevelopment, poverty, and unhealthy living conditions of people in a society. It invariably leads to decay, hunger, violence and even death. It is truly

---

[11] Šumah, "Corruption, Causes and Consequences."

[12] "Corruption has a disproportionate impact on the poor and most vulnerable, increasing costs and reducing access to services, including health, education and justice. Think, for example, of the effect of counterfeit drugs or vaccinations on the health outcomes of children and the life-long impacts that may have on them. Empirical studies have shown that the poor pay the highest percentage of their income in bribes. For example, in Paraguay, the poor pay 12.6 percent of their income to bribes while high-income households pay 6.4 percent. The comparable numbers in Sierra Leone are 13 percent and 3.8 percent respectively. Every stolen dollar, euro, peso, yuan, rupee, or ruble robs the poor of an equal opportunity in life and prevents governments from investing in their human capital," in The World Bank Group, "Combating corruption," https://www.worldbank.org/en/topic/governance/brief/anti-corruption (25/04/2020).

[13] "Corruption Could Costs Lives in Latin America's Response to Coronavirus," Transparency International Report 31 March 2020 (Updated 24 April 2020), https://www.transparency.org/news/feature/corruption_could_cost_lives_in_latin_americas_response_to_the_coronavirus (27/04/2020).

said, "Corruption is deadly." Corruption denies people from becoming a truly God intended persons and from enjoying abundant life (John 10:10).

A Theological Response to Corruption

Theology by definition is a critical reflection on the faith experiences of the people in a given context. It includes a critical examination of the way people live and practice in society and the way people relate to one another in the light of the Kingdom values. Theological reflection includes examining the relational dimension of humans with God, with fellow human and the whole of God's creation in the way we live and practice in our life.

Corruption is the one most critical issue of our time; it has always been of course. And therefore, it is a critical theological and faith concern for us. And this calls for a serious theological reflection and consideration.

Is God worried about corruption? Does God care about life? What does corruption with all its varied forms and manifestations do to the life of the created world? Does it promote life or destroy life? Obviously, corruption is anti-life; it corrupts human hearts and breaks relationships; it leads to destruction and death.

The Flood: God's Experiment in Uprooting Corruption

God is the source of life. Corruption is antithesis to all that is about life and ultimately to the nature of God. In the Bible, we see that God is so concerned about the well being of the people and creation. God was so abhorred by the corrupt life of the people. God did try to eradicate corruption from the face of the earth. We find that an initial teaching on how God deals with corruption in the book of Genesis. The world corruption provoked flood. The flood could be seen as an experiment in uprooting corruption. But God failed! "It shows God repenting of having created His decision 'to start again.'"[14] Though Naoh and his family were saved from the flood, his sons continued the history of sin and division. "And Babel was the result, followed by Babylon,... and eventually by Rome and anti-Christ. The story continues, though the epicenter of corruption has shifted from the Semitic world to wherever empires and cities are built: to Rome, London, New York, Berlin....Eventually Beijing and Delhi...?"[15] We might add as well, Guwahati, Kohima, Imphal, Aizawl, Shillong...?

Corruption as a Crime and Sin

First and foremost ethically and theologically, corruption is a crime and sin. Whatever definition we follow or in whichever way we understand corruption one thing is very clear: Corruption "is anti-social behavior that portends danger

---

[14] George Gispert-Sauch, "God's Handling of Corruption," in Francis Gonsalves and Shalini Mulackal, eds, *Corruption in Public Life: A Theological Response* (Bangalore: Indian Theological Association and Asian Trading Corporation, 2013), 54.

[15] *Ibid.*, 55.

to the cohesive fabric that holds a society together and to the integral growth and development of any society." Corruption is therefore immoral and prevalence of corruption betrays a latent decay in our moral values and orientation.

> It shows our futile attempts to build a political society without a foundational reference to the religious-ethical principles of justice, transparency, altruism, accountability and service–oriented notion of leadership. It shows a leadership praxis that promotes the selfish interests of a selected few at the expense of the common good which have generally been acclaimed by philosophers as the essence of the formation of political society.[16]

Ethically and morally, corruption is wrong. Corruption is a crime. Any organized society considers as misuse of power, an injustice, a violation of basic human rights of others, and hence punishable by law. Every organized society has a legal system or structure to deal with issues of corruption and the consequent punishment to be awarded to the guilty/parties. However, we are painfully aware of the fact that such legal systems are often marred by corruption; the system itself is corrupt. As a result, the big fishes are often let off and only the culprits of petty corruptions are sometimes punished according to the law of the land. Those of grand-scale corruption, which includes politicians, people in authority, bureaucrats and rich businessmen and firms are rarely punished. This is especially true in India.[17]

In religious and faith consideration corruption is sin. Corruption as a human act, done by a morally responsible agent carries with it a moral guilt, because it goes against the established moral standards accepted generally or by a particular society.[18] The question of corruption then assumes a status of philosophical importance; because it proceeds from the metaphysical nature of human as a being imbued with rationality and freedom. In other words, it proceeds from human as a moral agent. Therefore, corruption, because of its social effects hits at the foundation of the human being.[19]

As a moral being, corruption has a devastating effect on the person who is the agent of corruption. Sin leads to the moral disintegration of the person, leading

---

[16] A. F. Uduigwomen, *Introducing Ethics: Trends, Problems, and Perspectives* (Calabar: Jochrissam Publishers, 2006), 201.

[17] In recent years, though a few ministers have lost their positions and have even been arrested due to allegations (often with evidences) of large scale evidences) of large scale corruption, they easily escape, and often after a short break they return to the public office, often with greater power and vigor.

[18] George Gispert-Sauch, "God's Handling of Corruption," 76.

[19] Chinenye Leo Ochulor and Edet Patrick Bassey, "Analysis of Corruption from the Ethical and Moral Perspectives," in *European Journal of Scientific Research* 44/3 (2010), 470.

him/her away from living a life in accordance with her/his dignity as a person.[20] Corruption, as it is against the values of integrity, justice, truthfulness and honesty that each person is supposed to live, is an alienation from oneself, leading to the disintegration of oneself as person. Corruption violates many categories of justice. Corruption is a violation of commutative justice since a corrupt in realizing act involves deliberate transgression of obligations freely undertaken by an agent to a principle. Corruption is also an infraction of legal justice as a corrupt act directly affects the state's ability to assist its citizens the common good.[21]

At the personal level, therefore, corruption infects the heart of the greedy with an insatiable need to gratify the egoistic self without limits. It is an evil that exercises a seductive and addictive power over the morally weak. In the words of Jojo Fung, "Corruption constitutes an affront against the gratuitous God who freely offers all that is created for a good life that promotes human flourishing for all citizens, especially the suffering poor and powerless."[22]

Corruption as a Social-Structural Sin

I have deliberately decided to deal with the social and structural dimension of sin separately from personal sin, since this has been a neglected subject in our theological discourse. Often sin is considered at the personal level and regarded as individual sin. While individual sin is given so much of consideration, the institutional and structural nature of sin, grace and conversion is hardly given a serious attention. While deliberating on the issue of corruption one cannot bypass this enormously important dimension of structural sin because the nature of corruption is structural and systemic as well. According to S. Arokiasamy, a "Theology of sin should clearly include a challenge to, and conscientization about, the societal dimensions of sin, virtue, conversion and reconciliation. The 'hardness of hearts' spoken in the Bible is not a matter of the heart of individuals alone, but also of the compulsions and oppressions which get embodied in laws, customs and structures of society."[23]

In the New Testament, sin is viewed not merely as a personal failure of the person in his/her relationship with God, but also as something preventing the Kingdom of God becoming a reality.[24] That is, sin appears not only in the

---

[20] Osvaldo Schenone and Samuel Greeg, *A Theology of Corruption, The Theology of Economics of Sin,* ed. Gloreia L. Süńga, Christian Social Thought Series, no. 7 (Grand Rapids: Action Institute, 2003), 17.

[21] *Ibid.,* 92.

[22] Jojo M. Fung, "The Menace of corruption: An Accursed malaise and a Systemic Evil," in Asian Horizons 6/1 (March 2012), 52.

[23] S. Arokiasamy, "Sinful Structures in the Theology of Sin, Conversion and Reconciliation," in S. Arokiasamy and F. Podimattam, eds, *Social Sin: Its Challenges to Christian Life* (Bangalore: Claretian Publications, 1991), 111.

[24] Jon Sobrino, "Jesus' Relationship with the Poor and Outcasts: Its Importance for Fundamental Moral Theology," in *Concillium* 130 (1979), 16.

heart of humans, but is also incarnated in social structures and situations that contradicts and subverts the Kingdom of God.[25] A greater understanding of the call to conversion to the Kingdom of God and the relationship between the person and the society "reveals forces and structures that work to the detriment of justice and of the freedom and dignity of the people."[26] Though human persons are the agents of sin, sin is often mediated through social institutions and structures. Consequently, these structures attain a kind of autonomy and cause evil without conscious participation of individuals. Hormis Mynatty powerfully articulates this view:

> Even though human persons are the agents of sin, sin mediated through institutions and structures. The veil effects of sin often get embedded in social structures both ideological and operational. In the long run, these structures and institutions attain quasi-autonomy and produce evil without conscious participation of the individuals. Individuals and society as a whole internalize such unjust structures and institutions without much critical consciousness and thus reproduce them, and perpetuate evil in the society out of proportion.[27]

This powerfully demonstrates how individual persons and the structures and institutions help in perpetuating corruption in the society. While on the one hand, individuals are determined by these unjust structures, but on the other, they maintain and perpetuate them. In this sense, social sin is the conscious and willful participation of a group or a society in co-operating with the sinful social structures thus maintaining and perpetuating them and failing to do anything to change them when it is possible. Mynatti goes on to state, "Consciously or unconsciously people perpetuate evil through unjust social structures, where some values other than the human person have become the organizing and dominating value of a system or the society."[28]

What is vitally important for us is to recognize, "Sin is a negative and destructive relationship with society, resulting either in the breaking of positive relationships or refusal to develop them, hindering both the personal development and that of the society."[29] "Our Christian vocation requires that we become aware

---

[25] Hormis Mynatty, *Proposals for a Comprehensive Moral Methodology* (Bangalore: Asian Trading Corporation, 2008), 147.

[26] S. Arokiasamy, "Sinful Structures in the Theology of Sin, Conversion and Reconciliation," 90.

[27] Hormis Mynatty, *Proposals for a Comprehensive Moral Methodology,* 146.

[28] *Ibid.*, 149.

[29] Shaji George Kochuthara, "Indian Ethos and the Culture of Corruption: Moral/Psychological Perspective," in Francis Gonsalves and Shalini Mulackal, eds, *Corruption in Public Life: A Theological Response* (Bangalore: Indian Theological Association and Asian Trading Corporation, 2013), 82.

of the structures of sin around us and within us, and of our responsibility for their removal."[30] A deeper understanding of sin includes its expressions not only in intra-personal and inter-personal relationships, but also in the socio-economic, political and cultural life. The call to conversion includes all this whole fabric of the reality of sin.

Corruption is Worse than Sin?

According to Pope Francis, Corruption is worse than any sin because it hardens the heart against feeling shame or guilt and hearing God's call for conversion.[31] "Situations of sin and the state of corruption are two distinct realities, even if they are intimately linked to one another," In his book, "Corruption and Sin: Reflections on the Theme of Corruption," Pope Francis argues that while many sins can lead to corruption, sinners recognize their own weakness and are aware of the possibility of forgiveness. "From there, the power of God can come in." People who are corrupt, on the other hand, have become blind to the transcendent, replacing God with their own powers and abilities. "A sinner expects forgiveness. The corrupt, on the contrary, don't because they don't feel they have sinned. They have prevailed," he said.

The pope referred to many biblical passages to offer concrete examples. Most notably, the corrupt, like the scribes and the Pharisees who criticized Jesus for healing on the Sabbath, launch "a reign of terror" to discredit, attack or eliminate anyone who tries to criticize, question or contradict them.

One might ask shouldn't corruption be regarded as sin rather than making distinction between the two? One might disagree with Pope Francis and his view on corruption and sin. After all, corruption cannot be seen as being different from sin. Corruption is sin. However, Pope underscores the seriousness as well as the pervasiveness of corruption in the world today; people so blatantly practice and treat corruption as a way of life. It has become very normal so much so that people do not see the need for seeking repentance and forgiveness as "sinners" would do. In like manner, critiquing against the Euro-American Christians, Standing Rock Sioux (American Indian) scholar Vine Deloria, Jr, has this to say, "It is impossible to sin today because all of the really good sins have become Christian virtues, much as Greed, once one of the Seven Deadly Sins, has become chief American and Republican virtue."[32]

---

[30] S. Arokiasamy, "Sinful Structures in the Theology of Sin, Conversion and Reconciliation," 90.

[31] "Corruption is worse than sin," in http://www.catholicnews.com/services/englishnews/2013/corruption-is-worse-than-sin-because-heart-hardens-to-god-pope-says.cfm (18/02/2016).

[32] Vine Deloria, Jr, *Red Earth, White Lies: Native Americans and the Myth of Scientific Fact* (Golden: Fulcrum Publishing, 1997), 9.

Integrity as Antidote to Corruption

Corruption is everywhere. As noted above, Christians are equally corrupt as any other person is. In as much as we recognize the seriousness of corruption, there is a serious need to look for ways to root out corruption. And we know that there are different and many ways to fight against corruption at different levels – personal, social, corporate and institutional levels. Addressing the issue of corruption in the context of Christians and Christian organizations, Manfred Kohl in his article "Do We Care About Corruption: How Integrity Can Tame the Beast of Bribes and Extortion," argues that the antidote to corruption is integrity because looking from another side of the issue, "Corruption is simply the reflection of a lack of integrity."[33] There is therefore a serious need for Christians to have self examinations – the need to examine ourselves. Etymologically the term integrity derives from the Latin word, *integratem* meaning "wholeness," "soundness" "perfect condition." Corruption is therefore antithesis to integrity. Kohl appeals to Christians to learn from Jesus and that is the sure way to free ourselves from corruption.

> Jesus himself was tempted by the idols of power and pride, popularity and success, and wealth and greed, and he resisted the temptation. With his help we can distance ourselves from all of these idols that tempt us, often on a daily basis. Integrity is the integrating element that unifies character, conduct, and one's composite lifestyle. To address corruption and integrity one must begin with the condition of one's own life.[34]

King David as well prayed to God for integrity: "May integrity and uprightness protect me, because my hope, LORD, is in you," (Psalm 25: 21).

Conclusion

Corruption is, first and foremost, a personal act that has social consequences. It is a form of stealing – fueled by greed for wealth and power. Money that is meant to benefit the people – especially the poor — is diverted to the pockets of corrupt government officials and their conspirators. It can lead to death and damage of property when corrupt government officials allow corporations to destroy the environment that causes flooding, air pollution, and climate change.

It can lead to murder when the corrupt try to silence those who try to denounce them or in order to perpetuate themselves in power. Those involved

---

[33] Manfred Kohl, "Do We Care About Corruption: How Integrity Can Tame the Beast of Bribes and Extortion," in *Laussane Global Analysis,* Vol. 8, Issue 3, May 2019. https://www.lausanne.org/content/lga/2019-05/do-we-care-aboutcorruption?gclid=CjwKCAjwv4_1BRAhEiwAtMDLsn6yCQHBH0O_rNBityLFUxmteZpGPa7OjSGSl9hxyjrdTUuNxhCDSBoCqucQAvD_BwE (25/04/2020).

[34] *Ibid.*

in corruption end up losing their soul, even if they make it appear that they are pious.

Corruption is not only a personal act – a personal sin which has harmful social consequences. It is also the manifestation of social sin. Sin is not just found in the hearts of individuals, but embedded in systems and structures of society – in political, economic, social structures. It has become a way of life – part of culture. It has become the dominant environment.

It is part of the Church's prophetic mission to denounce corruption as a moral evil and social sin. It is her duty to call people to personal conversion. This is the fruit of new evangelization. But, calling individuals to personal conversion is not enough to overcome corruption since it is already embedded in the structures and systems of society.

Social and political transformation is necessary. This means awakening the moral conscience of the people vis-à-vis corruption. Thus, the struggle against corruption is waged not only within the hearts of individuals but also in the systems and structures of society. Christians talk about God's forgiveness as the remedy for our sin and corruption. Though God's experiment in uprooting corruption by flood failed, God kept trying through the prophets, and ultimately by sending His only begotten son, Jesus Christ. The cross of Jesus and the resurrection of the risen Lord conquered the sin and evils of the world.

> God deals with corruption not by mere forgiveness as forgiveness is normally understood in religious language, but by a divine-human joint act of reconciliation that implies a will to affirm the evil of injustice, the will to undo it, and a restoration to our dignity as children of God. And because corruption causes death and suffering, restoration involves the 'obedience' to history by dying to ourselves in love. By whatever word we call this miracle, it will imply a sacrificial act. The final word is hope.[35]

Robert Osburn, Jr. concludes his book *Taming the Beast: Can We Bridle the Culture of Corruption?* with a paraphrase of the Beatitudes (Matt 5:2-11),[36] and I find appropriate that we reproduce here by way of concluding.

- If you suffer poverty, corrupt wealth is utterly inferior to living under God's eternal rule and reign (v. 3: Blessed are the poor in spirit, for theirs is the kingdom of heaven).
- If you must suffer loss in your pursuit of an honest life, your sorrows will always be met by the comforting, encouraging friendship of those you have

[35] George Gispert-Sauch, "God's Handling of Corruption," 66.

[36] Robert Osburn Jr., *Taming the Beast: Can We Bridle the Culture of Corruption?* (St. Paul: Wilberforce, 2016), 225-226.

treated kindly and honestly (v. 4: Blessed are those who mourn, for they shall be comforted).

- Although, you could manipulate people with your money, how much greater is the restrained use of your power ("meek") for others' good; the result will be that people will demand that you become their leader ("inherit the earth") (v. 5: Blessed are the meek, for they shall inherit the earth).
- Whereas greed and corruption are never satisfied, the deep, passionate desire for justice and holiness always satisfies, day after day (v. 6: Blessed are those who hunger and thirst for righteousness, for they shall be satisfied).
- Rather than making demands for bribes, showing mercy and kindness to people makes them want to shower you with the same mercy and kindness (v. 7: Blessed are the merciful, for they shall receive mercy).
- Those who are not corrupt have nothing to hide and will not only never fear others but also never fear the face of God (v. 8: Blessed are the pure in heart, for they shall see God).
- Those who help others to be reconciled with each other will be wealthy beyond imagination, for as God's children they will inherit the wealth of his kingdom (v. 9: Blessed are the peacemakers, for they shall be called sons of God).
- If, in your pursuit of godliness, the corrupt make your life miserable, remember what the poor person knows so very well: nothing can compare with the glories of living under God's rule and reign (v. 10: Blessed are those who are persecuted for righteousness' sake, for theirs is the kingdom of heaven).
- If you are mercilessly attacked for living a life of honesty and purity, take great joy in two facts: 1) The Old Testament prophets suffered similarly, and that means you are in good company; and 2) You will have a greater reward than the richest corrupt leader could ever imagine (vv. 11-12: Blessed are you when others revile you and persecute you and utter all kinds of evil against you falsely on my account. Rejoice and be glad, for your reward is great in heaven, for so they persecuted the prophets who were before you).

14

The Pertinence of Ethics in Development Debates

Introduction

Ban Ki-moon, the then Secretary-General, United Nations states that the objective of the Millennium Development Goals (MDG) of 2000 is to "spare no effort to free our fellow men, women and children from the abject and dehumanizing conditions of extreme poverty."[1] The Millennium Development Goals report 2015 further states, "At the beginning of the new millennium, world leaders gathered at the United Nations to shape a broad vision to fight poverty in its many dimensions. That vision, which was translated into eight Millennium Development Goals (MDGs), has remained the overarching development framework for the world for the past 15 years."[2] The report lists the following eight goals:[3]

- eradicate extreme poverty and hunger;
- achieve universal education for all;
- promote gender equality and empower women;
- reduce child mortality;
- improve maternal health;
- combat HIV/AIDS, malaria and other diseases;
- ensure environmental sustainability; and
- develop a global partnership for development.

[1] "The Millennium Development Goals 2015 Report Summary Pdf," https://www.un.org/millenniumgoals/2015_MDG_Report/pdf/MDG%202015%20Summary%20web_english.pdf (6/04/2020), 2.

[2] *Ibid.*, 3.

[3] *Ibid.*, 3-6.

The report concludes:

> Although, significant achievements have been made on many of the MDG targets worldwide, progress has been uneven across regions and countries, leaving significant gaps. Millions of people are being left behind, especially the poorest and those disadvantaged because of their sex, age, disability, ethnicity or geographic location. Targeted efforts will be needed to reach the most vulnerable people.[4]

It is interesting to note that millions of people, especially the "poorest and those who are disadvantaged" have been left behind for reasons such as "sex, age, disability, ethnicity and geographic location." Whereas, the report falls short of naming the real cause for leaving behind the poorest and the disadvantaged people in the world.

In his book, *Winners Take All*, Anand Giridharadas powerfully names structural-systemic injustices as the root cause of social inequality in the world and those elites – the rich and powerful - who hypocritically position themselves as fighting for equality and justice through their market friendly initiatives are actually the ones perpetuating the inequalities in the world.[5] They harp for change without willing to change the status quo they are so comfortably entrenched with and yet they portray themselves as champions for social equality. Giridharadas describes the contradictory images of the elites thus:

> There is no denying today's elite may be among the more socially concerned elites in history. But it is also, by cold logic of numbers, among the predatory in history. By refusing to risk its way of life,.. it clings to a set of social arrangement that allow it to monopolize progress and then give symbolic scraps to the forsaken…the connection between these elites social concern and predation, between the extraordinary helping and the extraordinary hoarding, between the milking – and perhaps abetting – of unjust status quo and the attempts by the milkers to repair a small part of it.[6]

The bottom line is this: the system and the structure of the corporate world which is based on capitalist ideology and which promotes development as growth and maximizing benefits is the one root cause of the inequalities in the world.

At the backdrop of the MDG report, and the Corporate Scandals that have rocked the economic systems of the US and the world, it is crucial to look at the importance of ethics to development. In its special report, "The Biggest Corporate Scandals of the Decade," the 24/7 *Wall St.* lists innumerable corporate

---

4 *Ibid.*, 7.

5 Anand Giridharadas, *Winners Take All: The Elite Charade of Changing the World* (New York: Alfred A. Knopf, 2018).

6 *Ibid.*, 7.

scandals involving a number of powerful corporations and companies in the world, especially in the US in the decade between 2010-2019.[7] India is no stranger to such corporate-corruption scandals either. In recent years, several corruption scandals involving several corporations and companies including Hawala scam, the infamous Coalgate scam, 2G Spectrum scam, Satyam Computer Services scandal, Sarada Chit Fund scam, Punjab National Bank fraud scandal, Yes Bank fraud and money laundering scams, to name a few, have shook the nation and its economy. In all these, it is the ordinary masses and the poor who have been worst hit and affected.[8]

Ethics and Development

What is the pertinence of ethics to debates about development? This question inevitably begs the related question "what is development?" The answer to this question is determined and shaped by one's worldviews and beliefs about the nature of human beings. Our perceptions about life, creation, and the world are deeply influenced by the way we understand ourselves, our communities and the world.

If you understand the nature of human being to be inherently egoistic - as it is understood by the neo-classical theorists - then your idea of ethics and development will be shaped and influenced by that view.[9] The neo-classical theory is based on the premise of individual freedom and their goal is the maximization of individual satisfactions. They understand development in terms of economic growth and production. Driven by the ideal of greed for individual satisfactions they work toward accumulation of wealth employing every possible means available. And their understanding of ethics is predicated on the valuation of individual

[7] Evan Comen & Thomas C. Frohlich, "The Biggest Corporate Scandals of the Decade," 24/7 *Wall St.* https://247wallst.com/special-report/2019/12/20/the-biggest-corporate-scandals-of-the-decade/ (07/04/2020). The list includes BP Deepwater Horizon oil spill 2010 estimated to be the largest marine oil spill in history had catastrophic economic and environmental impacts; Foxconn suicides 2010 due to long-hour shifts and less pay; Libor scandal 2012 in which several major banks — including Deutsche Bank, Barclays, and UBS — colluded to illegally manipulate interest rates for profit; Turing Pharmaceuticals HIV drug price gouging 2015; Mossack Fonseca and the Panama Papers 2016 which revealed a global network of offshore bank accounts and shell companies used by the world's elite to conceal wealth and avoid taxes; WeWork IPO disaster 2019 laid off 2,400 employees — nearly one-fifth of its workforce; Probe on opioid makers 2019 crisis involving six pharmaceutical companies; and many more others rocked the world's economy.

[8] "According to a recent study by Transparency International — a Berlin-based NGO working against corruption, India is the 'Most Corrupt Country in Asia-Pacific Region', and seven out of 10 people in India, pay a bribe to access public services." https://www.educationworld.in/10-corruption-scandals-that-shook-the-nation/ Cf. https://www.business-standard.com/article/companies/india-s-top-5-corporate-scams-stuck-in-judicial-quagmire-113103000230_1.html (8/04/2020).

[9] George F. DeMartino, *Global Economy, Global Justice: Theoretical Objections and Policy Alternatives to Neoliberalism* (New York: Routledge, 2000), 38.

freedom and worth. It is ethical for them so long as your actions are geared toward achieving yourself-serving egoistic goal. This is certainly not a development that is centered on the well-being of all, and the ideal for sharing the natural resources and wealth goes against the very fabric of their idea of development. As Herman Daly and John Cobb point out, individual-centered economy "has no place for fairness malevolence, and benevolence, nor for the preservation of human life or any other moral concern."[10]

We live today in a world where the ideals of capitalism - or in the language of Frederic Jameson, "the cultural logic of late capitalism" - is in total control and its triumph over communism/socialism is being claimed as justifying the validity of capitalism.[11] Globalization, which is the direct extension of the cultural logic of late capitalism spearheaded by the powerful Multinational Corporations (MNC), World Bank (WB) and International Monitory Fund (IMF), has become the order of the day in the contemporary world. The globalizing effects of capitalism especially on the Third World and the Two-Third World are undeniably alarming. Unfortunately, whether we like it or not the process of globalization has become unstoppable; it has touched upon every continent of the earth and its effects are felt everywhere. Of course, undeniably it is the Two-Third World nations and the indigenous people who are the most affected. The gaps between the rich and the poor nations around the world are widening every day. The harsh reality is that in the capitalist world the rich are becoming richer while the poor remain poor if not poorer. According to the recent Oxfarm study report, "India's richest 1 per cent hold more than four-times the wealth held by 953 million people who make up for the bottom 70 per cent of the country's population, while the total wealth of all Indian billionaires is more than the full-year budget."[12] In its study, "Time to Care," released ahead of the 50th World Economic Forum (WEF) at Davos, the Oxfarm also stated that the "world's 2,153 billionaires have more wealth than the 4.6 billion people who make up 60 per cent of the planet's population."[13]

The "free market" economy, which has been aggressively pursued and promoted by the multinational corporations, has become the dominant economy of the contemporary world.[14]

It is in this extraordinary context that the pertinence of ethics in development comes to play a crucial role. If ethics is concerned with the critical reflection on the moral duties of the people in the context of human relationships then we need

---

[10] Herman E. Daly & John B. Cobb, *For the Common Good: Redirecting the Economy: Toward Community, the Environment, and a Sustainable Future (*Boston: Beacon Press, 1989), 159.

[11] Frederic Jameson, *Post Modernism Or the Cultural Logic of Late Capitalism (*Duke: Duke University Press, 1991), xviiif.

[12] https://economictimes.indiatimes.com/news/economy/indicators/wealth-of-indias-richest-1-more-than-4-times-of-total-for-70-poorest-oxfam/articleshow/73416122.cms?from=mdr (6/04/2020).

[13] *Ibid.*

[14] DeMartino, *Global Economy, Global Justice*, 2f.

to challenge the ethics that promote individualism. If humans are social beings then we are primarily relational beings. We belong to one another and we belong to the human community. Ethics then is concerned with critical reflection on the ways how political, social and economic privileges and resources are shared and distributed among the people in the community.[15] Ethics is concerned with issues of distributive justice, equal distribution of resources and the decision making process as well.

Recognizing the importance of relating development to ethics, Amartya Sen develops a theory of development that places freedom as the core value. In fact, Sen defines development as freedom- freedom in terms of human capabilities to choose and function.[16] By freedom of choice, Sen means the individual's ability to choose. While Sen may be criticized for situating freedom at the individual level, unlike the neoclassical theorists, Sen clearly recognizes individual freedom as a social commitment. For Sen freedom is both "the primary end and the primary means of development."[17] For Sen, unlike the neoclassical economics, development has to do with the well - being of the people and not merely the individual person. The goal of development is to improve the quality of human life - for the individual as well as for the community. The function of development is the removal of unfreedoms that prevent people from enjoying the quality of life. And Sen identifies a number of the forms of unfreedom including poverty, undernutrition, denial of clean water and sanitation, health care and education, political and civil liberty and so on.[18] Sen further clearly sees the deep complimentarity between individual agency and social arrangement and the linkages between different types of freedoms. He rightly argues that economic freedom and political freedom help reinforce one another in enhancing the life quality of the people.

This holistic perspective of looking at the human situation is in sharp contrast with most western scholars who tend to compartmentalize things and treat them as though they are not related to each other. Here I have in mind particularly the way human rights is conceived and understood. Western theorists give priority to civil and political rights over social and economic rights rather than treating them as equally important components of human rights.[19] Sen

---

[15] The need for emphasizing and renewing community has been recently stated by Michael Walzer when he asserts that "the idea of distributive justice presupposes a bounded world within which distribution takes place: a group commute to dividing. exchanging, and sharing social goods, first of all among themselves that is the political community" (Quoted by Daly and Cobb, 164).

[16] Amartya Sen, *Development as Freedom* (New York: Anchor Books, 1999), xii.

[17] *Ibid.*

[18] *Ibid.*, 15.

[19] William F. Schulz, *In Our Best Interest: How Defending Human Rights Benefits Us All* (Boston: Beacon Press, 1999), 15.

clearly and rightly recognizes the interactions among and between political, social and economic freedoms in shaping and improving the qualities of life.

Martha C. Nussbaum, following Sen's capability theory argues that this human capability approach is qualitatively a better approach than other systems such as Gross National Product (GNP) per capita for quality of life assessment,[20] which, while presents an attractive overall statistical achievement, overlooks the harsh reality of the enormous inequalities that exists among the people. Further, such approaches fail to "examine human goods that are not reliably correlated with the presence of resources: infant mortality, for example, or access to education, or the quality of racial and gender relations, or the presence or absence of political freedoms."[21]

Sen and Nussbaum are critical of neoclassical economics for the very reason that it benefits the few rich individuals while majority of the world populations especially from the poor nations become poorer and poorer. These are certainly questions of ethics. In the words of Sen, poverty is deprivation of freedom and quality of life. In the language of Nussbaum poverty is "a threshold of capability to function beneath which a life will be so impoverished that it will not be human at all."[22]

I started by claiming that the idea of ethics or development is influenced and shaped by the worldview one holds or by the way one perceives human self to be. Accordingly I cited that the ethics of the neoclassical economists are shaped by the way they perceive the nature of human being as "egoistic." The neoclassical theorists claim that their view of human nature is universally true for all people, which is of course committing a huge general assumption and thereby committing a serious mistake. If this is true how do we explain those societies and communities that practice subsistence economy based on reciprocity and sharing? For these societies humans are essentially relational being whose existence depend upon the interdependence of each other. Their ethics is based on such human conception that humans are relational beings and that everyone in the community works for the good of the community. Working for the good of the community includes taking care of each other and sharing the resources that are available among the people.[23]

---

[20] Martha C. Nussbaum, "Human Capabilities, Female Human Beings," Martha C. Nussbaum & Jonathan Glover, eds. *Women, Culture, and Development: A Study of Human Capabilities (*Oxford: Claredon Press, 1995), 90.

[21] *Ibid.*

[22] *Ibid.*, 81.

[23] Very often when such practices of the indigenous community are cited people tend to dismiss them as a case of romanticizing. The fact is that even this day most indigenous peoples continue to live based on their communitarian values in spite of the tact that they are also affected by the modern cultures.

Now in being critical of the neoclassical theorists I am simultaneously trying to argue that universalism or moral objectivism as it is represented by the neo-liberals does not work for everybody. In saying so, I am taking the position of the anti-essentialists or the cultural relativists who rightly argue that there can be no ethical foundation that can claim universal validity for all. All that we do is culturally conditioned and bound and hence the ethical values and practices have to emerge out of the worldviews and practices of the particular people. Of course, this view is not without its problems, either. As DeMartino rightly argues, there is no pure culture as such, every culture is contingent and is affected by cross-cultural interaction.[24] As a result all cultures undergo certain revision, modification and change in the process. Further, "Given our multiple, overlapping and contradictory subject positions, we do not belong to culture - and certainly not to any unitary culture - in the traditional sense that Walzer embraces."[25] He thus proposes for a normative ethics of development which he calls as "an internationalist ethic - global harmonization of capabilities"[26] following Sen's principle of human capabilities. DeMartino further argues that unlike the neoclassical theory's commitment to welfarism, this principle emphasizes sufficiency, attainability and sustainability. Further, the equalization of capabilities, while functions under a certain agreeable normative for all, it represents an approach to substantive equality that respects the diversity of human and social aspirations. Most of all this "approach is agnostic with respect to the metaphysical foundation of ethical judgments" because it provides rooms for both moral objectivists as well as for relativists "who refuses an objective or universal basis for normative judgments."[27]

A similar approach is proposed by Nussbaum who rejects extreme positions associated with moral objectivism on the one hand and cultural relativism on the other although she claims herself to be a universalist or essentialist. Nussbaum recognizes the distinctive features of concrete histories and seeks a subtle balance between perception of the particular and recognition of the common while pursuing public policy.[28] Likewise, DeMartino concludes that the egalitarian equality approach offers "a far better ethical basis for constructing a new global economic policy regimes in a world of egregious and crushing inequalities."[29]

Indigenous-Tribals, Development and Economic Life

The idea of economy is often understood in a narrow sense of management of finance and financial resources. Economy in its broader sense is about management of all forms of resources including human relationship with fellow human as

[24] DeMartino, *Global Economy, Global Justice*, 139.

[25] *Ibid.*, 142.

[26] *Ibid.*, 143.

[27] *Ibid.*, 147.

[28] Nussbaum, "Human Capabilities, Female Human Beings," 70.

[29] DeMartino, *Global Economy, Global Justice*, 147.

well as with the whole of God's creation. Economy of life pertains to the art of maintaining harmonious relationship at the individual level as well as social level including humans relationship with the nature. It means giving importance to life, life of every being and working towards promoting life and the values of life.

Traditionally, indigenous-tribal people follow subsistence economy; they follow a simple and transparent system of economy. Their primary objective is for their survival. Agriculture is their main occupation. They cultivate and tilt the land for their livelihood and not for any commercial purpose. Profit making is unknown to them. Commercialization of goods and profit making business is a recent phenomenon among the indigenous-tribal people in North East India. In the past, they follow a well regulated agricultural calendar throughout the year. They would cultivate and harvest the crops just enough to feed the family for the year. They did not work year long. That's the reason why they have plenty of time for socializing, recreation and merrymaking. Once the harvest is over they would go visiting their relatives and friends, hunting, fishing, picnicking, etc. The indigenous-tribals love feasting and merrymaking and their yearly calendar is filled with festivals. In a way, time was in their hands; they always had time for anything and everything.

True to their worldview, they give priority and importance to quality of life and building relationship. Under this subsistence economy, everyone is given a fair share. The poor are also given the necessary care and protection. It used to be in the past, every time the crop is harvested, certain quantities of the crops were left un-harvested setting aside for the poor people. This is also clearly demonstrated by the fact that tribal society did not have beggars among them. On the whole, the community is known for taking care of the poor and the needy.[30]

Indigenous-tribal people are as well known for their hospitable and welcoming nature. Generosity and culture of sharing are the hall marks of tribal community life. They loved to share with others whatever they have. Monetary exchange of goods is again a recent phenomenon. Of course, this day, things are changing rapidly. Influenced by modern capitalist ideology of profit making, people have become highly commercialized. The culture of consumerism has taken over people's life and their life styles have been greatly influenced by this culture.

Development, Biological and Cultural Diversity and Indigenous Knowledge

For most indigenous peoples land means life. Not only because they depend on it for their daily subsistence, but because their whole cultural, social and spiritual identity is connected with it. It is widely recognized that indigenous peoples due

---

[30] This does not mean tribal community is free from the poor and needy people, as well as people's experiences of discrimination and exploitation. What is being underscored here is the communitarian spirit of the people and caring attitude towards people in need.

to their ways of life, their attitude towards nature and their ecological knowledge have played a crucial role in the conservation of biological diversity on earth.

According to a study from World Wildlife Fund (WWF) by Gonzalo Oviedo, there is a strong correlation between areas with high biological diversity and areas with high cultural diversity. Eighty percent of the Global 200 eco-regions (areas identified as richest in biological diversity) is inhabited by one or more indigenous people(s). The study goes on to say, "In their long history of managing the environment, indigenous peoples have accumulated vast amounts of ecological knowledge, which is embodied in their languages. Local knowledge is a pillar of traditional medicine and health systems." According to the United Nations Environmental Program up to eighty percent of the non-industrial world's population rely on traditional forms of medicine.[31]

Conclusion

If by development we mean improving the quality of human life in all aspects then ethics is concerned with critical reflection on how development works toward achieving that goal. Any development projects that do not serve the well-being of the people concerned but rather benefits only a few individuals at the expense of the majority has to be challenged for ethical fairness. And while undertaking any developmental policies and projects the concrete concerns of the people and their aspirations including their cultural values should be given utmost importance. The people themselves are the best judge of their life destiny and aspirations. Of course, there is always a room for engaging in a critical interaction between the local and the global values so long as they are compatible to the aspirations of the community. Finally, any development projects that do not take the ecological/ environmental concerns into serious consideration will always be deficient and lopsided. There is today a growing concern for recognizing our human relatedness to creation and the need for developing ethics that is centered on creation. A globally responsible ethics will therefore include caring for creation and working toward eco-justice. After all our human existence greatly depends on the bounteous blessings we receive from nature.

[31] http://indigenouspeoples.nl/indigenous-peoples/about-indigenous-peoples (06/04/2016).

15

Baptist Churches Response to Globalization in North East India
Action Plan

Introduction

Globalization, as we all know, is and has been an all pervasive force impacting our world and society. And of course, it has always been the poor and the weak, who are the worst affected lots. However, churches' response to the challenges of globalization has not been that encouraging at all. The responses range from no action to making or adopting resolutions/statements against forces of globalization. This paper briefly examines the responses of the Baptist churches in the region, argues that the problems confronting us is at the core a spiritual problem, and that any solution or action plan we propose must be based on the faith and moral values of the people. The paper ends with some proposals of action plans for responding to the challenges of globalization.

Baptist Churches in NEI and their Responses to Globalization

Baptist churches in NEI comprises mainly of the Council of Baptist Churches in North East India (CBCNEI), Baptist Church of Mizoram (BCM), Lairam Baptist Church of Mizoram (LBCM), and North Bank Baptist Christian Associations (NBBCA), etc. The Council of Baptist Churches in Northeast India ("CBCNEI" or the "Council") is the largest Baptist group in the region. It is a conglomeration of Six Baptist Conventions, namely: Arunachal Baptist Churches Council, Assam Baptist Convention, Karbi Anglong Baptist Convention, Garo Baptist

Convention, Manipur Baptist Convention, and Nagaland Baptist Churches Council and their Associations and Churches. There are three Associate Members as well.

Looking at the ministerial activities of the churches, not much can be said on this front. So far, looking at and examining the ministerial activities of the CBCNEI and the BCM from their official websites, we find that "mission" and evangelism activities are the main thrust of their ministries. Social and justice concerns are given less emphasis.[1] While the CBCNEI has a desk on Justice and Peace, and BCM Relief and Development department, they are like an appendix compared to "Mission" and Evangelism. Moreover, there are no specific responses to the challenges of globalization, which is the main concern of our seminar today.

Theological Rationale and Resources

Before we can begin to talk about action plan, there is a need for us to deal with people's attitude, mindset and most of all people's understanding of church's mission and Christian spirituality. Very often, we hear people say, why we should be concerned about issues of globalization. Why concerned about human trafficking? Why concerned about issues of corruption? Why be bothered about big companies polluting our air, water and food? These are common responses we receive from the so called Christians – "devoted Christians?" Spirituality and mission are always regarded as matters of "heavenly things" and "winning the lost souls" respectively. Such narrow and dualistic understandings have led people to view anything that has to do with social and physical aspects negatively.

An objective observation of contemporary tribal Christian life and its spirituality tells us entirely a different story. Influenced by the Western Christian worldview, which tends to maintain sharp distinction between the secular and the sacred, earthly and spiritual life, tribal Christians have compartmentalized their Christian life into secular and religious lives. In other words, tribal Christians assume that what we do in the Sunday worship life has nothing to do with the day-to-day life activities of the week. Regretably, there are many contradictions in the ways tribal Christians live and behave. It is important for the church to remind tribal Christians that true spirituality makes no distinction between what is secular and sacred, what is worship life and outside the Sunday worship life. We need to recognize that the tribal worldview is not necessarily evil, that rather it goes in line with the Kingdom values that Jesus proclaimed and exhorted His followers to live by. True spirituality must be understood as a way of life – a way of living inspired by the power of the Holy Spirit.

---

[1] Visit their official websites for detail information on their ministries: www.cbcnei.in; www.mizobaptist.org.

Spiritual Problem

The problems and crises of our society is therefore primarily and fundamentally a spiritual problem. It is a spiritual crisis.

For this we need to turn to the biblical prophets and the teaching of Jesus Christ as well as tribal spirituality.

Traditional understanding of spirituality that emphasizes on individual conversion is not enough; we need a spirituality that would lead personal transformation to social transformation as well. A spirituality that would not run away from the reality of the world rather that engages with the world for bringing social transformation.

What Jim Wallis said about the American conservative Christians and liberal Christians could be helpful for our context too:

> In the most materialistic culture in history, conservative religion has produced a gospel of prosperity. In a society whose inequitable distribution of resources has become obscene, conservative religion has become a defender of the wealthy. Within the greatest military superpower in the world, conservative religion has become a primary advocate for extending American hegemony and a consistent defender of the nation's every war....
>
> Liberal religion has lost its spiritual center. It has become captive to the secular culture. Liberal activism has often lacked any real dynamic of personal conversion and, therefore, transformative power. With liberal religion, social action in the world can become severed from its roots in faith, producing a language and practice that seem more bureaucratic and ideological than spiritual.[2]

What we need today is therefore a return to the prophetic traditions of our faith; a return to the prophetic spirituality.

Prophetic Spirituality

- relates biblical faith to social transformation;
- personal conversion to the cry of the poor;
- theological reflection to care for the environment;
- core religious values to new economic priorities
- the call of community to racial/ethnic and gender justice;
- spirituality to politics.

[2] Jim Wallis, *The Soul of Politics: A Practical and Vision for Change* (New York: The New Press; Maryknoll: Orbis Books, 1994), 36-37.

Prophetic spirituality is a dynamic spiritual movement not a static spirituality. In the words of South African Archbishop Desmond Tutu it is "the spirituality of transformation."

Biblical Prophets

Biblical prophets had the power of the Spirit. And they had twofold tasks:

- first, empowered by the Spirit they were bold in telling the truth and proclaiming the justice that is rooted in God; they denounced kings and rulers for their corrupt practices and evil deeds, social evils, named the idols they worshiped, called the people to return to God. E.g. Prophet Nathan before king David; Amos, Isaiah, Hosea, Joel and others were highly critical of the rulers and the powerful.
- second, they often called for an alternative vision; they helped the people "to imagine new possibilities."

Jesus Christ and His Teaching

The Nazareth Manifesto in Luke 4:18ff. Jesus proclaimed that the Spirit of the Lord upon him and that He had come to proclaim good news to the poor; liberty to the captives; sight to the blind and; to release the oppressed and; to proclaim the year of the Lord's favor.

Jesus proclaimed the good news of the Kingdom of God. Jesus denounced and condemned the religious leaders – Pharisees, Scribes. They compared them with the whitewashed tombs, etc.

Jesus lived and moved among the people listening to their stories and ministering to them; while at the same time challenging the systems that oppressed and marginalized the people.

Spiritual Resources of the Tribal People

Tribal spirituality emphasizes on the wholeness of life and interconnectedness of all. It is basically a spirituality of relationship; our connectedness to one another and the whole of God's creation and the spirit world. Tribal worldview makes no distinction between what is the spiritual and physical, material and immaterial, sacred and secular; heavenly and earthly, etc.

Honesty, sincerity, speaking the truth and dignity of labor are all important spiritual values of the people. Hospitality, communitarian spirit, respect for one another are the hallmarks of tribal people. They practically lived out these values in their life.

Theirs is a spirituality that is centered on community, social justice and peace. They lived and worked for maintaining balance and harmony in the community as well as for the whole of creation. We need to learn a great deal from our fore-parents.

Some Action Plans

Making people to recognize that opposing forces of globalization that threaten and destroy life is intrinsically connected to our spirituality is paramount. And I believe, making people to understand this is the most challenging task confronting us. The success and failure of some of the action plans outlined below will greatly depend on how people view their spirituality to be. Secondly, it will also a great deal depend on how the church leadership view Christian mission to be and therefore accordingly prioritize the churches' ministry.

Seminar on Holistic Mission/Spirituality

This may sound redundant and inappropriate. People might think we have done enough on this front. We need to move on. But again, I ask, have we really done enough on this front? There is rather ever greater need for us to be concentrating on this now. Providing proper education on the meaning of mission and spirituality is therefore a necessity. And this cannot be a onetime deal; it has to be continuous efforts of educating the people. I strongly believe that our society will remain the same if not degenerate further unless we are prepared to get right from the very beginning the core values of our faith and what it means to be true believers and followers of Jesus Christ.

It reminds me of the just concluded Assembly elections of Nagaland and Meghalaya states. Most of us are aware of the circumstances and consequences of the election; how the elections played out to be. The Nagaland Baptist Church Council (NBCC) campaigned for clean and fair election; but would it be right to say that money and muscle powers ultimately triumphed? I think it is appropriate to ask whether they reflect the spiritual conditions and moral/ethical values of the people.

What it reminds us is that in our fight against the forces of globalization, we need to be informed and motivated by our spiritual and faith experiences. We need to go out empowered by the Holy Spirit.

A Pastor who is engaged in the ministry against globalization asked the following: "How can the Christian church influence Monsanto, Nike or Allan Greenspan? How can we stop George Soros from selling the rupiah? Preaching sermons against globalization...will not change anything. The people who need to hear are not there to hear. We need to take the message of justice to those in the market who are prepared to listen to such a message."[3] Then the author went on to propose five major methods the church can adopt to respond to the challenges of globalization. They are: public protest and use of the media; litigation; engage in dialogue and ethical appeal; churches' economic resources and investments; and political involvement.

---

[3] "The Church and the Challenge of Globalization," http://www.aibi.ph/tmk/tmk13_church_and globalization.htm (accessed on 23/03/2013).

In line with the pastor's proposals, I would like to outline few of the action plans the churches can look for in responding to the challenges of globalization.

Awareness Programs and Campaigns

There is no alternative to providing awareness campaign to the people on the problems and negative impacts of globalization. The church must relentlessly and intentionally promote such campaigns. The church must regard this as an integral missional program rather than treating it as otherwise. Problems of children working in big cities and towns; HIV/AIDS; human trafficking; child abuse and labor; etc. The most affected are the people in rural areas who have become easy victims to such abuses.

Protests and Rallies

Individual or public protests, they all matter. Taking the concerns of the people to the concerned authorities in the form of protests and rallies, letter writings, opposing the policies of the government or private agencies are critical. This days, with the help of media, social networking, etc. things can be brought to the notice of the people in no time.

Networking with Others

There are a number of anti-globalization networks and groups the church can tie up with and work together. It is good to learn and understand the issues from those groups who are engaged in opposing those firms and companies or even governmental agencies for their inhuman and exploitative practices. Furthermore, to join hands with them in the protest movements and so on.

Perhaps, when it comes to litigation, there is no other option but to work with those legal experts and groups who knows the laws and issues.

Of course, when it comes to legal matters, churches are not that comfortable with and it is certainly a contested issue. But, what happens when cases of human trafficking and human rights abuse take place; which are of course, an everyday happening. E.g. of 52 women and men children case in Jaipur, Rajasthan just a month ago.

There is no other way but to deal with and work with the groups as well as government agencies.

Partnership of Various Churches

The churches of various denominations must come together and jointly work as a united force. There must be an intentional effort to make this a possibility; simply making an occasional appeal for such partnership will not help. The church leaderships of various denominations must commit themselves to such partnership. This requires, intentional commitment for financial and personnel resources as well as sharing the logistics.

Partnership is also required for setting up rehabilitation centres and training centres for those people who have been affected by various forms of exploitations and abuses.

Research Undertaking

One area where churches can make impact is in research work. We need proper understanding of the issues confronting us. To study the causes and consequences of projects that are undertaken either by Government or private sectors are critical.

We are told there are a number of theological institutions in the NEI. In Dimapur, Nagaland alone there are over 40 Bible colleges and still counting? They are either individually funded or church funded. It makes me to question whether, we really need to have so many seminaries/colleges in our region? Would it not be sensible to have few colleges that are well funded and can provide quality theological educations in the region? Secondly, it is also proper that churches' resources can be pooled together to set up quality research institutions. For example, research can be undertaken to study the impact of globalization in our region, etc.

Pressure Group

Churches can also work as pressure groups. For this churches need to set up groups who could concentrate their time and energy working towards this cause. They will act as pressure groups to the concerned authorities including Government, private, etc.

Dialogue with Decision-Makers

Taking the issues directly to the decision-makers are always helpful. And it is important that we take a constructive practical and solution-focused approach rather than simply raising oppositions to their initiatives. The author of the "Church and the Challenge of Globalization" suggests that it is always helpful to prepare a one to two page handout to be given to the concerned authority. And I find this suggestion helpful for our context as well. The handout may consist the followings:[4]

What I Want? Specifically and Constructively in One Sentence

Why I Want It – three to four paragraphs.

How It Can Be Done? Practical, solution focused, one paragraph.

How You Can Help It To Be Done? What you want the politician to do in specific terms e.g. Refer to parliamentary committee on XYZ and so on....

---

[4] *Ibid.*

Economic Investment

Some of the churches in Northeast India are pretty wealthy and rich as well. It is significant to ask how and where the funds are invested. We all know that money is powerful. We know that money speaks and speaks loudly indeed. Setting up ethical investment funds that do not invest in questionable businesses and firms are critical. Firms that exploit and abuse workers and people, destroy and pollute environment and ecology, etc. must be questioned and rejected.

I am reminded of the Church of England withdrawing its investments with the VEDANDA company when the exploitative practices of the company in India was made known.

Conclusion

The challenges of globalization to our society are very real and at the same time highly pervasive. Dealing with these challenges cannot be an option any more. The church has no option but to deal with them. The church must recognize the social problems confronting our society as spiritual problems and accordingly respond to the challenges. We need a spirituality that would not run away from the reality of the world rather that engages with the world for bringing social transformation – a prophetic spirituality!

"Prophetic spirituality will always fundamentally challenge the system at its roots and offer genuine alternatives based on values from our truest religious, cultural, and political traditions."[5]

Prophetic spirituality will challenge our addiction to wealth and power; our consumeristic culture and corrupt practices; help people to work for change and transformation.

Empowered by the Spirit, people will be encouraged to work toward social justice and peace; work toward the good of the community.

Our broken relationship with God's creation must be restored. The Psalmist Declares, "The earth and everything in it belongs to God."

Our ethic of profit can be transformed by an ethic of sharing and community as the foundation of our economic system.

Prophetic spirituality can help us overcome our addiction to materialism. It can free us from the falsehood that the accumulation and consumption of things could give us happiness.

---

[5] Wallis, *The Soul of Politics,* 44.

Bibliography

Abraham, K. C. *Transforming Vision: Theological-Methodological Paradigm Shifts*. Tiruvalla: Christava Sahitya Samithi, 2006.

Alem, O. *Tsungremology*. Mokokchung: Clark Theological College, 1994.

Alfred, Taiaiake *Peace, Power, and Righteousness: An Indigenous Manifesto*. Ontario: Oxford University Press, 1999.

________. *Wasáse: Indigenous Pathways of Action and Freedom*. Peterborough: Broadview Press, Ltd., 2005.

Ahlstrom, Sydney. *A Religious History of the American People*. London: Yale University Press, 2004.

Aleaz, K. P. "Gospel and Culture: Some Indian Reflection." In *Indian Journal of Theology* 36, no. 2 (1999), 64-79.

Alemchiba, M. "Problems of Readjustment to New Situation with Special Reference to Naga Tribes." In *Highlander*. Vol. 4, 1 & 2. March-April, 1972.

Ahlstrom, Sydney E. *A Religious History of the American People*. New Haven: Yale University Press, 1972.

Anselm of Canterbury. *Proslogion*. Translated by M. J. Charlesworth in *The Major Works*. Eds. Brian Davies and G. R. Evans. New York: Oxford University Press, 1998.

Arokiasamy, S. "Sinful Structures in the Theology of Sin, Conversion and Reconciliation." In S. Arokiasamy and F. Podimattam. Eds, *Social Sin: Its Challenges to Christian Life*. Bangalore: Claretian Publications, 1991.

Augustine, Saint. *Four Anti-Pelagian Writings: On Nature and Grace*. Trans. John A. Mourant and William J. Collinge. Washington, D.C.: The Catholic University of America Press, 1992.

Aveni, Anthony F. "Archaeoastronomy in the Maya Region: A Review of the Past Decade." *Archaeoastronomy* 3 (JHT 12): 51-66.

Jonathan Baer, "Book Review: Blessed: A History of the American Prosperity Gospel, by Kate Bowler."

Babba, Homi K. *The Location of Culture*. London and New York: Routledge, 19194.

Bailey, Garrick A. Ed., *The Osage and the Invisible World: From the Works of Francis La Flesche*. Norman: University of Oklahoma Press, 1995.

Bean, Lowell John "Symbolic Representation of Cahuilla Women." In Williamson, Ray A. and Farrer. Williamson, Ray A. and Claire R. Farrer. Eds., *Earth and Sky: Visions of the Cosmos in Native American Folklore*. Albuquerque: University of New Mexico Press, 1992.

Bear, Leroy Little. "Foreward." In Gregory Cajete. *Native Science: Natural Laws of Interdependence*. Santa Fe: Clear Light Publishers, 2000.

Bergquest, James A. *The Ten Commandments and Responsible Freedom*. Delhi: ISPCK, 1971.

Berry, Thomas. *The Dream of the Earth*. San Francisco: Sierra Club Books, 1990.

Bevans, Stephen B. *Models of Contextual Theology*, revised and expanded, Faith and Cultures Series. Maryknoll: Orbis Books, 2002.

Boff, Leonardo. *Ecology and Liberation: A New Paradigm*. Maryknoll: Orbis Books, 1995.

Bonino, José Miguez. *Doing Theology in a Revolutionary Situation*. Philadelphia: Fortress Press, 1975.

________. *Towards a Christian Political Ethics*. London: SCM Press, 1983.

Bosch, David J. *Transforming Missions: Paradigm Shift in Theology of Mission*. Maryknoll: Orbis Books, 1991.

Bowler, Catherine "Blessed: A History of the American Prosperity Gospel." PhD. Dissertation, Graduate School of Duke University, 2010.

Brown, D. W. "Pietism." In *New Dictionary of Theology*. Leicester: InterVarsity Press, 1988.

Brown, R. The Tangkhul Nagas: Statistical Accounts of the Nature State of Manipur, 1973. In *The Tangkhul Nagas in the Nineteenth Century*. Ed. Verrier Elwin. Oxford: Oxford University Press, 1969.

Burton, Tara Isabella. "The Prosperity Gospel, Explained: Why Joel Osteen Believes that Prayer Can Make You Rich: The long, strange history of a quintessentially American theology."

Cain, Clifford Chalmers *An Ecotheology: Reunderstanding Our Relation to Nature*. Toronto Studies in Theology, Vol. 98. Lewiston: The Edwin Mellen Press, 2009.

Cajete, Gregory. *Native Science: Natural Laws of Interdependence*. Santa Fe: Clear Light Publishers, 2000.

Chauduri, Sarit K. "Folk Belief and Resource Conservations: Reflections from Arunachal Pradesh." In *Indian Folklife: A Quarterly Newsletter from National Folklore Support Centre*. Serial No. 28, January 2008.

Childs, Brevard S. *Introduction to the Old Testament as Scripture*. Philadelphia: Fortress, 1979.

Clark, M. M. *A Corner in India*. Guwahati: Christian Literature Center, 1978.

Cone, James H. *God of the Oppressed*. Revised Edition. Maryknoll: Orbis Books, 1997.

________. *A Black Theology of Liberation*. Twentieth Anniversary Edition. Maryknoll: Orbis Books, 1990.

________. *A Black Theology of Liberation*. Second Edition. New York: Orbis Books, 1986.

Deloria, Jr, Vine. *Spirit & Reason: The Vine Deloria, Jr., Reader*. Eds. Barbara Deloria, et al Golden: Fulcrum Publishing, 1999.

________. *God is Red: A Native View of Religion*. 2nd Ed. Golden: North American Press, 1992.

________. *Red Earth, White Lies: Native Americans and the Myth of Scientific Fact*. Golden: Fulcrum Publishing, 1997.

________. *The Metaphysics of Modern Existence*. San Francisco: Harper & Row Publishers, 1979.

Daly, Herman E. & John B. Cobb. *For the Common Good: Redirecting the Economy: Toward Community, the Environment, and a Sustainable Future*. Boston: Beacon Press, 1999.

DeMartino, George F. *Global Economy, Global Justice: Theoritical Objecttions and Policy Alternatives to Neoliberalism*. New York: Routledge, 2000.

Downs, F. S. *The Mighty Works of God: A Brief History of the Council of Baptist Churches in North East India: The Mission Period 1836-1950*. Guwahati: Christian Literature Center, 1971.

________. *Christianity in North East India: Historical Perspectives*. Delhi: ISPCK, 1983.

________. "Identity: The Integrative Principle." In *Asia Journal of Theology* 6 (1980). 238-249.

________."Tribal Ecumenism in Northeast India: The Christian Role in Tribal Solidarity." In Renthy Keitzar. Ed. *Good News for North East India: A Theological Reader*. Guwahati: Christian Literature Center, 1995. 8-21.

________. "Christianity as a Tribal Response to Change in Northeast India." In *Missiology: An International Review* 8, October 1980. 407-416.

________. "The Christian Role in Tribal Solidarity Movements in Northeast India." In *Bangalore Theological Forum*. Vol. 20, 1988.

Drenen, Tomas Sundnes. "Weber, Prosperity and the Protestant Ethic: Some Reflections on Pentecostalism and Economic Development." *Swedish Missiological Themes,* 100, 3, 2012.

Duchrow, Ulrich and Gerhard Liedke, *Shalom: Biblical Perspective on Creation, Justice and Peace*. Geneva: WCC, 1989.

Dunn, Edmond J. *Missionary Theology: Foundations in Development,* Foreword by Richard P. McBrien. Washington D. C. University of America, 1980.

Elwin, Verrier. *Nagaland*. Shillong: Adviser's Secretariat, 1961.

________. Ed. *The Tangkhul Nagas in the Nineteenth Century.* Oxford: Oxford University Press, 1969.

Enger, Trond "Pietism." In *The Oxford Companion to Christian Thought*. Oxford: Oxford University Press, 2000.

Fanon, Franz. *Black Skin White Mask*. New York: Grove Press, 1967.

Farrer, Claire R. "... by you they will know the directions to guide them:" Stars and Mascalero Apaches." In Williamson, Ray A. and Farrer. Williamson, Ray A. and Claire R. Farrer. Eds., *Earth and Sky: Visions of the Cosmos in Native American Folklore*. Albuquerque: University of New Mexico Press, 1992.

Freandenberger, C. Dean *Global Dust Howl: Can* We *Stop the Destruction of the Land Before It's Too Late?* Philadelphia: Ausburg Fortress Press, 1990.

Fung, Jojo M. "The Menace of Corruption: An Accursed Malaise and a Systemic Evil." In *Asian Horizons* 6/1. March 2012.

Fürer-Haimendorf, Christopher von. *Return to the Naked Nagas: An Anthropologist's View of Nagaland, 1960-1970*. New Edition. London: J. Murray, 1976.

________. *The Naked Nagas*. London: Methuen, 1939.

Gispert-Sauch, George. "God's Handling of Corruption." In Francis Gonsalves and Shalini Mulackal. Eds, *Corruption in Public Life: A Theological Response*. Bangalore: Indian Theological Association and Asian Trading Corporation, 2013. 54-67.

Goodman, Ronald. *Lakota and Star Knowledge: Studies in Lakota Stellar Theology*. Rosebud: Sinta Gleska University, 1992.

Griffin-Pierce, Trudy. "The Hooghan and the Stars." In Williamson, Ray A. and Farrer. Williamson, Ray A. and Claire R. Farrer. Eds., *Earth and Sky: Visions of the Cosmos in Native American Folklore*. Albuquerque: University of New Mexico Press, 1992.

Gutierrez, Gustavo. *A Theology of Liberation*. 15th Anniversary Edition with a new Introduction. Maryknoll: Orbis Books, 1988.

________. *We Drink from Our Own Well: The Spiritual Journey of a People*. Maryknoll: Orbis Books, 1984.

________. *A Theology of Liberation: History, Politics, and Salvation*. Revised edition with new introduction. Translated and edited by Sister Caridad Inda and John Eagleson. Maryknoll: Orbis Books, 2000.

Jones, Gordon "Good News for North-East India." In Renthy Keitzar. Ed. *Good News for North East India: A Theological Reader*. Guwahati: Christian Literature Centre, 1995.

Hallman, David G. Ed. *Ecotheology: Voices from South and North*. Geneva: WCC Publications, 1994.

Hardgerink, Virgil "The Protestant Ethic of Prosperity."

Horam, M. *Nagas Old Ways New Trends*. Delhi: Cosmos Publications, 1988.

________. *Naga Insurgency: The Last Thirty Years*. New Delhi: Cosmos Publications, 1988.

________. *Social and Cultural Life of the Nagas: The Tangkhul Nagas*. Delhi: B.R. Publishing Corp., 1977.

Hümtsoe-Nienu, Eyingbeni *God of the Tribes: Christian Perspective on the Naga Ancestral Idea of the Supreme Being*. Mokokchung: Clark Theological College, 2014.

Hutchinson, Dawn "New Thoughts Prosperity Theology and Its Influence on American Ideas of Success." In *Nova, Religio: The Journal of Alternative and Emergent Religions*, Vol.18, Issue 2, 2014.

Hutton, J. H. *The Sema Nagas*, Foreword by Henry Balfour. London: MacMillan and Co., Ltd., 1921.

Imchen, Panger. *Ancient Ao Naga Religion and Culture*. Delhi: Har-Anand Publication, 1993.

Inglis, Nathanael L. "The Importance of Gordon Kaufman's Constructive Theological Method for Contemporary Anabaptist-Mennonite Theology." *The Conrad Grebel Review*, 34 no 2 (Spr 2016).

Jacobs, Julia. *The Nagas: Hill Peoples of Northeast India: Society, Culture and the Colonial Encounter*. New York: Thames and Hudson, 1990.

Jajo, Champhang. *Christian Life in Tribal Context in Manipur*. Ukhrul: Published by the author, 1990.

James, Lovely Awomi. *Tribal Theology: Reviewing the Naga Traditional Worldview*. Christian Heritage Rediscovered – 48. New Delhi: Christian World Imprints, 2017.

Jameson, Frederic. *PostModernism Or the Cultural Logic of Late Capitalism*. Duke: Duke University Press, 1991.

Kaufman, Gordon D. *Systematic Theology: A Historicist Perspective*. New York: Charles Scribner's Sons, 1968.

________. *In Face of Mystery: A Constructive Theology*. Cambridge: Harvard Univ. Press, 1993.

________. *The Theological Imagination*. Philadelphia: The Westminster Press, 1981.

________. *An Essay on Theological Methods*. Missoula: Scholars Press, 1979.

Keitzar, Renthy. *In Search of a Relevant Gospel Message*. Guwahati: CLC, 1995.

________. "Developing Tribal Theology." A Paper Presented at the Theological Consultation for Northeast India. Council of Baptist Churches in North East India, Guwahati, Assam, November 5-8, 1988.

Keller, Catherine Michael Nausner, and Mayra Rivera. Eds. *Postcolonial Theologies: Divinity and Empire*. St. Louis: Chalice Press, 2004.

Khamrang. Khayaipam "Towards an Eco- Theology: Resources in the Primal Religion of the Tangkhul Nagas." M.Th Thesis. Madras: Gurukul Lutheran Theological College & Research Institute. 1992.

Khan, Haider. *Technology, Development and Democracy*. Cheltenham: Edward Elgar, 1998.

Kidwell, Clara Sue. "Archaeoastronomy as the Key to Human Intellectual Development and Social Organization." TMs,

Knitter, Paul F. *One Earth, Many Religions: Multifaith Dialogue and Global Responsibility* Maryknoll: Orbis Books, 1995.

Kochuthara, Shaji George "Indian Ethos and the Culture of Corruption: Moral/ Psychological Perspective." In Francis Gonsalves and Shalini Mulackal. Eds, *Corruption in Public Life: A Theological Response*. Bangalore: Indian Theological Association and Asian Trading Corporation, 2013. 68-88.

Kohl, Manfred. "Do We Care About Corruption: How Integrity Can Tame the Beast of Bribes and Extortion." In *Laussane Global Analysis*. Vol. 8, Issue 3, May 2019.

Konyak, A. Yanang. *From Darkness to Light: A Story of the Baptist Work among the Konyak Nagas*. Guwahati: Christian Literature Center, 1986.

Koyama, Kosuke. *Waterbuffalo Theology*. New York: Orbis Books, 1989.

LaDuke, Winona. *Recovering the Sacred: The Power of Naming and Claiming.* Cambridge: South End Press, 2005.

Lasetso, Razouselie and Yangkahao Vashum. Eds. *Tribal Christian Theology: Methods and Sources for Constructing a Relevant Theology for the Indigenous People of North East India.* Tribal Study Series no. 15. Jorhat: Tribal Study Centre, 2007.

Lee, Shayen "Prosperity Theology: T. D. Jakes and the Gospel of the Almighty Dollar." In *Cross Currents*, 57 no. 2, Summer 2007. 227-229.

Longchar, Wati. *Returning to Mother Earth: Theology, Christian Witness and Theological Education: An Indigenous Perspective*. PTCA Series no. 4. Tainan: PTCA; Kolkatta: SCEPTRE, 2012.

________. *An Emerging Asian Theology: Tribal Theology: Issue, Method and Perspective*. Tribal Study Series no. 8. Jorhat: Tribal Study Centre, 2000.

________. *The Traditional Tribal Worldview and Modernity*. Jorhat: Eastern Theological College, 1995.

________. *The Tribal Religious Traditions in North East India.* Jorhat: Assam, ETC, 1991.

________. Comp., *Contextual Theologies: Method and Perspectives*. Kolkatta: SCEPTRE, 2013.

________. "An Assessment of the Tribal Theology: Trends and Challenges for Future." In Shimreingam Shimray and Limatula Longkumer. Eds, *Tribal Theology On the Move*. Tribal Study Series No. 14 (Jorhat: Tribal/Women Study Centres, 2006), 1-14.

________. "Myth: A Source for Conceptualizing Tribal Theology." In Shimreingam Shimray. Ed. *Tribal Theology: A Reader*. Tribal Study Series no. 12. Jorhat: Tribal Study Centre, 2003.

________. "A Creation-Poem of the Ao Nagas: A Theological Exploration." In *The Tribal Worldview and Ecology*, Tribal Study Series No. 2. Eds. A. Wati Longchar and Yangkahao Vashum. Jorhat: Tribal Study Centre, 1998.

Luikham, R. *Folktales and Tales of the Nagas.* Delhi: Immanuel Publishers, 1983.

Luther, Martin. *The Bondage of the Will.* Tr. J. I. Packer & O.R. Johnston. Grand Rapids: Fleming H. Revell, 1957.

Macquarrie, John. *Principles of Christian Theology*. London: SCM Press Ltd, 1966.

Malstrom, Vincent. *Cycles of the Sun, Mysteries of the Moon*. Austin: University of Taxes Press, 1997.

Mann, Michael "'Torch Bearers Upon the Path of Progress:' Britains Ideology of a 'Moral andMaterial Progress' in India: An Introductory Essay." In Harald

Fischer-Tine and Michal Mann. Eds. *Colonialism as Civilizing Mission: Cultural Ideology in British India*. London: Wimbledon Publishing Company, 2004.

Marem Khullen Baptist Church. *The Marem Baptist Church History-cum-Golden Jubilee Programme* Marem, Manipur: Marem Baptist Church History Committee and Golden Jubilee Committee, 1992.

Mboya, Imas, J. B. "Gift Challenges and Transforms Prosperity Gospel." In *African Ecclesial Review,* Vol. 58, Nos. 1 & 2, 2016.

McCluskey, Stephen C. "Science, Society, Objectivity and the Astronomies of the Southwest" in *Astronomy and Ceremony in Prehistoric Southwest*, no. 2. Eds. John B. Carlson and W. James Judge. Albuquerque: Maxwell Museum of Anthropology, 1987, 205-217.

Medom, Noulezhalie Ricky. *The Relevance of the Theological Motiff of Exile to the Naga's Struggle for Sovereignty as a People.* Delhi: ISPCK, 2002.

Memmi, Albert. *The Colonizer and the Colonized.* Expanded Edition, Introduction by Jean-Paul Sartre. Boston: Beacon Press Books, 1967.

Mills, J. P. *The Rengma Nagas*. London: Macmillan, 1937; Reprint New York: AMS, 1979.

________. *The Lhota Nagas: With an Introduction and Supplementary Notes by J. H. Hutton* London: Macmillan and Co., Ltd., 1922.

Minz, Nirmal. "Tribal Perspective on Ecology," in Wati Longchar and Yangkahao Vashum. Eds. *The Tribal Worldview and Ecology*. Tribal Study Series No. 2. Jorhat: Tribal Study Center, 1998.

________. "Primal Religious Perspective on Ecology." In *Ecology and Development Theological Perspective.* Ed. Daniel D. Chetti. Madras: Gurukul Lutheran Theological College and Research Institute, 1991.

Moltmann, Jürgen. *On Humanity: Political Theology and Ethics*. London: SCM Press, 1984.

________. "Human Rights, the Rights of Humanity and the Rights of Nature." In *Ethics of World Religions and Human Rights* Eds. Hans Kung and Jürgen Moltmann. Philadelphia: Trinity Press International, 1990.

Monroe, Jean Guard and Ray A. Williamson. *They Dance in the Sky: Native American Star Myths.* Boston: Houghton Mifflin Company, 1987.

Montgomery, John W. *Human Rights and Human Dignity*. Grand Rapids: Zondervan Publishing House, 1986.

Mulackal, Shalini. "Christian Witness in a Corrupt World." In Francis Gonsalves and Shalini Mulackal. Eds, *Corruption in Public Life: A Theological Response.* Bangalore: Indian Theological Association and Asian Trading Corporation, 2013.111-130.

Mynatty, Hormis *Proposals for a Comprehensive Moral Methodology*. Bangalore: Asian Trading Corporation, 2008.

Naga International Support Center (NISC), Amsterdam. Press Release. November 15, 2004.

Nagaland Baptist Church Council. *From Darkness to Light: A Publication of the Nagaland Baptist Church Council on the Celebration of the 125 years of Christianity in Nagaland*. Kohima: Nagaland Baptist Church Council, 1997.

Nandy, Ashish. *The Intimate Enemy: Loss and Recovery of Self under Colonialism*. Delhi: Oxford University Press, 1983.

Nussbaum, Martha C. "Human Capabilities, Female Human Beings." Martha C. Nussbaum & Jonathan Glover, eds. *Women, Culture, and Development: A Study of Human Capabilities*. Oxford: Claredon Press. 1995.

Niebuhr, Reinhold. *The Nature and Destiny of Man*. Vol. I. Upper Saddle River: Prentice Hall, 1964.

________. *The Nature and Destiny of Man*. Vol. II. New York: Charles Scribner's Sons, 1943

________. *The Essential Reinhold Neibuhr: Selected Essays and Addresses*, ed. & int. Robert McAfee Brown. New Haven: Yale University Press, 1986.

Nirmal, Arvind P. *Heuristic Explorations*. Madras: Christian Literature Society, 1990.

Nuh, V. K. Ed. *In Search of Praxis Theology for the Nagas*. New Delhi: Regency Publications, 2003.

Ochulor, Chinenye Leo and Edet Patrick Bassey, "Analysis of Corruption from the Ethical and Moral Perspectives." In *European Journal of Scientific Research* 44/3. 2010.

O'Grady, Joan. *Early Christian Heresies*. New York: Barnes and Noble Books, 1985.

O'Grady, Ron. *Bread and Freedom: Understanding and Acting on Human Rights*. Geneva:World Council of Churches. 1979.

Osburn Jr., Robert. Taming The Beast: Can We Bridle the Culture of Corruption? St. Paul: Wilberforce, 2016.

Pettigrew, William. "Report for the Years 1907-1909." In *Rev. Pettigrew's Mission Reports and Letters,1891-1932*. Comp. and reproduced by Champhang Jajo. 20-29. Ukhrul: Phila Jajo, n.d.

Pinxten, Rik and Ingred van Dooren, "Navajo Earth and Sky and the Celestial Life-Force." In *Earth and Sky: Visions of the Cosmos in Native American Folklore*. Eds. Ray A. Williamson and Claire R. Farrer. Albuquerque: University on New Mexico Press, 1992.

Planning Commission, *The Report of the Working Group on the Land System Among Tribals in the North Eastern India*, May 1984.

Presler, H. H. *Primitive Religions of India*. Madras: Christian Literature Society, 1971.

Pui-lan, Kwok. *Postcolonial Imagination and Feminist Theology*. Louisville: Westminster: John Knox Press, 2005.

Rad, Gerhard von. *Old Testament Theology*. London: SCM Press, 1975.

Rahner, Karl. "Theology," in *Encyclopedia of Theology: The Concise Sacramentum Mundi*, ed. Karl Rahner. New York: Seabury Press, 1975.

Raveena, "Anatomy of Insurgency," *North East Sun*. Vol. I, No. l. July 29, 1995.

Rayan, Samuel "Reconceiving Theology in the Asian Context." In *Doing Theology in a Divided World*. Eds. Virginia Fabella and Sergio Torres. Maryknoll: Orbis Books, 1985.

________. *Ecological Dimensions of Our Eaith: To Care for the Earth-Towards a Theology of Nature*. Kunchala Rajaratnam Endowment Lectures. Series 1. Madras: Gurukul Lutheran Theological College and Research Institute, 1991.

Rieger, Joerg. "Christianity, Capitalism, and Desire: Can Religion Make a Difference." In *Union Seminary Quarterly Review*. 64, No. 1, 2013.

Ruether, Rosemary Radford. *Sexism and God-Talk: Toward a Feminist Theology*. Boston: Beacon Press, 1983.

Rustomji, Nari *Imperilled Frontiers: India's North-Eastern Borderlands*. Delhi: Oxford University Press, 1983.

Rymbai, R. Tokin Roy. "Evolution of Modern Khasi Society (Babu Jeebon Roy)," in J. N. Chowdhury. Ed. *The Khasi Canvas: A Cultural and Political History*. Shillong: Srimati Jaya Chowdhury, 1978.

________. "The Traditional Ecological Concepts of the Khasi-Pnars," in *The Tribal Worldview and Ecology*, Tribal Study Series No. 2, Eds. A. Wati Longchar and Yangkahao Vashum. Jorhat: Tribal Study Centre, 1998.

Said, Edward. *Orientalism*. New York: Vintage Books, 1979.

Sangma, Milton S. *History of American Baptist Mission in North-East India (1836-1950)*, vol. 1. Delhi: Mittal Publications, 1987.

Satter, Beryl. *Each Mind a Kingdom: American Women, Sexual Purity and the New Thought Movement, 1875–1920*. Berkeley: University of California Press, 1999.

Schenone, Osvaldo and Samuel Greeg, *A Theology of Corruption, The Theology of Economics of Sin*. Ed. Gloreia L. Süñga, Christian Social Thought Series, no. 7. Grand Rapids: Action Institute, 2003.

Schreiter, Robert J. *Constructing Local Theologies*. Maryknoll: Orbis Books, 1989.

Schulz, William F. *In Our Best Interest: How Defending Human Rights benefits Us All.* Boston: Beacon Press, 1999.

Sedmak, Clemens *Doing Local Theology: A Guide for Artisans of a New Humanity.* Maryknoll: Orbis Books, 2002.

Sen, Amartya. *Development as Freedom* New York; Anchor Books, 1999.

Shakespear, L. W. *History of Upper Assam, Upper Burma and North-Eastern Frontier* London: Macmillan and Co. Ltd., 1914.

Sharma, Suresh *Tribal Identity and Modern World.* New Delhi: Sage Publications, 1994.

Sherman, Ben "Watchers of the Ancient Skies." In *Winds of Change,* Vol. 13 No. 3. Summer 1998. 20-25.

Smart, Ninian. *Worldviews: Crosscultural Exploration of Human Beliefs.* Third Edition. Upper Saddle: Prentice Hall Inc., 2000.

Smith, David L. *Theologies of Success: Handbook of Contemporary Theology.* Illinois: Victor Books, 1992.

Snaithang, O. L. *Christianity and Social Change IN Northeast India (A Study of the Role of Christianity in Social Change among the Khasi-Jaintia Tribes of Meghalaya).* Shillong: Vendrame Institute; Calcutta: Firma KLM Pvt. Ltd., 1993.

Sobrino, Jon "Jesus' Relationship with the Poor and Outcasts: Its Importance for Fundamental Moral Theology." In *Concillium* 130, 1979.

Soelle, Dorothee and Shirly A.Cloys, *To Work and Love: A Theology of Creation.* Philadelphia: Fortress Press, 1984.

Solo. Jonah M. and K. Mahangthci. Eds. *Forty Years in Manipur Assam: An Account of the Work of Rev. & Mrs. William Pettigrew.* Imphal: Privately published by Mrs. M. Asenath and Mrs. K. Ruth, 1986.

Song, C. S. *Tell Us Our Names: Story Theology from an Asian Perspective.* Indore: Satorakashan Sanchai Kendra, 1986.

Spivak, Gayatri Chakravorty. *Critique of Postcolonial Reasons: Toward a History of the Vanishing Present.* Cambridge: Harvard University Press, 1999.

Sugirtharajah, R. S. *Postcolonial Reconfigurations: An Alternative Way of Reading the Bible and Doing Theology.* St. Louis: Chalice Press, 2003.

Taylor, John V. *The Primal Vision Christian Presence Amid African Religion.* London: SCM Press, 1977.

Taylor, Mark L. "Spirit and Liberation: Achieving Postcolonial Theology in the United States." In Catherine Keller, Michael Nausner, and Mayra Rivera. Eds. *Postcolonial Theologies: Divinity and Empire.* St. Louis: Chalice Press, 2004.

Thanzauva, K. *Theology of Community: Tribal Theology in the Making*. Bangalore: Asian Trading Corporation, 2004.

________. *Transforming Theology: A Theological Basis for Social Transformation*. Bangalore: Asian Trading Corporation, 2002.

________. "Issues in Tribal Theology." In Shimreingam Shimray, ed., *Tribal Theology: A Reader*. Tribal Study Series no. 12. Jorhat: Tribal Study Centre, 2003. 17-39.

The Tangkhul Naga Shiyan-Yanza, compiled and prepared by the Tangkhul Naga Long. Ukhrul, Manipur, 1988.

Thomas, M. M. "Primal Vision and Modernization." National Seminar on Theological Implications of the Primal Vision Sponsored by the Board of Theological Education Senate of Serampore College and the Gurukul Lutheran College and Research Institute. Madras, 9-12 September, 1993.

Thomas, Owen C. *Introduction to Theology*. Revised edition. Serampore: The Indian Theological Library, Senate of Serampore College, 1989.

Thumra, Jonathan H. "The Naga Primal (Traditional) Religion and Christianity: A Theological Reflection," in V. K. Nuh. Ed. *In Search of Praxis Theology for the Nagas*. New Delhi: Regency Publications, 2003.

________. *Impact of Christianity* on the Socio-cultural Ethos of the Tangkhul Nagas." In *Souvenir: TBL Centenary 1996.* Ukhrul: TBL Centenary, 1996. 44-50.

Tillich, Paul. *Systematic Theology*, vol. 1. Chicago: University of Chicago Press, 1951.

Tinker, George E. *Spirit and Resistance: Political Theology and American Indian Liberation*. Minneapolis: Fortress Press, 2004.

________. *Missionary Conquest: The Gospel and Native American Cultural Genocide*. Minneapolis: Fortress Press, 1993.

________. "The Stones Shall Cry Out: Consciousness, Rocks and Indians." *Wicazo Sa Review* 19(2). January 2004, 105-125.

________. "Spirituality and Nature of American Personhood: Sovereignty an Solidarity.'" In *Spirituality of the Third World*. Eds. K. C. Abraham & Berndetta Mbuy-Beya. Maryknol: Orbis Books, 1994. 127-128.

________. "God, Gods, Goddesses, and Indians." TMs.

"Together Towards Life" – The New WCC Affirmation on Mission and Evangelism Commission on World Mission and Evangelism (CWME), 2013.

Tracy, David. *The Analogical Imaginations: Christian Theology and Culture of Pluralism.* New York: Crossroad, 1981.

Treat, James ed. *Native and Christian: Indigenous voices on Religious Identity in the United States and Canada*. New York: Routledge, 1996.

Tüngoe, Merithung. *Administrators Missionaries and a World turned Upside Down.* Delhi: ISPCK; Jorhat: ETC, 2000.

Uduigwomen, A. F. *Introducing Ethics: Trends, Problems, and Perspectives.* Calabar: Jochrissam Publishers, 2006.

Vansina, Jan. *Oral Tradition as History* (Madison: University of Wisconsin Press, 1985.

Vargas-Hernández, José G. "The Multiple Faces of Corruption: Typology, Forms and Levels." In *Studies of Changing Societies: Corruption Study*, Vol. 1, (6) 2012, 1-27.

Vashum, Yangkahao. *Christology in Context: A Tribal-Indigenous Appraisal of North East India*. Christian Heritage Rediscovered – 49. New Delhi: Christian World Imprints, 2017.

________. "Sources for Studying Tribal Theology." In Shimreingam Shimray. Ed. *Tribal Theology*. A Reader. Tribal Study Series no. 1. Jorhat: Tribal Study Centre, 1997. 67-78.

________. "Emerging Vision of Indigenous/Tribal Theology," In Massey, James and Shimreingam Shimray. Eds. *Dalit-Tribal Theological Interface: Current Trends in Subaltern Theologies*. Jorhat: TSC/TWC, 2007. 16-55.

________. "Theology of Land: A Naga Perspective." In Wati Longchar and Yangkahao Vashum. Eds. *The Tribal Worldview and Ecology*, Tribal Study Series 2. Jorhat: Tribal Study Center, 1998.

________. "The Stars are Our Relatives: Some Musing of Indigenous People's Stellar Theology." In *JTCA: The Journal of Theologies and Cultures in Asia* . vol. 6, 2007. 111-130.

________. "Colonialism, Missionaries, and Indigenous: A Critical Appraisal," in *Journal of Tribal Studies*. Vol. XII, no. 2. July-December 2007, 1- 22.

________. "A Tangkhul Creation Myth: Implication for a Holistic View of Human Rights." In *The Tribal Worldview and Ecology*. Tribal Study Series No. 2. Eds. A. Wati Longchar and Yangkahao Vashum. Jorhat: Tribal Study Centre, 1998. 34-40.

Vashum, Yangkahao Peter Haokip and Melvil Pereira. Eds., *Search for a New Society: Tribal Theology for North East India*. Guwahati: North Eastern Social Research Centre, 2012.

Wallis, Jim. *The Soul of Politics: A Practical and Vision for Change*. New York: The New Press; Maryknoll: Orbis Books, 1994.

Ward, W. R. *The Protestant Evangelical Awakening.* Cambridge: Cambridge University Press, 1992.

Wilfred, Felix. *Margins: Sites for Asian Theologies*. Delhi: ISPCK, 2008.

Williamson, Ray A. and Claire R. Farrer. Eds., *Earth and Sky: Visions of the Cosmos in Native American Folklore*. Albuquerque: University of New Mexico Press, 1992

Williamson, Ray A. "The Celestial Skiff: An Alabama Myth of the Stars." In Williamson, Ray A. and Farrer. Williamson, Ray A. and Claire R. Farrer. Eds., *Earth and Sky: Visions of the Cosmos in Native American Folklore*. Albuquerque: University of New Mexico Press, 1992.

Zvobgo, Eddison J. M. "A Third World View." In *Human Rights in American Policy. E*d. Donald P. Kommers and Gilburt D. Loescher. Notre Dame: University of Notre Dame Press, 1979.